Maria Edgeworth and the Public Scene

Maria Edgeworth
and the Public Scene

Intellect, Fine Feeling and Landlordism in the Age of Reform

MICHAEL HURST
Fellow in Modern History and Politics, St John's College, Oxford

MACMILLAN

First published in 1969 by
MACMILLAN AND CO LTD
Little Essex Street London W C 2
and also at Bombay Calcutta and Madras
Macmillan South Africa (Publishers) Pty Ltd Johannesburg
The Macmillan Company of Australia Pty Ltd Melbourne
The Macmillan Company of Canada Ltd Toronto
Gill and Macmillan Dublin

Library of Congress catalog card no. 70–88024

Printed in Great Britain by
WESTERN PRINTING SERVICES LTD
Bristol

to Arthur Bell

'Les grandes pensées viennent du cœur.'

LUC DE CLAPIERS, MARQUIS DE VAUVENARGUES,
Réflexions et Maximes

Contents

List of Plates	8
Preface	9
Acknowledgement	10
Maria Edgeworth's Family	11
List of Abbreviations	13
Introduction	15
1 The Path of Tolerance	29
2 Rents and Repealers	54
3 A Bleak Outlook	90
4 O'Connell Contained	112
5 Good Works *versus* Self-help	141
6 Repose and Death	174
Epilogue	181
Appendixes	
1 Maria Edgeworth's Thoughts on her Profession	186
2 Isaac D'Israeli on Maria Edgeworth	188
3 Ministries of the Period	190
Bibliography	192
Index	201

List of Plates

1 Maria Edgeworth in old age   *facing page* 32

2 A view of Edgeworthstown House   33

3 A corner of an Irish market   64

4 Irish peasants at work   65

5 Irish peasants at play   65

The illustrations were made available by Mrs H. M. Colvin to whom I offer my thanks.

Preface

THIS is not a history of Ireland from the beginning of Daniel O'Connell's big Catholic Emancipation agitation to the passing of the Great Famine. It is an attempt through the life of one highly intelligent and observant woman to pinpoint many of the problems of those times, not only from a particular United Kingdom angle, but from a general one relevant to a wider context then and now. Maria Edgeworth's angles were usually acute and seldom obtuse. Her comments on the matters within her experience are almost always worth recording – be they on topics of vast and obvious public importance, on those of general relevance to some widespread phenomenon, or even on those of an ostensibly pettifogging nature apparently peculiar to herself or at most to her district. The last often contribute to the understanding of the rest in very significant ways. And the rest contribute to the understanding of human society in a wide range of countries as well as of that in Regency and early-Victorian Ireland. It should perhaps be added, however, that no attempt has been made to deal with her activities in circles like that of the Royal Irish Academy and related bodies.

The method has been to set the scene for the comments she made, dividing up the time span according to the most fundamental shifts in politics, the economy and the Irish ways of life. That done, the comments have been presented as nearly as possible in strict chronological sequence and interspersed with the author's comments upon them. A narrative approach enabled the interaction of the numerous subjects of discussion and the development of Maria Edgeworth as a person to be brought out most forcibly. Division into topics such as religion, the Poor Law and party politics would have killed all sense of entering into the atmosphere of life in county Longford and destroyed all idea of the central character as a complete human being. Atmosphere and personality study constitute two of the most vital commodities in the historian's cupboard. Without them logic and imagination are severely hamstrung. A false foundation cannot be overcome by good logic and inspired guesses. Only a whole atmosphere and a proper appreciation of character and convictions can lead to the best results.

One of the most gratifying and attractive features of the Edgeworth family generally was its capacity for comment of high quality where news and views were often separated. Where an Edgeworth comment is not followed by one from the author it can be taken as meaning that so far as he is concerned that comment has stood a comprehensive test for historical reliability. It should not be assumed that because the Edgeworth approach has been taken so seriously that any axe is being ground. The book is merely a bid to tackle something of undoubted interest.

ACKNOWLEDGEMENT

I wish to thank all those who, either directly or indirectly, helped me in the preparation and production of this book, especially Mrs H. M. Colvin, whose contribution was invaluable. The views expressed are entirely my own.

St John's College, Oxford   MICHAEL HURST
August 1968

Maria Edgeworth's Family

Richard Lovell Edgeworth (1744–1817) married four times, the first time while he was still up at Oxford, and he had, in all, twenty-two children.

(1) By his first wife, Anna Maria Elers, his children were:
Richard (1764–96), who was born before his father's twentieth birthday.
Lovell I (1765, died after a few days).
MARIA (1767–1849).
Emmeline (1770–1847).
Anna (1773–1824).

(2) By his second wife, Honora Sneyd, whom he married in July 1773, four months after the death of Anna Maria:
Honora I (1774–90).
LOVELL II (1775–1842).

(3) By his third wife, Elizabeth Sneyd, sister of Honora, to whom he was married on Christmas Day 1780, nine months after the latter's death:
Elizabeth (1781–1800).
Henry (1782–1813).
Charlotte (1783–1807).
Sophia (1784, died after a few days).
CHARLES SNEYD (1786–1864), known as Sneyd.
William I (1788–90).
Thomas Day (1789–92).
HONORA II (1791–1858), who married in 1837 Francis

Beaufort, brother of the fourth Mrs R. L. Edgeworth, and ultimately an admiral.

WILLIAM II (1794–1829).

(4) By his fourth wife, Frances Beaufort, whom he married in May 1798, seven months after his third bereavement:

FRANCES MARIA (1799–1848), known as Fanny, who married Lestock Wilson in 1829.

HARRIET (1801–89), who married in 1826 Richard Butler, a Church of Ireland clergyman, and lived in Trim, county Meath.

SOPHIA II (1803–37), who married in 1824 Barry Fox of near-by Fox Hall.

Lucy Jane (1805–98).

FRANCIS BEAUFORT (1809–46).

MICHAEL PAKENHAM (1812–81).

The fourth Mrs Edgeworth's brother the Rev. William Beaufort and her sisters Harriet and Louisa Beaufort also feature in the story.

List of Abbreviations

CHR	*Catholic Historical Review*
CSE	C. Sneyd Edgeworth
EcHR	*Economic History Review*
EHR	*English Historical Review*
FE	Frances (Fanny) Edgeworth (Mrs Lestock Wilson)
HE	Harriet Edgeworth (Mrs Richard Butler)
HJ	*Historical Journal*
IHS	*Irish Historical Studies*
JMH	*Journal of Modern History*
ME	Maria Edgeworth
Memoir	Mrs R. L. Edgeworth, *A Memoir of Maria Edgeworth* (1867)
NLI	National Library of Ireland
P&P	*Past and Present*
RLE	Richard Lovell Edgeworth
Mrs RLE	the fourth Mrs Richard Lovell Edgeworth
TRHS	*Transactions of the Royal Historical Society*
TSR	Thomas Spring-Rice

Introduction

I R E L A N D in the nineteenth century provides a splendid example
from which all manner of general themes about modern nationalism, race relations, religious strife, democracy, liberalism, class
warfare, economic problems, the role of the state and, not least,
individual human nature can be successfully extracted. Materials
abound for their development and illustration, but are usually
exploited for exposition at a less general level. Most writers on
Ireland, whether or not they are Irish, tend strongly to treat
their subjects as strictly Irish affairs and neglect to consider them
within the wider contexts of world history or political, social
and economic problems of general significance.

Maria Edgeworth is, of course, interesting as Maria Edgeworth. When so acute and penetrating an observer with her
environment and set of well-worked out principles has left
behind so illuminating a set of letters and memoranda as she
did, the historian is certainly justified in regarding them as
worthy of presentation and discussion. Then, too, her purely
literary side would necessarily be further revealed by such
treatment, not to mention the help it would give to those with a
mainly antiquarian approach to Ireland. But this is only a part
of the story. There remains Maria Edgeworth the player of an
historical role – one to be found in so many countries before,
during and since her time. She was cast for the part of an enlightened member of a ruling class who wished it to deserve its
power and privileges through devotion to what she considered
its obvious duties towards the rest of the community. Great

though its shortcomings undoubtedly were, she never wavered from the conviction that any alternative was quite unthinkable. It was all very well to support the Catholic Emancipation campaign of the 1820s. Its object was absolutely in accord with the notion of justice under the Ascendancy. Repeal, however, was a vastly different kettle of fish. Admittedly Richard Lovell Edgeworth had voted against the Act of Union,[1] but his objections had centred round the methods employed to secure its passage, not the major principles behind the plan. Indeed he and Maria both regarded the United Kingdom idea as the great opportunity for taking Ireland ahead. Father and daughter were well aware of how the power structure of the country functioned, yet were hopeful that the Irish aristocracy and gentry would have the intelligence and virtue to realise their good luck. Behind the shelter of British power they could live up to the Edgeworth ideal of benevolence and yet impose salutary reforms upon a mass peasantry vastly more feckless than they themselves had ever been. London would provide that very breathing-space so clearly lacking under the state of semi-independence set up in 1782. Good treatment of tenants, the spread of education and better agricultural methods, genuine religious toleration for Catholics and Protestants alike, the improvement of the standard of justice at all levels – these would in Edgeworth eyes lead to peace and prosperity. Not altogether a hopelessly impractical scheme, but unhappily one highly unlikely to be adopted and in fact never taken up by those it was intended for. As things turned out, the failure to grant Catholic Emancipation at the time of the Union almost paled into oblivion before the long series of errors into which Ascendancy intransigence led the British Government. Blind selfishness had long been a political characteristic of the Irish ruling class. Nothing new in it arose after 1800. The great shame was that a chance to turn over a new leaf was missed. Direct self-interest lay behind slack as well as Draconian features of the land system. Absenteeism among landlords and the permissive administration of estates, with an absurd amount of sub-letting

---

[1] For RLE's attitudes at this time, see RLE and ME's *Memoirs of R. Lovell Edgeworth*, 3rd ed., pp. 384–92. On the whole problem of the passing of the Act of Union, see Bolton, *The Passing of the Irish Act of Union* and Ingram's *History of the Legislative Union of Great Britain and Ireland*.

to please the Catholic peasant's passion for a plot of his own; bad land-utilisation; and overconcentration upon the potato (even poor versions of it, such as the 'lumper') – all sprang from indolence and disillusionment.[1]

Bitter racial and religious differences in the south and west of Ireland between a Protestant possessing class of predominantly British or pseudo-British origin and a mass of Catholic peasants, making up what had always constituted the lower orders of the country, were bound to leave their mark. One aspect of it was oppression; another complaisance. Both were selfish. A troublesome people has to be coerced in politics and perhaps in religion, but in other spheres the line of least resistance is often a conqueror's most profitable course, even in the long run. From the time when the old Irish Catholic upper class was either dispossessed and fled as 'Wild Geese' to the Continent, or went over to the enemy lock, stock and barrel, or remained to face almost total degradation, the Catholic peasantry had become the sole repository of the profound sense of national distinctness felt in Celtic Ireland. Not unnaturally they associated the soil of Ireland with the nation of Ireland, and possession of any of its surface was for them something of a sop to their yearning for the native land-customs destroyed by British conquest and a partial satisfaction of their national pride. Leaving the estates to agents saved landlords a lot of bother. Allowing those agents to fall in with 'native' sentiment got in the rent with fewer troubles and aborted a substantial proportion of rural agitation in a land-hungry people with a very high birthrate.

Spit, polish and kindness would undoubtedly have gone a long way had it been applied on a national scale. But, and it is a very big but, the Protestant idealists suffered from several enormous drawbacks if the solution, as opposed to the easing, of the Irish predicament was the aim. And this even in the event of a hundred

---

[1] *Two Centuries of Irish History*, ed. Bryce, has a good account of conditions generally in part III, ch. I by J. H. Bridges. A detailed account of events during the first decade of the Union is to be found in Plowden, *History of Ireland*, and interesting sidelights upon Irish religious life abound in Milner, *An Inquiry into Certain Vulgar Opinions*. Salaman's *The History and Social Influence of the Potato* is an interesting introduction to the vexed question of Irish popular diet and a substantial output of academic articles (listed in the bibliography) has illuminated the topic most thoroughly.

per cent response from their allegedly wayward fellows.
Maria Edgeworth and her like represented the conquest whether
they liked it or not. Almost invariably landowners and Protestants, their pedigree was just wrong for gaining the love and
confidence of the Catholic masses. Moreover, apart from the
barrier of the Catholic priesthood, there were other more
extreme Catholic lay figures to outbid the reformist top dogs.
These popular leaders might or might not, and generally did
not, have a proper social programme in Maria's time, yet their
emotional contact with the masses was automatic and immediate,
engendered by countless unspoken elements of history and
kept alive through the great agency of their religious faith;
whereas those like the Edgeworths had to rely upon local links
to bring them close to the people. An enormous number of
pleasant contacts would have had to have been manufactured
with startling rapidity to approach within striking distance of
O'Connell and his like. As a rule the reformist Establishment
of any country with a social and economic structure like Ireland's during the first fifty years of the Union would have stood
little or no chance of converting their own group, let alone
moving off to implant their ideas into the hearts and minds of a
basically hostile mass. Ireland at this time therefore provides
the student of public affairs with a fascinating essay in failure,
and Maria Edgeworth, as a highly intelligent and voluble
instance of the upper-class reformer with limited ends, serves
as a well-nigh classic illustration of the general dilemma of her
kind.

The Irish land-system might have been based upon English
real property law, but the local variations were of such a nature
as to put a heavy premium upon landlord power. Conquest and
land-hunger both pushed justice farther and farther into the
background. The result was that what the Catholic masses
lacked as strictly legal rights never came to them by custom.

The landlord was not, as in England, a partner in agricultural
production, investing capital in fencing, drainage, farmhouses, and
cottages, and bound to the cultivator by social and prescriptive
ties, but simply the receiver of a rent-charge. From time to time
this increased, as the labour of others or the increase of population
made occupation of the soil more valuable; but in respect of it,
with few exceptions, no obligations were recognised beyond those
of neighbourly feeling, where this might happen to exist. In fact

Irish landlords are to be compared, not with English squires, but with the ground landlords of London.[1]

In such circumstances the differences between good, bad and indifferent landlords ranged round whether or not they exploited the immense power in their hands. Throughout the period of Maria's active concern with the Edgeworth estates most landlords delegated much of this authority to middlemen.

> With the exception of that part which the owner or his agent had parcelled out in forty shilling freeholds for political purposes, the land was held in leases of from twenty to one hundred and fifty acres, granted for varying periods, but very commonly for twenty or thirty-one years, with one or more lives. The land so held was sometimes cultivated by the lessee. But it was a far more rapid road to wealth to parcel it out in patches of five, three, or even one acre, at extravagant rents to cottiers on yearly tenancy, or to let larger tracts on the same terms to groups of families in village partnership.[2]

In counties Monaghan, Roscommon and Tyrone there were many noteworthy examples of the first practice; in counties Cork, Galway, Kerry, Mayo and Sligo even more of the second.

Usually the top landlords commanded handsome rents from the middlemen, who in turn almost invariably extracted amazingly exorbitant ones from the cottiers. Vast rises in the population and an act of 1778 allowing Catholics 'to take, hold, and dispose of lands in the same manner as the Protestants'[3] had led to a considerable rise in overall land values. What was worse, the strong preference for easy access to a certain income more often than not resulted in actual cultivation being left in the hands of those with the smallest holdings, whose obligation to middlemen frequently exceeded double the rack-rent and whose resources generally fell lamentably below the level desirable for a satisfactory working of the soil. To ensure the highest money return, these unfortunates had overmuch recourse to corn crops – a habit which led, naturally enough, to the widespread exhaustion of their land. Still more astounding was the fact that during the earlier stages of our story those on the bottom rung of the landholders' ladder and actually tenants-in-possession were sometimes obliged to pay their rents twice over.

[1] *Two Centuries of Irish History*, ed. Bryce, p. 207.
[2] Ibid. p. 209.
[3] Ibid.

When anyone between the top landlord and the possessor defaulted and failed to pay up, the top landlord was entitled to demand the amount due from the hapless and fully paid-up possessor. Refusal to pay led either to distraint or eviction. Legislation of 1816 intended to suppress the abuse had had little effect. As late as 1825 it was still very common. Then, too, even quite substantial lessees were often obliged as part of very hard bargains to work off the amount of their rents with poorly rewarded labour, or abandon work on their own land for some on their landlords' whenever the demand came. But more dreadful than any other hardship was that of eviction for non-payment of rent. In Ulster evicted tenants usually received compensation under the custom known as Tenant Right,[1] but elsewhere sheer destitution stared them unrelentingly in the face. Such a fate was almost bound to have profound social repercussions in areas where it was common form. Peasant secret societies, indiscriminately referred to by many writers as 'Whiteboys' and 'Ribbonmen' sprang up with the one basic idea of either preventing eviction altogether, or, failing that, of depriving the offending landlords of new tenants. The problem had not begun with the Union, and agrarian unrest would have been rampant had there been neither eviction nor periodic famine, for the simple reason that the land-hunger meant many families depended upon plots that were quite incapable of yielding them a profit. When famine did come – and 1845–8 was merely the worst of several between the Union and Maria's death – the subsistence-economy structure of much of the south and west served to aggravate the situation most tragically. Small wonder then that public order became a chronic problem. To the Catholic peasantry, hardship on top of 'foreign' rule was adding untold injury to an unforgivable insult. During the first half of the nineteenth century some forty-six government measures sought to establish 'Coercion' in the land.[2] The life of the Anglo-Irish remained as ever the life of the frontiersman. 'Whitefeet' rural terrorists could ruin peace of mind every bit as effectively as 'Blackfoot' Red Indians.

[1] A clear explanation of Ulster Tenant Right is to be found in Richey, *The Irish Land Laws*, at pp. 103–7.

[2] A full list of the measures can be found in Fox, *A Key to the Irish Question*, p. 225.

Even for those tenants making both ends meet there were other irritations. At the markets where their produce had in most cases to be sold there was often the burden of tolls to be met. As at Edgeworthstown, the markets were frequently to be found only in an urban area under direct top-landlord surveillance. And for Catholics there were the crowning annoyances of payments due to the clergy of the Church of Ireland. Church rates and tithe were grievances of no mean order. Emigration was heavy, but it still left Ireland with all her problems, and, whoever was to blame, there was no denying their terrible and well-nigh insoluble nature. Nevertheless Maria Edgeworth was undoubtedly right in one thing – that the initial changes of attitude would have to come directly from the ruling class. Only by good leadership can severe political, social and economic tension be mitigated. In Britain a mixture of firmness and reform, coupled with the accidents of industrial and market prospects, had done much to undermine the force of Chartist agitation. In Ireland, of course, no corresponding weakening of O'Connellite agitation for Repeal, nor any diminution of a sense of separate nationality would have been accomplished by public any more than by private enlightenment, but local friction could well have been deprived of at least some of its edge. Landlords such as the Edgeworths and John Hamilton of St Ernan's, Donegal,[1] accomplished much. Yet the whole of their success in bringing spiritual and material amelioration was made possible by the great fact of British control. Without the authority of Dublin Castle their little 'paradises' would rapidly have succumbed to the inroads of irreconcilable disruptive forces. Even had the landlords embraced the Edgeworth approach to a man, British power would have been necessary, both to hold the situation steady while they got to work and to discourage outbreaks based on more strictly sentimental grounds once their task approached completion.

The virtually total association of Protestantism with the ruling and colonial minorities naturally worsened the political strain. Indeed the two factors were inextricably interwoven. With the vast population-increases of the nineteenth century the Catholic majority got bigger and bigger. In 1834 the

---

[1] John Hamilton committed his thoughts and memoirs on landlordism to paper, entitling them *Sixty Years' Experience as an Irish Landlord*.

Catholic population was estimated at just under 6,500,000, while Protestants of all denominations were said to number a trifle over 1,500,000. Of these, only 850,000 were members of the established Church of Ireland. O'Connell always claimed not to be questing for disestablishment, yet it is very hard to credit that with all the lesser religious grievances out of the way he would have rested content with the establishment in fact had he lived on into the fifties and sixties. At any rate the attack upon the privileges of the Church of Ireland that succeeded the fulfilment of nominal Catholic Emancipation suggests things would not have stood still. And this was the interpretation put upon prospects by the overwhelming proportion of the Ascendancy – Maria Edgeworth included. The same sense of insecurity which characterised attitudes on religious reform lay behind a deal of the intransigence upon land rights. It was more than a belief that 'Tenant's Right is Landlord's Wrong'. It was one that 'Tenant's End is Landlord's End' – that alien land ownership should be swept away and be replaced by a peasant proprietary system. Ireland, like many poor countries, conquered and unconquered alike, brought out an 'All or Nothing' attitude in rulers and ruled. The cause of religious reform got further because a minority Church could be deprived of privileges with less damage to the British hold on the country than any substantial shift towards Tenant Right over land in the south and west of it would have involved. The Protestants had never succeeded in holding the peasant mass in thrall, but in many ways landlordism was the Union and the Union landlordism. Here lay much of the trouble. Ostensibly the Union had offered Ireland justice between the factions. So bound up with the Orange side, however, did the British governments come to be – partly by design, partly because of disloyalty among the Greenites, and partly through the force of circumstances connected with the overwhelming respect for property felt in London – that the Union soon came to represent nothing but existing grievances writ larger for the Catholic majority, not only in political, but in economic and social matters as well.[1]

[1] McCulloch, *A Descriptive . . . Account of the British Empire*, ii 308, provides the 1834 denominational statistics. In his *Orangeism in Ireland and Britain*, H. Senior provides a full account of ultra-Protestant activity for much of our period.

John Hamilton of St Ernan's, Donegal, used interdenominational evangelism as the way through to his people on the
spiritual plane. His success in getting Catholic and Protestant
to joint Bible classes in the pre-Emancipation years was
nothing short of remarkable. His ability to bring parson, priest
and presbyter into friendly social intercourse was an achievement much after Maria Edgeworth's heart. Nevertheless she
never even dabbled in that kind of thing, let alone made it a
prime concern. Her religious neutrality betokened more than
the quest for tolerance – it signified her penchant for the rational
and Rousseauistic. Apart from the impossibility of getting the
Catholics and Protestants of Edgeworthstown to sit at the feet
of a common pastor, and apart from her complete unwillingness
to undertake any bid for that unenviable role on practical
grounds, her approach was essentially that of the lay educator.
With true eighteenth-century-style intellectualism she rejected
the path of unreflecting enthusiasm, preferring instead that of
education – academic, moral and practical. Catholicism was to
her something the intelligent person just had to look down upon.
Tolerance of it was an economic, political and social matter,
not expected to impinge upon the realms of the mind. For them
it was rank superstition – and so indeed were the most emotional
forms of Protestantism. And, as if this wasn't enough, her
cultural standards led her into disapproval of the bulk of the
priesthood – a body sadly beneath her requisites for gentlemen
made by birth or education. The truth of it was she saw her
role as something between a colonial civil servant and a
missionary rescuing the masses from inferior material and
spiritual practices. Priestly witch-doctors and the mumbo-
jumbo of the old Irish language she regarded with the same
scorn as Macaulay did the customs of the 'Hindoos'. But while
the people was to be saved from degradation, the landlord class,
in true James Mill style, was to go on ruling the roost as the
Lord's anointed. In the ultimate analysis, like Albert Schweitzer,
she was always aiming to remain a 'Friend of the People' and
its untiring guide rather than the instrument of profound social
revolution leading on to a transference of political authority into
'native' hands. She made the very best of being an 'intelligent
insider',[1] and dreamed of what today would be called racial

[1] See p. xxii of Watson's Introduction to his edition of ME's novel *Castle Rackrent*.

integration with all the essential features of the old order fundamentally unchanged.

The 'model' school at Edgeworthstown managed for long to fulfil the same socially unifying purpose as Hamilton's Bible classes. Far from being a breeder of potential Jacobins thirsting after the republicanism the Edgeworths themselves had briefly entertained back in the 1780s, it aimed at the production of solid citizens well versed in the things their station at the lower end of society would demand of them. 'The education of the lower classes', wrote Maria, 'must obviously in many respects differ from that of the higher.' Moreover the Three R's alone would not suffice.

> Without you inspire a general spirit of industry [she insisted] you may in vain distribute meat, drink and clothing to a few mendicant pensioners. Without you inspire a taste for cleanliness and order, it is in vain you build or plant for your cottagers . . . in vain you expect that the poor should neither be discontented or seditious, unless you teach them how their happiness is connected with their obedience to the laws and how those laws which are beneficial to society in general were advantageous to them in particular.

Latin and the intricate methods of bookkeeping, Pye's *Commentary upon Aristotle* and Dryden's 'Alexander's Feast' were not for the shoemakers, chimney-sweepers and butchers of county Longford. Misplaced instruction served only to aggravate a dangerous situation, but well-conceived curricula would inculcate labourers' children with the spirit of 'obedience, truth and honesty'. In a country like Ireland it was very necessary too that they should also come to perceive 'the horror of murder and the inevitability of punishment'. Industry and ingenuity in their betters would arouse eager emulation among them.[1]

That Maria combined much sense with her sensibility is well known. Nothing illustrates the fact better than a passage from her piece 'On the Education of the Poor' upon the theme: we must educate our servants.

> The enemies of liberty [she argued] would take advantage of the tide in public opinion, and would insinuate that all potential power should be taken from the people and that they should be kept in ignorance that they may be held in subjection. But it is too late to

[1] ME 'On the Education of the Poor' – an unpublished short memorandum, written during her father's lifetime and reiterating much of what had been said in *Practical Education* in 1798 (Edgeworth Papers).

uphold this system of mental coercion. The operations of thought are invisible to the eye of power, and no force can counteract them but that of reason. The press is a more powerful engine in society than the cannon, and all attempts to restrain the freedom of opinion will only endanger instead of preserving public tranquillity.

Why, she asks, should it be supposed that false doctrines should prevail if writings circulate freely? Surely prohibited matter acquires a special and unjustified value? As the poor were vastly influenced by the 'thinking part of the community', it was of the greatest consequence 'that the judgement of the middle classes of society should have free exercise'. Yet men could not live by enlightened principles, and the practical side of life required sustained treatment in educational establishments. Enthusiasm certainly led her badly astray when she claimed 'Those who cultivate the earth are independent in a great measure of others and all commodities are at the command of those who have a surplus of food to exchange for the labour and ingenuity of the artist or manufacturer', especially in the Irish context. Nevertheless it was true 'good husbandry' was essential to the national well-being and likely to foster good qualities among those engaged in it. Simple peasants would undoubtedly thrive upon happiness as well as upon good crops.[1]

Family enterprise coped with education at Edgeworthstown. Heart and mind were drawn to better things at all levels. As was to be expected, those at the lower ones received first priority. In Ireland generally, private schemes had long provided what education the masses were fortunate enough to undergo. In 1812, however, the annual report of the commissioners for education recommended state monetary support for the Kildare Place Society (founded the previous year), which aimed at 'promoting the education of the poor in Ireland' without attempting 'to influence or disturb peculiar religious tenets of any sort or description of Christians'.[2] Their idea was adopted, and the society grew accordingly, only to be displaced by a state system of education with the same ostensibly nonsectarian ends in 1831. From 1832 all pupils in its schools were supposed to receive religious instruction of the kind appropriate to their respective faiths quite separately from the bulk of the

[1] Ibid.
[2] *Two Centuries of Irish History*, ed. Bryce, p. 294.

education – something supposedly entirely drained of theological content. In practice one denomination or another came to dominate particular schools, and from the very beginning the most ardent sectarians had done their very best to stultify the overall aim. During the first stages Presbyterians rather than Catholics tended to come out most strongly as the villains of the piece. Later, all – Church of Ireland men included – spared few pains in the quest for denominational advantage. Another fine idea of the Edgeworth brand was wrecked on the rocks of Irish bigotry and, in the last analysis, on those compounding the great Irish question. Nor were things better at the university level. Official backing for 'godless institutions' – the Queen's Colleges of 1845 – led to endless sectarian chuntering. This time it was primarily Catholic, but Maria Edgeworth had nothing to say on the topic. Trinity College, Dublin, and the village school made up her picture of what was required in Irish education. In 1845 she was very old and not prepared to take up fresh enthusiasms. She already had enough causes on her hands to last most people a dozen lifetimes; so many of them had faltered and needed her zestful backing most urgently. Even had she felt inclined, therefore, the scope for added activity would have been painfully narrow and inadequate for the purpose.

At the time of the Union the Irish House of Commons had three hundred members. Of these county Longford had ten members – two for the county and two each for the four boroughs of Granard, Lanesborough, Longford and St Johnstown. Richard Lovell Edgeworth was sitting for the last of these in 1800. Before the readmission of Catholics to the franchise in 1793 the electorate had been very small indeed, but the changes of that year had meant that in all counties and some boroughs substantial increases had taken place.[1] Under the Union Ireland lost two-thirds of its members; county Longford four-fifths, keeping only its county members. Until the passing of Catholic Emancipation in 1829 the franchises remained unchanged. Then, however, the substitution of the ten-pound for the forty-shilling freeholder as the basis of the county electorates played havoc with Catholic strength – something not fully made up for by the changes of 1832 admitting ten-pound leaseholders with

[1] See the maps facing p. 116 of Johnston, *Great Britain and Ireland*.

twenty-one-year leases in the counties and the reform of the boroughs on a ten-pound occupier, freeholder and leaseholder basis.[1] Nor even by those of 1850, increasing the county electorate from a paltry 32,000 or so to 135,000.[2] County Longford contained about 700 electors in all prior to 1793. Just after the first Reform Act it mustered nearly 1300 on its county roll – its sole remaining electorate.[3] Potential Catholic power was increased there by leaps and bounds in 1793 alone, but with the abolition of the Protestant-dominated boroughs in 1800 the trend was quickened yet more. Only in 1829 did the Protestant potential increase again, but if landlord control broke down that meant little in a predominantly Catholic area. The 'Patriot' party could oust Ascendancy men at will if the Catholic electoral majority broke loose. At one time it was generally supposed that nothing in the nature of an important Catholic electoral 'revolt' occurred anywhere until 1826. Now the subject would appear to be open to argument.[4] For our immediate purposes, however, there is no need to resolve the point. County Longford's period of 'revolt' began in the 1830s. Local attitudes to Emancipation had been such as to deny opportunities for carpet-bagging Protestant landlords or fiery 'Patriot' Catholics before the cause was won. Only with Repeal did 'Patriotic' politics get powerfully on the move.

For Irish society in the last quarter of the eighteenth century the novels of Maria Edgeworth provide a truly excellent source of information and intelligent comment. In *Ennui* the role of the ideal estate-manager is thoroughly explored; in *Ormond* the churches and education are discussed at considerable length with great sympathy and understanding; in *Rosanna* elections get their due notice; and in *Vivian* again politics and the people is an important theme. To some extent the views expressed are

---

[1] See Gash, *Politics in the Age of Peel*, pp. 50–64.

[2] Whyte, *The Independent Irish Party*, p. 63.

[3] *General Register of Ireland, 1834*, p. 190.

[4] In his article 'Irish Parliamentary Elections and the Influence of the Catholic Vote, 1801–20' in *HJ* x (1967), P. J. Jupp argues that the readiness of Catholic voters to exert pressure upon their Protestant landlords has been underestimated. Maybe, but the overall impression given by the evidence produced suggests no more than that even in conditions of limited political freedom the rulers have to take the views of the ruled into account from time to time. A distortion has been corrected. It would, however, be nothing less than the creation of a new one to maintain that Catholic voters had formidable power in these years.

relevant and more than relevant to the themes of this book. And in the disapproval she feels for Thady Quirk's son, Jason, in *Castle Rackrent* there is an excellent example of how the principles of the later years were foreshadowed at an early stage.[1] Nevertheless what was written, albeit generally under the Union, about a period before it and what is not directly geared to situations as they actually came upon her are in many ways less valuable as evidence about the Ireland of the first half of the nineteenth century than letters and memoranda composed spontaneously from day to day. In these and these alone one can see best the Canute-like quality of so many of her thoughts and actions; the curiously Louisa M. Alcott quality transferred into some place reminiscent of the western frontier; the dilemma of the liberal 'White' in a quasi-colonial situation and the quest for integration of the deserving 'native' into 'White' society along lines still trodden by bodies such as the South African Progressive Party. So too one can make out the bold design of the Repealers in an age groping towards democracy for the United Kingdom. With the Repealers in this game were the Chartists, the Anti-Corn Law League and even the much neglected yet fascinating Anti-League of the protectionist tenant-farmers. Among a bunch of failures the Repealers came off best. Just why, shouts from the pages of Maria's correspondence. By 1849 the world of the novel *Patronage* was over and done with as surely as that of its fellow *The Absentee*. Often in the 1790s Maria claimed politics were 'above' her 'capacity and information'.[2] Experience made it impossible for her to say that and ring true about the 'now' of the 1820s and on, whatever had been the case during the 'then' of the Grattan régime. Working as a 'Friend of the People', above and alongside, but not merged in with it, she recorded her 'As it Happened'. This should belong to posterity.

[1] See the 1832 *Collected Edition* of her novels.
[2] ME to her aunt Mrs Ruxton, Oct 1796 (Edgeworth Papers).

1

The Path of Tolerance

FOR all her literary effort and enthusiasm, Maria Edgeworth very seldom thought of herself primarily as a writer. The force of tradition and the habits of mind engendered by social position, both in Ireland and elsewhere, made her prefer the role of Miss Edgeworth of Edgeworthstown in county Longford.[1] By 1821 the vital portion of her writing was done and most of her ideas on politics and society clearly formed.[2] At fifty-four she was coasting along on her reputation and largely immersing herself in the life of the Irish midland countryside, the ins and outs of which had long been engraved upon her heart and mind. The combination of feeling with thought is crucial to the understanding of both her views and actions. Quite rightly, she argued that what was desirable for any community resulted from the application of reason tempered by a sympathetic morality. What was generally true had an especially powerful relevance to Ireland, a country where bad feeling abounded and reason usually never went beyond the systematic quest for supremacy by mutually antagonistic sections of the community. To Maria, the ideal instrument for revolutionising Irish conditions was an enlightened governing class, by which

[1] See ME to the 6th Duke of Devonshire, 14 Aug. 1837 (Devonshire Papers). This letter is discussed in Appendix 1.

[2] *Helen*, of course, was published in 1834, and *Orlandino* in 1848. There were, moreover, other projects on hand during the ostensibly non-productive years that never saw a printing works. Among these were three novels: *Nora*, *Take for Granted* (a two-volume affair burnt by ME) and *Travellers*. Books for children still appeared up to 1826.

she meant the aristocracy and gentry made aware of their duties and willing to mitigate the full rigour of their technical rights. The greatest single influence on the formation of her outlook had been her father, whose death in 1817 was almost certainly the most important event of her whole life. From Richard Lovell Edgeworth were derived all her basic convictions about and plans for her public and private worlds. Only through an understanding of his thoughts, words and deeds can the daughter be truly fathomed and her thoughts, words and deeds have their full meaning revealed. Only through the end of one century can the beginning and course of the next be accurately interpreted.

The Edgeworths had owned land in county Longford since the reign of Elizabeth I, but, although part of his school and university education had been acquired in Ireland and although he had visited it many times, it was not until 1782 that Maria's father settled there.[1] She was then fifteen and had not previously spent any considerable time at Edgeworthstown, the little capital of the domain. Edgeworth was a man with a mission and straightway began that long, uphill, yet partially rewarding battle for improvement and enlightenment that was to bring him and his family so much fame and to become so ably recorded in works of fact, or what purported to be fiction.

When on a visit to his estates some nine years before, he had found the people there 'in a wretched state of idleness and ignorance'.[2] English servants had been necessary for putting the 'big house' into apple-pie order. The land required urgent attention, and conditions generally were such as would have daunted a lesser man. But in this case the response turned out to be as impressive as the challenge. 'Axe and plough were presently at work. The yew hedges and screens of clipped elms and hornbeam were cut down to let in air and the view of green fields. Carpenters and masons pulled down and built up.'[3] Straitened circumstances soon obliged a return to England and progress was halted, eager though Edgeworth was to carry out his plans. Because, however, he was a man of immense resilience, the passage of time did not sap his enthusiasm one iota. He returned to Ireland 'with a firm determination to

---

[1] ME was born in 1767 at Black Bourton, Oxfordshire.
[2] *The Black Book of Edgeworthstown*, ed. H. J. and H. E. Butler, p. 150.
[3] Ibid.

dedicate the remainder of his life to the improvement of his estate and to the education of his children; and further with the sincere hope of contributing to the melioration of the inhabitants of the country from which he drew his subsistence'.[1] Before long the people said 'His Honour anyway is good pay'.[2] Yet that was a small part of it all. Good tenants found themselves accorded *de facto* Tenant Right, sub-division was drastically curtailed, duty fowl and duty work were abolished, tenants were forbidden to act in partnerships or in common, many fines and penalties were omitted from leases (though the ones concerning alienation or sub-letting always remained unmitigated), a year's rent was left in the tenant's hands and the driver was forbidden to threaten seizure of goods or take money on account. In future all rents were to be paid over to him at his house and the day of the middleman thus came virtually to a close.

So uncommon was this English approach that his fame rapidly spread far and wide. Few landlords of the time were so just and gentlemanly, and scarcely any so unbiased in political and religious affairs. Lack of bias against men for their opinions does not, of course, denote in this case any indifference to public matters. Edgeworth's progress was all aimed at the improvement of the social system, not its replacement by something revolutionary. Enlightened conservatism meant higher profits and more benefit all round. Such a development consolidated him and his in the 'big house'. Justice went far towards bringing Catholic tenants to accept a Protestant landlord. Yet this was not all, for in the very year of Edgeworth's return to Ireland the Irish Parliament had acquired a greater degree of independence from Britain, and the aristocracy and gentry began a series of moves designed to create a unified feeling of Irish nationality in place of faction and, through it, conditions in which the past could be forgotten. The régime, known as Grattan's Parliament,[3] also hoped better economic conditions resulting from freer overseas trade would help the process along. The tragedy was that only by a comprehensive

[1] Ibid. p. 156.
[2] Ibid. p. 157.
[3] For a thorough treatment of this arrangement, see Johnston, *Great Britain and Ireland*, passim.

type policy, such as that applied at Edgeworthstown, could something substantial be achieved. Social conditions would in any case have been difficult in Ireland. A large and under-privileged Catholic majority, including very few landowners or wealthy business or professional men, could only be reached by the leaders of the privileged Protestant minority through quite striking policies. Straightforward measures of equality before the law, falling short of complete emancipation of Catholics and opportunities for the educated minority amongst them, were not going to smooth over the consequences of the Williamite victory at the Boyne. The Catholic Church was to remain dissatisfied, and the sufferings feeding rural discontents led in freer conditions to the outbreaks culminating in the 1798 rebellion.[1] Once the Grattanite policy was shown to be bank-rupt, the sole hope for the enlightened aristocracy and gentry lay in a legislative Union with Great Britain (together with a completion of Catholic Emancipation) and rural reforms admini-stered with understanding. Edgeworth conquered his peasants' prejudices for things such as sub-division through kindness and suggestion, rather than by command. Example more than precept carried his points. Unhappily for Ireland most of the enlightened did not want a Union, full Catholic Emancipation did not accompany its fulfilment, and social policy generally remained static. A great chance was provided in 1800. Ireland's level of civilisation could certainly have been raised, her sectarian feuds much mitigated and her agrarian troubles considerably eased by a government with courage and the right convictions. The king (George III), the problems of foreign affairs and undue reliance upon selfish Tory interests in Ireland when faced with disorder and difficulties all led the British into a political cul-de-sac.

The greatest irony of Edgeworth's position was that in the last analysis his place was behind the Government. Whatever

---

[1] A large literature exists on this rebellion. Among the most useful works on it are RLE's own memoirs (begun by himself and finished by Maria); *A Memoir of Maria Edgeworth* by her stepmother, the fourth Mrs RLE, who outlived her; and several books of a general nature or dealing with areas outside the county Longford: Dickson, *Revolt in the North*; Madden, *Antrim and Down in '98* and *Ireland in '98*, ed. Daly; McHugh, *Carlow in '98*; and Ronan's edition of Cullen's *Insurgent Wicklow*. Maxwell, *History of the Irish Rebellion in 1798*, also provides much interesting fact.

Maria Edgeworth in old age

for synett.

my mother: ——— 1825

on the little sycamo

A view of Edgeworthstown House

his criticisms, he could not countenance rebellion, for his whole *raison d'être* in the country depended upon the Ascendancy remaining the Ascendancy and calling the tune of Irish politics. Yet amongst that Ascendancy his voice and the voices of those who thought like him carried little weight. His dilemma was a cruel one, and his daughter Maria first shared and then inherited it. Like the Moores of Moore Hall in county Mayo, Edgeworth regarded the Union as 'an indispensable step towards the civilisation of Ireland'. It would 'diffuse British customs and manners'.[1] Maria too accepted this as both valid and desirable. She had learned how to manage an Irish estate as early as 1791. Her novels were published either at the very end of the Grattan-ite period or under the Union. All but two appeared before her father's death and, *Castle Rackrent* apart, owe an enormous amount to his influence. They combine an intimate knowledge of the Catholic Irish masses with a didactic optimism, the basic assumption of which is that the aristocracy had it within its power to save Ireland from the 'horrible revolutionists'[2] and bring in a period of peaceful co-operation under Ascendancy guidance. When O'Connell's movement for Repeal finally convinced her that the ends she sought were a chimera, she ceased to publish material about Irish society in her usual manner. Indeed, she wrote hardly anything at all for publication. By 1834 she was complaining: 'It is impossible to draw Ireland as she now is in a book of fiction. . . . We are in too perilous a case to laugh, humour would be out of season, worse than bad taste.'[3] From 1817 until the Repeal movement got under way, Maria cherished her hopes, placing what often amounted to a naïve faith in the efficacy of the completion of Catholic Eman-cipation as a panacea for Ireland's social and political ills. She chose to forget the logic of her own convictions about estate-management and landlord–tenant relations with its inexorable conclusions on the needs for social changes. After this gigantic piece of self-deception the ultimate disappointment was all the more vexing. Bitter touches enter into her letters and conversa-tion. Fortunately for the historian, her small published literary output in these years is made up for in part by a voluminous

---

[1] J. Hone, *The Moores of Moore Hall*, p. 48.
[2] *Memoir*, I 145.
[3] *Memoir*, III 85.

correspondence, some of which was devoted to the discussion of public affairs. O'Connell's Emancipation and Repeal movements provided the first serious challenge to Ascendancy leadership in Ireland, and it is therefore from the revival of the Catholic question in 1821 that the story of her reactions to the stirrings from beneath can best be recounted.

Her activities were carried on in varying economic conditions. The vast majority of the 'downs' were due to the misdeeds of her well-intentioned but spendthrift and drunken brother, Lovell. His reckless stewardship as joint trustee under his father's will led to Maria having to take over full management of the estates from 1826 until 1839, when Francis Edgeworth relieved her. His decision to act released one, George Hinds, the agent appointed before the débâcle for work on his own estate. Maria had found him invaluable in coaxing the tenants into paying up old debts and handing over sums as they became due. Then it was that the good will built up by the father paid off handsomely, some tenants actually lending Maria money to meet pressing demands from creditors. Income from Edgeworth property in Ireland reached £3700 sterling by 1817.[1] Two decades later it was undoubtedly higher. Nevertheless a debt which stood at £26,000 sterling in 1826 was not easily wiped out, although it was more than halved in two to three years by an intelligent use of regular payment as an incentive to reduction of claims and by simple parsimony stepping up the rate of repayment. The strain for Maria must have been enormous, especially as she regularly used her private money to meet commitments before funds were forthcoming from the tenantry. A situation such as this did much to bind her affections to the farmers and peasantry still more. Interdependence was something in which she needed no instruction. After 1833, however, when C. Sneyd Edgeworth bought out Lovell, following another of his financial forays, the pressure on her must have eased. The more so as Lovell left for England and closed his famous but financially calamitous school. From 1818 until 1828 the school had brought more overall pleasure than pain. It had managed to abolish the gulf between Catholics and Protestants and thus had achieved at a local level what the Edgeworths

---

[1] Income from the 'trust estate' was £2500, and an estate worth £1200 had been settled on Lovell in his mother's marriage settlement.

wished to see as a national phenomenon. Religious instruction was given by the priest and parson to their respective flocks and the later Birmingham-inspired solution for the religious difficulty in English and Welsh education was simply a copy of this system. Just what happened when Ireland was treated to an attempt to follow the Edgeworth ideal during the 1830s has already been explained. The initial success also underlined interdependence. The disappointing sequel depressed Maria still more at a time when her political ideals were being shattered. A little material comfort from better-ordered finances hardly provided an adequate recompense in such circumstances.[1]

The Irish political system into which O'Connell launched his thunderbolts proved very vulnerable.[2] At the Union most of the closed boroughs had been swept away and no fewer than sixty-four of the hundred allotted to Ireland in the United Kingdom House of Commons belonged to the counties. These had quite a wide electorate, a high proportion of which were humble forty-shilling freeholders. Most of these were Catholics, except in the north-east, but almost everywhere they served largely as election fodder for their landlords. Provided they could be persuaded to risk opposing their social superiors, the old order would not weather the storm. When O'Connell contrived to link the patriotic and nationalistic self-assertion of the new Catholic middle class to the agrarian and nationalist discontents of the rural masses through the medium of the Catholic priesthood, a weapon was forged giving independence to the movement for Catholic Emancipation and reducing the import-

---

[1] The information presented above can be found in an appendix (dated April 1839) written on RLE's will by ME (Edgeworth Papers and *The Black Book of Edgeworthstown*, ed. Butler).

[2] The most useful works devoted to O'Connell's Catholic Emancipation and Repeal of the Union campaigns are: Gwynn, *Daniel O'Connell*; Lecky, *Leaders of Public Opinion in Ireland*, II; Machin, *The Catholic Question in English Politics*; MacIntyre, *The Liberator*; McCaffrey, *Daniel O'Connell and the Repeal Year*; Nowlan, *The Politics of Repeal*; Reynolds, *The Catholic Emancipation Crisis in Ireland*; *The Life and Speeches of Daniel O'Connell, M.P.*, ed. J. O'Connell; and *Daniel O'Connell: nine centenary essays*, ed. Tierney. Several learned articles are also of considerable value. They are: Blackall and Whyte, 'Correspondence on O'Connell and the Repeal Party', in *IHS* XII (1960); Graham, 'The Lichfield House Compact, 1835', in *IHS* XII (1961); Inglis, 'O'Connell and the Irish Peers, 1800–1842', in *IHS* VIII (1952); Large, 'The House of Lords and Ireland in the Age of Peel, 1832–50', in *IHS* IX (1955); Machin, 'The Catholic Emancipation Crisis of 1825', in *EHR* LXXVIII (1963); and Whyte, 'Daniel O'Connell and the Repeal Party', in *IHS* XI (1959).

ance of those like the Edgeworths who supported change from the angle of enlightened Protestantism. One essential thing the new Catholic Association of 1823 still needed was sympathetic Protestant parliamentary candidates, for it was towards gaining the right to sit in parliament that the first great O'Connellite campaign was directed. Technically speaking, a great deal of Catholic Emancipation had been won, or granted rather, before the Union. At the general election of 1826 several counties returned Emancipationist Protestants against the wishes of the local magnates. A serious forty-shilling-freeholder revolt had begun. Two years later O'Connell himself was illegally elected for county Clare and a civil war threatened. Early the next year the Government caved in – but a high price was exacted. In return for almost complete equality of rights O'Connell had to tolerate a narrowing of the franchise to exclude the forty-shilling freeholders, face the suppression of the Catholic Association and endure the prospect of other kindred organisations being dissolved in future.[1]

Throughout these years Maria Edgeworth preserved the political ideals of the optimist. It was as much because of as despite the disorders of the 1790s that, throughout the strife leading up to Catholic Emancipation and the diminution in the importance of tolerant Protestants on the Irish scene, she cherished her father's moderate Whig political beliefs: constitutional monarchy, based on the Rule of Law and equality of rights; mutual toleration between the social classes and religious denominations; the encouragement of high standards of public and private devotion to duty; and the elimination of chronic discontents through the regularly appointed channels with an eye to general satisfaction – all carefully planned and controlled by the 'Friends of the People', not the 'People' itself – these were the ideals near to her heart and acceptable to her mind.

Writing to her aunt Mrs Ruxton in 1796 she declared herself 'proud of the honor' of having been asked to 'criticise' on a political subject she felt to be 'far above' her 'capacity and information'. 'Were the subject any other than Politics', she adds, her aunt would find her 'pert and ready'.[2] Even as late

---

[1] See J. O'Connor, *History of Ireland*, I 178–83.

[2] ME to her aunt Mrs Ruxton (*née* Margaret Edgeworth, the sister of RLE), Oct 1796 (Edgeworth Papers).

as 1803 she writes of a politician that he spoke well, but whether 'on the wrong or right side of the question, like a true woman' she would not trouble herself 'to enquire'.[1] No such nonchalance held her back later, and in the novel *Helen*, published in 1834, the opinion is expressed in no uncertain terms that a young woman, 'as a rational being', could not 'go through the world as it now is without forming any opinion on points of public importance' and satisfy herself 'with the common namby-pamby little missy phrase, "Ladies have nothing to do with politics" '.[2] Maria practised what she latterly preached, even before her father's death, and during the Emancipation campaign she drew up, probably for use in a novel, a list of items under the headings of 'Evils of Ireland' and 'Remedies'.

She thought 'Party Spirit' derived from a want of confidence, of unanimity, of employment, of money and of honesty. Families of all ranks were living beyond their means. The country, she declared, was 'mortgaged twice over', a comment very likely made with deep personal feeling. Emigration of many good workers and the chronic absenteeism among landlords did untold harm, not to mention sectarian strife and inequality of political rights. The established Anglican Church had an excessively high income and with Catholic disabilities alongside made for serious and widespread trouble. And here she interposes a note making crystal clear the Edgeworth suspicion of Catholicism: 'Catholics *can* and should have equal rights. But *must* not have a *dominant* religion.' Again the basic contention is that the Protestant-dominated 'Quality' should control the country. All the masses – Catholic and Protestant alike – were unfitted for political authority. The Catholic masses might well replace Protestant, Old Presbyter by a New Priest writ large. An enlightened ruling *élite* was therefore the best guarantee for general liberties. The imperfections of the Union troubled her, not least the failure to achieve mutual liking and a 'Union of Hearts'. Jealousy of 'England' was far too rife, and 'opinion and law' were not going in the same direction. Part of the reason for these evils was the 'insolence of magistrates, who make the laws appear *all* on their side and *parties* concerned against the people'. This applied with an especial force to the controversies

[1] ME to Sophy Ruxton, 18 Dec 1803 (Edgeworth Papers).
[2] *Helen*, 1st ed. II 233.

surrounding application of the game laws. In her view a way
out of all this lay through making the Union one of hearts,
under which British industry and commerce would 'hazard their
capital in Ireland'; through rural good will whereby the
peasantry secured itself by joining with the 'Irish proprietors'
in agricultural enterprise; through the *élite* retraining the
peasantry; and through correcting the strong tendency towards
unpunctuality by *'paying* wages'.[1] Seldom can so telling and
comprehensive an indictment of a whole society have been made
with such a spirit of detachment, and the remedy proffered with
such simplicity and truthfulness. The whole grand solution was
based on the precept Maria's father had daily inculcated into his
children: 'He used to say that with this power of improving
they might in time be anything, and without it in time they
would be nothing.'[2] Perhaps an English education gave her the
capacity for a bird's eye point of view in Ireland. At all events
her comments hit the bull's eye. Moderation would have
accomplished much in Ireland, although its methods could not
have been spectacular. This and the prospect of perpetuating the
ascendancy of Protestantism made it doubly distasteful to most
Catholics of the middle and lower classes.

Although, strictly speaking, her ideal of Irish nationality
perished with the outbreak of the 1798 rebellion, the Union did
not bring Maria to abandon her feeling of being Irish. Despite
the hundred Irish members in the Commons and the Irish lay
and ecclesiastical peers in the Lords, she always referred to
Westminster as the 'English' Parliament. Most of her novels
display a distaste for politicians. After 1817, however, a change
took place in her outlook. The removal of her father's influence
undoubtedly played some part in bringing this about; so too
did her greater involvement with local affairs. But the greatest
single reason for the shift was almost certainly her increasing
contacts with men such as Lansdowne and Spring-Rice.[3] In

---

[1] From a notebook of ME's (Edgeworth Papers).

[2] Ibid.

[3] Henry Petty-Fitzmaurice, 3rd Marquess of Lansdowne (1780–1863), had
succeeded to the title in 1809, having served in the House of Commons for six
years. An active supporter of slave-trade abolition and liberal causes generally, he
was largely instrumental in creating the link-up between certain Whigs and the
followers of Canning upon which the Canning ministry of 1827 was based. Having
served as Lord President of the Council under Lord Grey from 1830, he held
office on and off up to 1841 and again between 1846 and 1852. Though in the

1818 she was down at Bowood,[1] and while in London she had
been a welcome visitor at many Whig houses. This is not to
say that she became in any way narrowly partisan. Being
committed to particular ends did not in any way necessarily
involve supporting a particular group to the exclusion of all
others. This was especially true with regard to Catholic
Emancipation, on which not only the Whigs, but a large proportion of the Tories were on the liberal side. Not for nothing
was the issue left an open one in Lord Liverpool's Cabinet. Her
attitude was, nevertheless, formed by profounder factors. At
bottom the willingness to accept what she regarded as improvements from any British quarter derived from something
amounting to an equivalent of a civil-service approach strongly
impregnated with missionary zeal. The very nature of her
attitude, though recognisable as a species of party political
commitment in Britain, was way up above the factions of
'emerald green' and 'bitter orange'[2] in Ireland. Like an administrator or missionary in many an Asian or African colony,
she represented in her aims and objects the powers-that-be
outside the country. The governments of Liverpool, Canning,
Goderich and Wellington, which held office in the 1820s, were
predominantly Tory, the last overwhelmingly so. Yet Maria's
object was always to get the measure. She never cared from
whom.

The early 1820s were exciting for her. She was in and out of
Ireland as never before, visiting England in 1820, 1821 and
1822, and Scotland in 1823. The result was that her general
political education went on apace. Meetings with Whig
notables were renewed and introductions to figures such as

Cabinet until 1863, he held no specific office during the last eleven years. His
doctrinal position had invariably been that of a very moderate Whig. In Ireland
he owned vast estates, especially in county Kerry.

Thomas Spring-Rice, 1st Baron Monteagle (1790–1866), first sat in the House of
Commons as Member for Limerick from 1820 and attempted to interest the
Canning ministry in Irish reforms. Under Lord Grey he was Secretary to the
Treasury, and Chancellor of the Exchequer in Melbourne's second administration
until 1839. Although responsible for the introduction of the penny post in that year,
he became rather unpopular, particularly with the extreme left, and was disappointed in his hopes for the Speakership. A peerage was given to him by way of
compensation.

[1] Lord Lansdowne's country house near Calne in Wiltshire.
[2] ME to CSE, 12 Feb 1835 (*Memoir*, III 168–71).

Ricardo[1] and Wilberforce[2] obviously did much to widen her outlook. Generally speaking the Edgeworth family was as one on politics at this time. A letter from Mrs Frances Edgeworth, her stepmother, to C. Sneyd Edgworth of 14 May 1821 can therefore be taken as a true reflection of Maria's views. 'Alas', she comments, 'when will the Catholic emancipation be granted? When will people's eyes be opened?' The last session of Parliament 'has been a dead one' and 'Year chases year. Decay chases decay. . . . Each succeeding year' she has 'lived, some right, some freedom has been torn from our once glorious constitution'. It seemed 'as if there was an impossibility of maintaining of government'.[3] Maria's tone the following spring was more buoyant. Time spent in London listening to parliamentary debates had lessened her tendency to regard 'country gentlemen' as the sole repository of political good. Despite Lord Londonderry's[4] 'grammatical blunders and malapropisms', for which the excellent performances of Peel[5] and Vansittart[6] for the Government and those of Brougham[7] and Denman[8] for

[1] David Ricardo (1772–1823), a leading economist of the period and the principal founder of the classical school of political economy.

[2] William Wilberforce (1759–1833), the leader of the anti-slavery movement and a prominent evangelical.

[3] ME to CSE, 14 May 1821 (Edgeworth-Beaufort Papers).

[4] Robert Stewart, 2nd Marquess of Londonderry, better known as Lord Castlereagh (1769–1821). He had been William Pitt the Younger's main agent in negotiating for the British–Irish Union and prominent as Foreign Secretary at the peacemaking in 1814–15. Commonly regarded as an arch-reactionary by his political opponents, he was in fact quite liberal on most fundamental matters in public life and a firm believer in the Concert of Europe. *Castlereagh*, by C. J. Bartlett, is the latest and best study of his life.

[5] Sir Robert Peel, 2nd Baronet (1788–1850), then out of office after serving 1812–18 as Chief Secretary for Ireland. The next year (1822) he became Home Secretary. For the earlier stages of his career, see Gash, *Mr Secretary Peel*; Lecky, *Historical and Political Essays*; and *Sir Robert Peel*, ed. Parker, vol. I.

[6] Nicholas Vansittart, 1st Baron Bexley (1766–1851), currently Chancellor of the Exchequer in the Liverpool Government.

[7] Henry Peter Brougham, Baron Brougham and Vaux (1778–1868), a leading Whig spokesman and ultimately Lord Chancellor. For him, see Aspinall, *Lord Brougham and the Whig Party*, and New, *Henry Brougham to 1830*. For his party at this time, see Davis, *The Age of Grey and Peel*, and Mitchell, *The Whigs in Opposition, 1815–1830*.

[8] Thomas Denman, 1st Baron Denman (1779–1854), Solicitor-General to Queen Caroline and instrumental in securing the withdrawal of the Government's Bill of Pains and Penalties against her. In 1831 he, as Whig Attorney-General, drafted the Reform Bill in 1831 and was raised to the peerage in 1834. Subsequently he became Lord Chief Justice.

the Opposition more than made up, she was left with a most favourable impression of Westminster. 'Upon the whole', she wrote, 'the speaking and the witness of the scene far surpassed our expectations. We felt most proud to mark the real difference between the English House of Commons and the French Chambre des Députés.' But while Whiggery caused her to rhapsodise about constitutional forms, it also provoked her mind into protest about public grievances and the need for remedying them through the proper use of these same forms. '*Nevertheless*', she went on, 'there are some disturbances in Suffolk and Lord Londonderry was obliged to get up from dinner to order troops to be sent there – before he had swallowed two mouthsful he rose after reading his despatches.'[1] Life in London had not left her uninformed, and the very next month 'a rush of blood took place in' her 'whiggish' body on entering Londonderry House as a guest. Calm was restored a little later, however, when the Tory prime minister's house proved 'wretched indeed' and its furniture 'shabby' 'when compared' to the *ménage* sported by the leader of the Whig Opposition.[2]

Great too was the satisfaction afforded by a visit to Spring-Rice. The fact was reported back to Mrs Edgeworth: 'We have just breakfasted with Spring Rice our Irish patriot, who has all the characteristic excellencies of his nation without, as far as I can see, any of those counterbalancing defects with which our countrymen are reproached. He has genius without imprudence and generosity without extravagance.'[3] A firm friendship soon sprang up between Maria and the Spring-Rices. He promised to visit Edgeworthstown and inspect Lovell's school,[4] and his wife invoked Maria's aid in searching for a children's governess.[5] Once contacts became firmly established the topics of discussion multiplied fast. Early in 1824 he is proposing exchanges with Maria on the subjects of 'flax, meal, schools, bog, priests and 150 other topics affecting our country'.[6] On 14 March Maria produced a gigantic missive packed with

[1] ME to HE, 11 March 1822 (Edgeworth Papers).
[2] HE to Harriet Beaufort, 1 April 1822 (Edgeworth Papers).
[3] ME to Mrs RLE 28 May 1822 (Edgeworth Papers).
[4] ME to TSR, 18 Aug 1824 (Monteagle Papers, NLI MS 13346).
[5] ME to TSR 25 Aug 1824 (Monteagle Papers, NLI, MS 13346).
[6] TSR to ME 19 Feb 1824 (Monteagle Papers, NLI, MS 13346).

comment on a plan of his for Irish rehabilitation.[1] He in turn
sent her a paper on Irish affairs with remedies for various
problems and declared she should have more information as it
became available.[2] In July Maria felt quite satisfied at the way
things were going at Westminster, stating:

> The discussions which have taken place in your Parliament res-
> pecting Ireland and the examinations before the Committee –
> though the evidence only on our side of the question in favour of the
> necessity of continuing this year the insurrection act is all that has
> yet come out fully – will be of essential service. More light has
> been thrown upon the state of Ireland than had ever reached English
> eyes in the course of several hundred years. . . . All now depends
> upon the sincerity of good government. *All*, no – but all for the
> present.[3]

Order had in her view to be fully maintained before law could
rule and useful change be implemented; pure charity avoided so
as to stimulate self-help and greater honesty in the peasantry;
and education and instruction on neutral lines energetically and
systematically pursued to raise the levels of prosperity and
civilisation. Here was no rabblerouser!

The year 1825 was one of high hopes and deep disappointment for liberals and Catholics alike. Spring-Rice kept Maria
informed of what was afoot, pursuing Emancipation and general
Irish reform with 'the warm heart of an Irishman and Irish
gentleman' and hoping for a major breakthrough.[4] Writing on
2 May to her American Jewish friend Mrs Lazarus (formerly
Miss Mordecai), Maria showed herself optimistic:

> We hope that we are this moment on the eve of a great national
> benefit. We hope that what is called Catholic emancipation will be
> granted this session by the English Parliament. If this be done the
> people will be contented and quiet. English capital, now overflowing
> will flow over here, set industry in motion all over this country
> and induce habits of punctuality, order and economy – virtues and
> happiness which have for centuries been unknown to the despairing
> oppressed Irish population. If this Bill do not pass, or if we have
> not reason to hope that it will be passed next Session, we shall have
> reason to fear more than ever from the disappointment of highly
> raised expectation. I seldom say a word on any political topic –
> but this comes home to every family, every cabin, every heart.

[1] ME to TSR, 14 March 1824 (Monteagle Papers, NLI, MS 13346).
[2] TSR to ME, 29 June 1824 (Monteagle Papers, NLI, MS 13346).
[3] ME to TSR, 10 July 1824 (Monteagle Papers, NLI, MS 13346).
[4] ME to TSR, 3 April 1825 (Monteagle Papers, NLI, MS 13346).

Certainly her family and heart were deeply engaged, and although the piece about comment on politics was undoubtedly untrue, all was profoundly sincere. So too were her concluding remarks, ridiculously fanciful or not. 'Vast companies of men of science and commercial enterprise', she averred, 'have been formed in England for working our mines, establishing manufactories – making canals – working slate quarries – mills etc. in Ireland. One of the companies begins its prospectus with these words: "Our capital is two millions." From this you may judge of the extent of the issues at stake and of the multitudes whose hopes and fears are set upon the cast.'[1]

A month later her mood had not changed so much as might have been expected after yet another failure to pass Emancipation. Spring-Rice had sent more official reports to Edgeworthstown and Maria was elated. 'They are most valuable. It is impossible but what they must do good – let the Duke of York[2] say, or do what he pleases. This body of evidence will spread among the people and counteract the prejudices of "John Bull" and his fear of the Papists – at least part of it, if he deserves Shakespeare's definition of Man, which Burke, you know, pronounces to be his best. "Man is a creature holding large discourse, looking before and after." "*John*" is of few words, but I think he is apt enough to look before and after.'[3] This same day, 6 June, another instalment was sent off across the Atlantic to Mrs Lazarus. Apparently the future was not going to be so black as originally anticipated. 'The Irish Catholics, whose hopes had been much excited by feeling their object almost attained' had 'borne their disappointment with great temper' and much was 'attempting now in Ireland by English mercantile companies who have capital and scientific skill. *If* the want of the habits of punctuality in the workmen and lower orders of my but half-educated countrymen do not frustrate these attempts to establish manufactories and keep industry in employment, Ireland will become a flourishing and happy country.' Her own family was involved in one such enterprise and Mrs Lazarus's interest had appeared so marked that an

---

[1] ME to Mrs Lazarus (*née* Mordecai), May 1825 (Edgeworth Papers 2).

[2] Frederick Augustus, Duke of York and Albany (1763–1827), second son of George III and an unsuccessful soldier—not to mention his exploits as a philanderer and reactionary.

[3] ME to TSR, 6 June 1825 (Monteagle Papers, NLI, MS 13346).

actual prospectus was enclosed for her perusal. William Edgeworth had been engaged as one of the engineers and was at that
time down at Valentia in county Kerry 'clearing out great slate
quarries and examining the capabilities of the harbour – a very
fine one.'[1] Two steam vessels had been ordered for 'Valentia
to trade with *America.*' Shortly afterwards William himself was
recording the arrival of O'Connell down at Cahirciveen. The
bonfires had burned on the Douglas mountains and the 'inhabitants had deserted their town to meet him on the road and
drew him in to his estate'.[2] Excitement was still mounting
despite the setback in Parliament. By December Spring-Rice
was trying to take his opponents from behind through arguing
for Emancipation solely 'on the highest Protestant principles'.[3]

The general election of 1826[4] passed off very quietly in
county Longford, but in neighbouring county West Meath
things proved much livelier. Violent death and violent drinking
marred the voting. Social cleavages between the liberal and
illiberal aristocracy and gentry went deep and from it the
revolutionary elements took considerable comfort. For Maria,
however, the immense peasant defections in such counties as
Louth, Monaghan and Waterford had been a painless process.
The triumph of liberal Protestants appeared all that was great
and good. Her quest for Emancipation therefore slackened not
one whit. Spring-Rice's claim that 'the safety of the Protestant
Establishment in Ireland requires Catholic Emancipation'[5]
called forth her enthusiastic approval. Not that her critical
faculty was asleep. Admittedly there was an element of the
'willing suspension of disbelief' in overlooking the more
sinister sides of Irish Catholicism, yet even at this point the
superiority of Protestant education and the bigoted attitude of
most priests towards mixed schools were prominent in her
mind.

Some signs of uneasiness in the family during the spring of
1827 concerned, not so much the risks of liberalism, as the

[1] ME to Mrs Lazarus, 6 June 1825 (Edgeworth Papers).
[2] William Edgeworth to FE, 30 Aug 1825 (Edgeworth-Beaufort Papers).
[3] TSR to ME, 13 Dec 1825 (Monteagle Papers, NLI, MS 13346).
[4] R. W. Greaves in his article 'Roman Catholic Relief and the Leicester Election
of 1826', in *TRHS* 4th ser. xxii (1940), sheds some interesting light upon the
effects of the Emancipation issue in one large English industrial town.
[5] ME to TSR, 14 Feb 1827 (Monteagle Papers, NLI, MS 13346).

ill-effects of its opposite. Mrs Edgeworth confided some of
them to her brother the Rev. William Beaufort on 27 March.
Illness had made it certain Lord Liverpool[1] would be replaced
as prime minister, and it was not at all certain at first that
Canning[2] would in fact succeed him. The great problem was the
split in the forces behind the Liverpool administration on the
Emancipation issue. Canning's liberalism was bound to cause
him enormous difficulties, yet Ireland would not stand still
while they were being ironed out. 'What', asks Mrs Edgeworth,
'will be the end of this same Catholic Question? And, still more,
what will become of this devoted island with all the differences,
religious and political, which keep the minds of the people in a
constant state of fermentation. All the bad passions finding
excuses and all the ungoverned spirits ready to explode! What,
think of the conversions. One even at Edgeworthstown. Have
you had any? . . . One clear thing is the making the breach far
wider, far more irreconcilable than ever.'[3] Nevertheless
Canning's becoming premier and the Lansdowne Whigs
joining him encouraged her much.[4] In April, again to her
brother, she wrote: 'The change in the Ministry is most
astonishing – the question is – will it last? I think the getting
Lord Lansdowne to join them will make a liaison with the real
Whigs that may steady them very much. . . . What is to be
done about the Catholics? Nous verrons.'[5]

At the Longford assizes of July 1827 C. Sneyd Edgeworth
actually encountered O'Connell, 'who was down special, made
a furious speech and won his cause'. After a meeting over the
dinner-table Sneyd adjudged him vain, entertaining and good-
hearted. A local crowd was less critical and chaired the great
man around the town before he left for Dublin – an experience
that cannot have helped to settle the turbot and lobster sauce

[1] For a good account of the last years of the Liverpool ministry, see Brock,
Lord Liverpool and Liberal Toryism.

[2] Rolo, *George Canning*, is a highly useful general account of its subject's
political career. Sir Charles Petrie's work with the same title is, however, still
well worth reading.

[3] Mrs RLE to the Rev. William Beaufort, 27 March 1827 (Edgeworth-Beaufort
Papers).

[4] Aspinall, 'The Canningite Party', in *TRHS* 4th ser. xvii (1934), provides the
background necessary for a proper understanding of this development.

[5] Mrs RLE to the Rev. William Beaufort, 27 April 1827 (Edgeworth-Beaufort
Papers).

partaken of as his fast-day dinner.[1] A little later the Edgeworth
links with the more respectable side of the Emancipation
movement was strengthened when Spring-Rice accepted office.
He wrote to Maria:

> It is not for me to guess how we may strengthen and consolidate, but
> I feel sanguine that we shall deserve success as far as motives can
> entitle us to do so. To me, individually, in my present position it is
> delightful that all my relations with Irish affairs are more intimate
> than ever and that I am placed with the individual for whom, of all
> public men, I feel the strongest respect and confidence.

As an ardent admirer of Canning, Maria accepted wholeheartedly
Spring-Rice's claim that he had become 'an office man' 'without
any sacrifice of public principle'.[2] Indeed on 6 August she went
further and sent him a veritable encomium of his chief.

> I hope [she stressed] Mr Canning's health will *last* and enable his
> temper to endure all it ought and *must* if he means to keep his
> painful preeminence. England may glory in the disinterestedness
> that has been shown in the last trials of the characters of her states-
> men and senators. While such public virtue lasts in any country
> that country may be certain of surmounting all difficulties – in
> time. . . . We in Ireland must and will have patience. We are a
> confiding people and you will deserve our confidence.[3]

Nearer home the less acceptable side of Catholicism was making
itself felt, not only through violence in politics, but by a
resurgence of educational bigotry. On the other hand the then
current Protestant proselytism could not have been expected to
remain unchallenged.

Despite concern about the state of the Irish Poor Law and the
police habit of blowing up minor tenant-affrays into outrages,
the mid-1820s offered Maria some crumbs of comfort on a
central question. When, during 1825, Walter Scott and Lockhart returned the visit she had paid to Abbotsford two years
earlier, they were able to record that at Edgeworthstown
'above all we had the opportunity of seeing in what universal
respect and comfort a gentleman's family may live in' Ireland,
'and in far from its most favoured district, provided only they
live there habitually, and do their duty as the friends and
guardians of those among whom Providence has appointed
their proper place. Here we found neither mud hovels nor

---

[1] CSE to Mrs RLE, 28 July 1827 (Edgeworth-Beaufort Papers).
[2] TSR to ME 3 August 1827 (Monteagle Papers, NLI, MS 13346).
[3] ME to TSR, 6 Aug 1827 (Monteagle Papers, NLI, MS 13346).

naked poverty, but snug cottages and smiling faces all about.'
Yet, of course, the very contrast between this oasis and most
of the country could not possibly have escaped Scott's eye. Lockhart remarked: 'Their factions have been so long envenomed,
and they have such narrow ground to do their battle in, that
they are like people fighting with daggers in a hogshead.'[1] Even
in Edgeworthstown the struggle for and against Emancipation
made itself felt and in 1828 ruined a state of educational neutrality.

Fresh hopes were, nonetheless, aroused in Fanny Edgeworth
that same year by the advantages likely to accrue from 'the
change of property' which was gradually taking place.

> Several estates [she claimed] have latterly been purchased by
> Dublin magistrates or lawyers – by people who will really reside
> and attend to the interests of their tenants – knowing this to be the
> wisest way of taking care of their own. Absentee and half-absentee
> landlords, who find themselves incompetent to get the good manage-
> ment of their property, will soon find it for their interest to get
> some certain sum for the sake of their estate from some businesslike
> person, who will know how to make the full value of the estate.
> In how many places in Ireland this seems all that is wanting to give
> occupation to the number of able and willing hands that are reduced
> to idleness during the greater part of the year.[2]

Just how facile her remedy for overpopulation was requires no
underlining, but there was much more to be said for the
concept, shared by the Edgeworths as a whole, that good
management would arrest Ireland's headlong rush along the
road to ruin. A hardworking *élite* could have minimised sub-
division, raised food production, lowered prices and increased
the respect for government at all levels. Coupled with Emancipation such changes would certainly have mitigated religious
friction and political unrest among the 'Patriots', but public
affairs had taken a most unfavourable turn in January 1828.
Canning had died just two days after Maria had written so warmly
of him. His successor as prime minister, Goderich,[3] showed scant
talent and all too soon the Tory right-wing under Wellington and
Peel elbowed his coalition of liberal Tories and moderate Whigs

---

[1] Quoted from Lockhart's *Life of Sir Walter Scott*, VIII 25, 57, in Flanagan, *Irish Novelists*, p. 102.

[2] FE to CSE, 31 Jan 1828 (Edgeworth-Beaufort Papers).

[3] Goderich was a somewhat insignificant character. Nevertheless, he has been deemed worth a recent study: W. D. Jones, *Prosperity Robinson: the life of Viscount Goderich, 1782–1859*.

out of office. Needless to say the new ministry was anti-Catholic.

Spring-Rice found himself liberated to fight for reform without the trammels of office. He had had, so he told Maria, no malicious motive in declining to support Wellington. Only his doubts as to the intention and power of the new Government 'of doing what' he considered 'right in the administration of Ireland' had forced him into giving up. Initially pessimism had led him into preparing for a trip to India. 'The formation of a government excluding all the friends of Ireland and admitting all its enemies' had made him 'despair of being able to do any *real* good' in Parliament. Then an appeal had been made to him 'on the part of almost all the principal persons connected with Irish politics in both houses, many of them' his 'opponents, but remonstrating with' him against his 'departure from Europe on public grounds'. So his 'hand' was 'therefore again' at the plough. He thought it 'important that' their 'Governors should be left for a few months to calm reflection. If they' could 'but feel the weight of responsibility that rests upon them they must cease to resolve upon resolving nothing; and if they see the necessity of moving at all, it is in advance only that they can go'.

> Many of our best authorities [he confided] are persuaded that the great Duke means to introduce some measure of concession. It may be so, but what I fear is that he may couple it with Bills of a very different tendency, depriving Emancipation of all its benefits. If, for instance, he were to legislate furiously against the [Catholic] Association he would only prevent its dissolution and would continue the present alarming system of irresponsible organisation. That constitutes the real danger of the case. If, on the contrary, he were to wait and try the effects of concession, resolved to act firmly and decisively should any future movement take place, he would break up the confederacy, and, if it revived, would have justice and policy both on his side.

Like Maria herself, and like the vast bulk of British and Irish liberals, he placed enormous stress on taking the plunge with Emancipation. He was not, however, blind to the possible dangers of the situation, commenting as he did: 'Is it not a curious illustration of popular movement that I should be among the Members *denounced* by the Catholic Association?'[1] In the following June the message intended by this development was to become painfully clear on the field of an election battle.

[1] TSR to ME, 1828 (Monteagle Papers, NLI, MS 13346).

Fear of a breakaway by the newly organised democracy from the guidance of the enlightened portion of the 'Quality' were voiced by Mrs Edgeworth in mid-March. She quoted with approval a statement by the local Catholic bishop to the effect that 'a popular meeting' was 'a very good tool, but a very bad master'.[1] In April Fanny reported 'a great registering of freeholds'[2] in anticipation of possible dissolution of Parliament. Doubtless the landlord class generally was very apprehensive since the creation of bogus forty-shilling freeholders, so long a cherished habit, had proved a boomerang in 1826. During the following weeks Maria perused the Press for parliamentary reports with unrelenting assiduity, not only for news of Irish politics in the narrow sense, but for any of educational reform. She informed Spring-Rice of how glad it made her that he would be in Parliament to press for the adoption of the admirableReport of the Committee of Education for Ireland and reported with undisguised glee of how a boy at Edgeworthstown school had answered 'I don't know' when asked the meaning of proselytism.[3] Surely one of the rare occasions when ignorance had struck her as a virtue?

Late that autumn her correspondence with a certain Captain Basil Hall put into a nutshell the abhorrence she felt for real democracy. After a recital of problems attending American politics she denies that the happiness of the people increases through its 'practising individually, and without being prepared for it by education, the office of legislators'. 'I am', she avers, 'as adverse, from reason and from aristocratic taste, as you can be to democracy; I feel as keenly as you do the monstrous, the disgusting absurdity of letting the many-headed, the greasy many-headed monster rule. The French Revolution gave us enough of the majority of the people.' Then there followed a plea for what she regarded as the major need in politics. 'But you must take care that your hatred of democracy does not touch, or seem to affect your love of liberty, your love of manly freedom – I mean, in short, your LIBERALITY, in the largest sense of the word. . . . You may attack the absurd system of universal suffrage as much as you will, provided you clearly and strongly show the advantages of just, representative

[1] Mrs RLE to the Rev. William Beaufort, 14 March 1828 (Edgeworth-Beaufort Papers).   [2] FE to CSE 19 April 1828 (Edgeworth-Beaufort Papers).
[3] ME to TSR, 29 May 1828 (Monteagle Papers, NLI, MS 13346).

government. Define well to yourself what you mean by loyalty.'[1]
Added poignancy had been given to all this by the victory of
O'Connell in the county Clare by-election of June. The events
of 1826 had been more than confirmed and a pro-Catholic
member of the Government rejected because he dallied with
Wellington. Spring-Rice had failed to deliver the necessary
goods of Emancipation. Now sympathy was not enough for the
Catholic Association. In its opinion actual success would be
better achieved by bold measures and extra-parliamentary non-
co-operation, not by talk and good will. 'Friends of the People'
and vague sympathisers had therefore to be condemned. The
'People' under O'Connell decided upon the way of 'self-help'.

Once the situation began to slip towards serious civil strife,
Wellington gave way. At the beginning of 1829 it was clear
that any limitations attached to Emancipation would have to be
very modest. In February a thoroughgoing scheme was pro-
pounded in the King's Speech, but Spring-Rice's worst fears
for the Catholic Association were fully confirmed. And there
was worse – the forty-shilling freeholders were to go. Maria
indulged herself in a somewhat simple-minded mood throughout.
The great day had come through 'Constitutional Agitation'.
Even the concomitant restrictions were all for the best. On St
Valentine's Day she informed her half-sister Fanny of her
admiration for the great Duke.[2] Six weeks later her aunt
Ruxton was told: 'You see that public affairs are going delightfully; I am glad you have lived to see the great measure carried.'[3]
In mid-April things still seemed perfect, especially as the agent,
Hinds, had just received '*all* the arrears and lodged them in the
Bank of Ireland!' 'The Duke of Wellington', she declared,
'must now indeed feel that he is a happy as well as a Great man.
He has certainly prevented a civil war and has by his civil
courage saved both England and Ireland. The Catholics in
their moment of triumph behave wonderfully well – with a
noble spirit that strikes . . . even those who were formerly
least favorable to their cause.'[4] The idea of any Ulster 'anti-
Catholics' having, albeit momentarily, let up on what Sir

[1] ME to Captain Basil Hall, 12 Oct 1828 (*Memoir*, III 19–22).
[2] ME to FE, 14 Feb 1829 (Edgeworth Papers).
[3] ME to Mrs Ruxton, 23 March 1829 (*Memoir*, III 30).
[4] ME to FE, 13 April 1829 (Edgeworth Papers).

Henry Holland termed their 'pure passion and malice'[1] is probably the most fanciful element in Maria's outlook just then, but others ran it pretty close. 'How wise of the Catholic Association to put themselves down'[2] was one current in February, and the way she clutched at straws about Catholic feeling suggests a desire to use her mind to feed her feelings. Again in February she wrote: 'All the Catholics of whom I have heard the sentiments receive this promise of emancipation in the best possible manner. "Yes, now every man may educate his son with the hope that he may get forward according to his merits. Curran's son was only a weaver." Harriet Butler told me this was said by some of the Catholics in their neighbourhood.'[3]

That this sentiment clashed with the desire for an essentially static society never seemed to have occurred to her and the approval given to the Abbé Langan's opinions on the forty-shilling freeholds hardly betokened belief in a more democratic way of life. This gentleman had apparently questioned many Catholics about their reactions to the whole affair. This she related to Fanny:

> The Abbé L. questioned several in Dublin, and on the coach top, and among people in this neighbourhood, who did not know and who did, about their opinions concerning the abolition of the 40/– Freeholders. Many of the freeholders were quite content, glad of it, for they knew they got nothing by the *freeholds* but trouble and just drinking, and getting into trouble for or against the landlord at Election time. They thought what was true, that they were driven like beasts, or cajoled and forced to be perjuring their souls and no thanks to their bodies, and the landlord reaping all the advantage throughout.[4]

[1] Sir Henry Holland to ME, 11 Feb 1829 (Edgeworth Papers). Sir Henry Holland, 1st Baronet (1788–1873), a prominent physician, whose contribution to Sir George S. Mackenzie's account of Ireland of 1810 was well known. Medical attendant to Queen Caroline as Princess of Wales, he later served as a doctor to both Queen Victoria and Prince Albert. An account of Protestant obduracy from the Union until Emancipation is to be found in Best, 'The Protestant Constitution and its supporters, 1800–1829', in *TRHS* 5th ser. VIII (1958).

[2] ME to FE 14 Feb 1829 (Edgeworth Papers).

[3] Ibid. John Philpot Curran (1750–1817) was latterly an Irish judge. Earlier in his career he had become very well known as a 'Patriot', and his services as counsel to various United Irishmen had earned him a fine reputation with all the 'Green' population.

[4] ME to FE 13 April 1829 (Edgeworth Papers). In his *Seventy Years of Irish Life*, W. R. Le Fanu records: 'I can well remember the exaggerated notions the peasantry had of all the benefits they were to derive from the measure [i.e. Catholic Emancipation]. Wages were at once to be doubled, and constant, well-paid employment was to be given to every man.' On the day Emancipation became law,

While much of what the abbé was told had been and was still
true, 1826 and the Clare by-election had shown that the *ancien
régime* was doomed. It is therefore very odd that the friend of
the old steward Langan and author of *Castle Rackrent* should
have swallowed whole the evidence of a man who had suffered
from the well-established Irish custom of telling someone what
he obviously wants to hear. The only conclusion to be drawn
is that Maria thought she had seen the Celestial City and there
was no discouraging her.

The vision was shortlived. Within a few days she was
retailing a passage, quoted by Lord Lansdowne from a speech
by a G. Knox, to the effect that the changes had satisfied the
Catholics, but not the constitution.[1] Disillusionment was hard
for her to bear and the ensuing decade and more proved that in
truth the Catholics generally were not satisfied, that her con-
ception of the Constitution could no longer be maintained and
that the most significant cleavage in Irish politics was between
the haves and the have-nots. The Irish Catholic masses seemed
to have felt enlightened Protestant guidance such as that of the
Edgeworths had become an undignified luxury. Like the liberal
'White' in an Asian or African colony in our own times, Maria
saw her function more than swallowed up by a militant mass
movement. Much Irish Whiggery made obeisance to the new
power. Accordingly her political position shifted rightwards
behind British authority and any determined defence of property
rights. By 1835 Edgeworthstown itself had been engulfed in
the great O'Connellite tide. Tenants voted contrary to the
family's wishes under the twin impact of patriotic Repeal of the

---

bonfires blazed on the tops of the mountains and hills surrounding the Le Fanu
mansion (at that time in county Limerick) and the Catholic peasants gave three
cheers for the Protestant tenants who had been in favour of the change. Especially
clear in Le Fanu's memory was a farmer named James Fleming, known generally
as Shamus Oge (Young James), who on being asked by 'someone in the crowd
what emancipation meant' replied: 'It means a shilling a day for every man so
long as he lives, whatever he does.' General wages in the district, and indeed in
much of Ireland, then stood at sixpence a day, and Le Fanu concluded: 'We little
thought on that night how soon we should see the same fires lighted all around us
when any of the clergy near us had suffered outrage, or how soon, without any
change on our part, we should be hooted and shouted at whenever we appeared.'
Doubtless disappointment over the failure of Fleming's shilling to materialise
as well as all the grand issues like Repeal, rents and tithes contributed to this
deterioration of landlord–tenant relations. See Le Fanu, p. 293.
[1] ME to an unknown correspondent, 21 April 1829 (Edgeworth Papers).

Union fervour and priestly intimidation. Some good came out of the evil, however, for Whig–O'Connellite co-operation in Parliament brought beneficial reform and no Repeal. The Union thus began to appear in a better light, and Maria's aims became partially fulfilled. But to what purpose? The idealistic conduct of affairs by her friend the Permanent Under-Secretary Thomas Drummond[1] did hold the balance between 'Orange' and 'Green', yet the masses of the centre, south and west regarded that as a second-best to Repeal, and those of the north detested it as an abomination. The neutral party in Ireland was busy falling between two stools. As E. M. Forster demonstrated so movingly of India, in his *A Passage to India*, one could not in such a deeply divided country run with the hare and hunt with the hounds.

The 1830s then saw the rise of the Repeal movement to immense power and counter-measures both liberal and illiberal. A game was begun later generations were to find the most frustrating of their lives. The long Tory supremacy ended in 1830. Apart from a brief interval during the winter of 1834–5, the Whigs held office right through to 1841. From 1835 their parliamentary security depended upon O'Connellite support. Ironically the 'Irish' party never had more constitutional influence than at the time when the acids of patronage, indifference and contentment born of secondary changes were eating into its vitals. Maria hated O'Connell and his party, but he and it represented the deepest feelings of the Irish Catholic masses. His appeal called to their instinct, whatever the irrelevance of much of his programme to their daily material needs or interests. It was the heart of O'Connell against the reason of Drummond. For all their 'education of the heart', even the tenants of Edgeworthstown fell from grace when faced with such a choice. In these circumstances it is hardly surprising that Maria feared new and far-reaching demands would soon be made: that the Church of Ireland would be disestablished and stripped of property and the Protestant aristocracy and gentry would be ejected from the country. Fast though the emergence of democracy was in Ireland compared with England, fright played havoc with judgement. Things were not as bad as that in her lifetime or for many years after.

[1] For his life, see O'Brien, *Thomas Drummond*.

2

Rents and Repealers

BEFORE the passing of the Great Reform Bill of 1832, political matters in Ireland remained fluid. O'Connell's first organisations for spreading the Repeal cause were dissolved, and he spent great energy upon demanding such things as the abolition of tithes, Church rates and vestry cess, reform of the Grand Jury, secret ballot, triennial parliaments and fair apportionment of patronage, rather than going all out for ending the Union.

In January 1830 Maria made a determined bid to sustain some family property rights. Doubtless economic exigencies forced her hand to some extent. Very probably though, to judge from her tone and temper, the threats to property and the position of the aristocracy and gentry contained in that O'Connellite programme had a great deal to do with this tough approach. The more so because the grass-roots interpretation given by the masses to O'Connell's doctrines was that the property of others (especially the rich or comfortable) was theft. Her immediate problem concerned the tolls and customs payable at Edgeworthstown fairs. She complained to Spring-Rice: 'It could scarcely be thought just that persons, even those in the discredited class of landlords or landholders, should give up altogether rights which they purchased, probably in former times, by good [or bad] service to the Crown, or by good money – rights at any rate granted by patents standing on the same foundation as right to landed property.'[1] Here was the old dilemma again – that even the most enlightened of the Protest-

[1] ME to TSR 6 Jan 1830 (Monteagle Papers, NLI, MS 13346).

ant Ascendancy had to base their case on the defeat of the
people they were attempting to conciliate. This is why a
blanket-seller from Navan, of whom she spoke so bitterly,
found such a ready response to his little handbills advising the
populace not to pay these dues.[1]

Happily the Reform agitation in Britain augured well for
more 'prudent' change, but here again she is all for a firm stand
on legitimate property rights. Mob demands in Kent had, she
felt, been yielded to quite unnecessarily and unjustifiably. 'To
say the truth, the farmers and middle gentlemen have acted like
cowards and fools hitherto – with few exceptions. I almost
suspect that they wish these disturbances to go on that they
may in their turn have an example for forcing all the higher
landlords and aristocracy to pay *all* in lowering rents and also in
forcing the clergy to lower tithes.' Her conviction was all the
more assured because of first-hand experience. As a climax
she harped back to the old issue of method. 'I have no doubt',
she assured Mrs Edgeworth, 'that something ought to be done
and must be done, but not by the mob. If any step be gained by
the mob all is lost, for there is no saying to the mob any more
than to the sea: "So far shalt thou go and no further." If the
Ministry change, as from this majority against them seems
inevitable, those who come in *must* see what they can do for
Reform and then all the grievances must come before Parliament in constitutional form.'[2] Just as horrific thoughts about
army loyalty were flashing through her mind, Spring-Rice
dropped in with a budget of comfort. As regards Britain his
news was sound. In Irish matters his optimism verged on the
pathetic. According to him the anti-Union party was going to
'die quickly'. Having already received 'adherence from one
prime opponent of the Union' the Whig Government was hopeful that 'the rustling of a silk gown' would 'have happy effect
upon another'.[3] The actual way of it was to be vastly different.

[1] ME to TSR 29 Jan 1830 (Monteagle Papers, NLI, MS 13346).
[2] ME to Mrs RLE, 17 Nov 1830 (Edgeworth Papers). For a recently published
account of British mob violence at this time and its importance in Kent (the
principal seat of the disturbance and an area where Sneyd Edgeworth, as a local
landowner, was involved), see Rudé, 'English Rural and Urban Disturbances', in
P&P no. 37 (1967). For a detailed treatment of disturbances in South-East
England at this time see E. J. Hobsbawm and George Rudé *Captain Swing*,
chapters 5 and 13.
[3] ME to Sophia Edgeworth, 8 Dec 1830 (Edgeworth Papers).

Given the neuroses of the Ascendancy, its members must certainly have regarded the death of the Repeal party as strongly reminiscent in one way of that of Charles II.

County Longford took the 1830 general election in its stride. The famine of the summer had soon passed and the 'brilliant foul-mouthed demagogue in whom the tribes of O's and Mac's'[1] had found a champion did not obtrude himself upon Maria's scene. Indeed, as 1831 opened, troubles poured in upon him. As Lecky remarked:

> The new ministry was quite as determined as that which preceded it to use every means to put down the repeal agitation. The public breakfasts, though they now professed to be for charitable purposes, were put down. The same fate attended other attempts at association, and O'Connell himself was prosecuted for an attempt to evade the King's proclamation under the recent Act, and also for conspiracy under the common law. With the consent of the Government the latter charge was withdrawn, and O'Connell, after some vacillation, pleaded guilty to the former. He was never called up for judgment, and the Act which he had broken soon after expired. It was in the course of this struggle that he retaliated by formally recommending that run upon gold which he had suggested in the preceding year.[2]

Over in London, Maria found herself in the midst of the official O'Connell-haters. The depth of their animosity can be seen from what was retailed to Mrs Edgeworth in a letter of 5 January. 'Spring Rice . . . says O'Connell is a much distressed man – executions etc. – and that money is at the bottom of his agitations, that he expects 50,000 pounds from this collection now making. Government are resolved to let him get it and glad that the people should see and feel that he taxes them. At the moment when he *has* pocketed this they mean to act.'[3] But the 'Liberator' and his Repeal campaign were far too big to be snuffed out by spite. While county Longford again remained demure at the polls in May 1831, the same could not have been said of neighbouring Meath, where Mrs Edgeworth's family, the Beauforts, lived.

This difference Maria interpreted in part as due to the Edgeworths and their like, though the future was to belie her. Longford was a small county and the reduction of the electorate

---

[1] *Memoir*, ii 511.
[2] Lecky, *Leaders of Public Opinion in Ireland*, ii 110.
[3] ME to Mrs RLE, 5 Jan 1831 (Edgeworth Papers).

from some 4000 in 1829 to a paltry 600 may well have had some influence on behaviour. Voting was then held solely in the county town and the landlords had generally escorted their people in to the poll. 'Were any facts necessary to convince me that the Irish tenants may be educated to act with firmness and decorum when brought to the stakes of popular odium the conduct of Lovell's freeholders would do so. But how can any landlord, who has made it a practice to oppress his tenants, or at best to disregard their interests, expect them to vote against their own prejudices and risk their own lives to oblige him? . . . A gentleman's estate should be a moral school and the moral education must depend on the justice or kindness with which the proprietor acts.'[1]

The moral lesson Lovell had taught in preparation for the election must certainly have baffled some, at least, of his tenants. He, a supporter of the Whig ministry, had asked them to support one of the retiring Tory members and exercise their own discretion as to what they did about the other, insisting at the same time that not a single vote be given to the O'Connellite side, despite its avowal of government policies on parliamentary reform. Nor can most tenants have found their 'prejudices' any easier to swallow and risking their lives the more enjoyable to face when frosts were well on the way to ruining the local potato crop. 'Black powder' (to which all potatoes then above ground had been reduced) would be a scant recompense for stifling their inmost inclinations at the behest of a 'moral' teacher, especially when he exploited good will in an attempt to perpetuate in essentials at least the very social system that in most parts of Ireland woefully failed to measure up to the standards Maria and other idealist landlords set it. The truth was that for Lovell and his family the election was about the very basis of the political system in Ireland, and not about the rights and wrongs of franchise extension in the United Kingdom as a whole. And then the position of the landed class had to be maintained pending necessary reform of abuses. The Tories were 'sound' on these two issues, the O'Connellites the very embodiment of 'error'. The course was therefore clear, and a great strain straightway put on the liking of the Edgeworthstown tenants for their 'master'. How and why the local

[1] ME to FE, 17 May 1831 (Edgeworth Papers).

notion of a landlord's position prevailed over the almost national popular view is very difficult to understand, even after making due allowance for family reputation. Only through examining the affair in some detail can the real truth be gleaned, and fortunately a very full account survives in the form of a long letter almost totally devoted to the election and written the day after it ended. Mrs Edgeworth evidently felt her daughter Fanny would want to know all, and accordingly obliged to nigh on the point of excess. Nevertheless, to her industry and enthusiasm we owe a fascinating picture of the relationship between a well-liked Irish landlord and his tenants, bearing all the marks of authenticity and bringing in the precise atmosphere of the times. Such evidence is unfortunately all too rare.

The two retiring members were Viscount Forbes, eldest son of the Earl of Granard of Castle Forbes in county Longford and a major-general in the army, and Anthony Lefroy, son-in-law of Viscount Lorton, another county magnate. Against them the O'Connellites nominated Luke White, a magistrate and a member of an up-and-coming county family, heirs of a Dublin bookseller said to have been the wealthiest man in Ireland, and one Mullins, a local canal engineer whom Mrs Edgeworth, for one, dubbed 'a vulgar fellow'. Though Lovell Edgeworth had been seriously under the weather, he had determined early on to take an active part in the election. In the Edgeworths' view Lefroy had scant claim on those far from sold on his Tory ideas, defence of the Union or no defence of the Union. Lefroy's family had acquired its fortune quite recently, through the law, and the imprimatur of men such as Thomas Pakenham, Earl of Longford, the Earl of Granard and Lord Lorton barely made up for his parvenu status. Forbes was different. Both pedigree and personal friendship made him preferable and worthy of support. Doubtless there was also an element of satisfaction at taking a semi-independent line and not falling in solidly behind the Tory banner, even in the face of the Repeal campaign. At any rate Lovell decided to plump for Forbes and to ask the tenantry to give a vote to him, leaving 'them at liberty to vote for Lefroy if they chose', but under strict instructions not to go for White and his crony.

For all their fine 'moral' training a good deal of doubt about what the right thing to do actually was would appear to have beset the tenants, especially the Catholics among them. However fine a body of men they were, it looked at one stage as though there might be many a slip between the cup of 'education' and the lip of the polling process. Mrs Edgeworth had soon become aware of their dilemma and reported accordingly: 'Now Lord Forbes and Lefroy both voted against the Reform bill – They were therefore equally below par in the opinion of the *people* and all their last year's love for Lord Forbes was turned to hate. Mr White was set up by the Catholics and the priests did take unwearied and unwarrantable pains to obtain and secure votes.'

One of the Catholic tenants – Garret Keegan – had come to her at the outset and asked how Lovell was going to vote. 'For his old friend Lord Forbes to be sure.' The answer had come pat, but Keegan wanted to know more. 'And will he be splitting in Mr Lefroy?' Mrs Edgeworth had been well briefed, and the following exchange took place.

'No, no,' I replied, 'he gives his plumper.[1] I hope all his tenants will do the same.' 'That is just what *I* wish,' said Mr Hinds. 'On faith,' continued Garret, 'it would not do to be putting up Lefroy. I am afraid anyhow he'll be hard set to keep any with him – for they are all for reform.' 'Who do you mean?' 'I mean the master's freeholders, and Mr Sneyd's – that's all the same.' 'You will vote Lord Forbes yourself Garret,' says I. 'That I will, but I am only one, you know. There is not another Catholic among them will vote for him especially. They never could abide him since he dispersed the Anti-Union meeting last January at Longford – and he finished himself by voting against this bill of Reform.' Then he slily added: 'I'm thinking the Allens, the Presbyterians, are not much fonder of his lordship'.

Apart from the curious piece of commentary upon how a purely political move by Lord Forbes had apparently disturbed the calm and approval with which he had apparently been regarded on the social and economic fronts in his own area, it is clear from the last remark that the tenants' unease was far from restricted to those whose birth and religion inclined them towards Repeal. Presbyterians like the Allens would in the normal run of things have been Whig stalwarts, and Keegan knew the news of their possible defection would not only be

[1] Plumper: a vote given solely to one candidate in an election, when one has the right to vote for two or more.

likely to disturb Lovell's calculations as to the election, but could possibly disturb his conscience and raise up bogies about actively campaigning for a Tory, whatever purely personal factors in his favour might exist. A new policy of neutrality would have let Keegan and his like off a very awkward hook. Abstention would enable them to say that they had followed Lovell without actively injuring Repeal or helping the Tory resistance to it and the Reform cause. The bid for an easy life failed, 'for Lovell never heeded all this'. Still, it had been a clever little try and a significant indication of how the tenantry were really feeling. All the stops had to be out for bringing off the result Lovell wanted and by using up vast reserves of good will to get it he made a full repetition of the process later on all the less likely.

The very day after all this Lord Forbes actually dined at Edgeworthstown and a little later Lovell bestirred himself enough to interview some of his people about the election. Choosing to seize the bull by the horns he went mainly to Catholics. One and all they said they 'had been applied to by each candidate and by their priest, but that they had given for answer but this – that they did not yet know how their landlord would vote and they wished to oblige him or some such thing'. A direct approach by Lovell had therefore revealed that the unease had not been directly communicated to the outside world and that in his presence at least no one had chosen to indulge it to the point of argument, familiar though the course he expected of his men was by that time to each and every one of them. Yet a direct approach was no small thing, and Lovell had not risked issuing a general statement of intention and desire without what amounted to a man-to-man canvass. The moral pressure exerted thereby was probably greater than any White and his key allies, the priests, had at their disposal just then. Failure now was, however, only a spur to intensified efforts thereafter – at a time when the Edgeworth appeal was less potent and the end to which it was directed more odious still to the generality of Catholics. And from what follows it is quite clear that Lovell had set out far from certain of success. 'So he thanked them very much', his stepmother reported, 'and really it has done him more good than any of the powders and pills and baths that have been prescribed for him.' On returning home he immediately set to and 'wrote, or caused to be written, notes to each freeholder inviting them to meet him at the turn to Allens' on the Longford road at 10 on Tuesday, when he would accompany them into Longford – and he invited himself to breakfast at John Allen's'. Having shored up his fortunes on the Catholic front, he had decided upon a thorough session with the Presbyterians just to be on the safe side. Keegan would seem merely to have provoked a reinsurance campaign all round. On the other hand he had been 'heeded', albeit in a sense he had not wanted.

Meanwhile the contest itself had hotted up with a vengeance. Lord Forbes had gone so far as to send a challenge to Luke White, and while Mrs Edgeworth was being subjected to a seventy-minute sermon by the Dean of Ardagh, her son-in-law Barry Fox and his brother Charles were dashing about the neighbourhood making sure all was ready for a duel. And that on a Sunday! Next morning Lovell set off early to call upon Lord Forbes, and together they went into Longford town. 'When the time came they . . . made their way through so dense a mob that the Sheriff and the Justices could hardly clear a passage for the gentlemen. At last they reached their places and as soon as the mob had filled the body of the courthouse silence was called for, but called [for] in vain. At last, when there was some interval of peace, Lovell went forward and in a neat and appropriate speech nominated Lord Forbes.' Here was commitment indeed. Things had certainly reached a pretty pass in Irish politics when such a thorough Whig as Lovell Edgeworth had been reduced to being the prime sponsor of a Tory candidate. Nor did he fulfil the task unchallenged. 'He says', commented Mrs Edgeworth, 'that he seemed more listened to than any of the succeeding speakers, but some people groaned and hooted him and called him turncoat.' After the nomination of Lefroy as the second Tory by an almost inaudible and halting member of the local gentry, Luke White was named by his younger brother, Colonel Henry White claiming his sole motive in the affair was to 'prevent the county being made into a mere "borough" '. Finally, 'some old man whom nobody knew stept forward and named Mr *Mullins*', virtually a man of straw, introduced into the election as a symbol of Repealer strength. 'When all this speaking was over the polling began and each person polled a few.'

Lovell retailed all this at dinner that night and prepared himself for the testing-time on the morrow. Tuesday was to be the crucial day, both in the election generally and for him as a landlord. Would the Catholics rat on him after all? Would he manage for sure to get the Allens fully round? At any rate he took no chances and 'was off at eight o'clock in good time for breakfast'. Apparently the potentially wayward Presbyterians felt themselves honoured by the visit, and it was with no fewer than nine Allen freeholders that he rode to the trysting-place. 'And there, contrary to the prognostics of Garret the sage, or James Woods the fearful, he found all his little and large Cath'lic boys.' He exploited his chances straightway, coming directly to the point in a courteous, clear speech such as could only have been made by a man very sure of his ground. 'Gentlemen', he declared, 'I feel very gratified, much gratified by your meeting me here. I am doubly and trebly obliged, for it shows that you have confidence in my not asking you to do what would be hurtful to your credit – it shows that you are ready and willing to confer an obligation on myself and I take your voting for Lord Forbes as a personal favor. And it makes me feel that you treat me as the representative of my father, who would not have asked you to do anything contrary to your political interests.' The good old days seemed firmly entrenched, · but the present and future were to deal harshly with the past and the whole occasion was in the nature of a swansong.

> Then asked one of them: 'You do not require that we should give our second votes to the man Lefroy?' 'No, indeed,' said Lovell, 'I don't vote for him myself and I do not ask you. Neither do I prevent you. Those who wish to do so have my free permission. I only desire and wish them *not* to give a vote to Mr White because he set up in a way that I cannot approve and under an influence that I will not submit to.' 'All's well then and we hope we shall do what you like – and we thank Your Honour very much.'

All the height of amicability, but there was a wealth of ominous meaning in the tenant's reply. It was all very well for Mrs Edgeworth to tell Fanny: 'This election has been of such use to him that I think an election once a fortnight would quite set him up in the world' and of how great was the 'satisfaction' he felt 'in the having succeeded with his tenants in so handsome and obliging a manner and in feeling that when he does assert himself he does get through business as well as anybody else'. In fact, however substantial the incident might have been as a temporary tonic to poor Lovell, the truth of the matter was that in securing adhesion to Lord Forbes he had gone to the furthest limit of his influence. Moreover the words employed by the tenant reeked of reluctance and the conditional. 'Provided that is your full demand we will meet it, but so far and no further' was the purport of his message. And for the Catholics it was so evidently a favour to a well-liked family, which pressure of events might all too easily make difficult, even impossible, to repeat in the near future.

The journey into Longford must have been quite a sight – a cavalcade of jaunting cars filled with the Edgeworth contingent of the Forbesian host. In the county town itself 'Lovell hired a room for them and to ensure that no priests came to meddle with them he sat down with them and waited patiently with their woolly coats till the time came for their polling'. As it happened, it was the Tories not the priests who sought to exert pressure at the last moment. 'Just as' the tenantry were going in came two of Lord Forbes' Committee in a great passion to reproach Lovell for not splitting his votes with Lefroy. "I told you I would not and could not from the first", said he, "so pray don't unsettle the minds of my people. They are all satisfied to give plumpers to Lord Forbes – and pray be content with that." ' Very sensibly the agents did not press their luck too far, 'Lovell was steady and his men voted the right way. His Catholics gave plumpers to Lord Forbes and his nine Allens' – now more convinced than the 'master' himself – 'voted for both'. Only two small flies had appeared in the ointment, and they made no attempt to hide their embarrassment. Two Catholic tenants had evaded contact with Lovell for as long as possible. One had felt impelled to prepare him for the worst and had explained himself the day before. Much though it was against 'his grain' to vote for White, the foul deed had to be done. '"I must", says he, "or my son who is going to be a priest never will be ordained." ' The other left apology until after having cast his votes and put the blame on local conditions. Neither had gone so far as to patronise Mullins, and both had supported Lord Forbes. But neither had accompanied Lovell

into town, and Mrs Edgeworth described them as the 'two
who went to the enemy'. Still, all save these had been fully
'loyal', and once their polling was done Lovell 'went into their
room to ask how it had gone on. "Oh, very smooth and asy –
only there were two priests shaking their heads at us all the
time and they said we were not loyal subjects." This was an
ingenious device of the priests. They said: "You take an oath of
allegiance to the King and the first thing – almost with the
same breath – is to vote contrary to his wishes. The King wishes
for a Reform and you are going to vote for a man who opposed
the bill for Reform and goes in opposition to His Majesty's
wishes." ' The 'new loyalty' was a trifle too subtle for most to
absorb, and they stuck to the devil they knew. As a reward
Lovell 'saw them all sit down to a good plain dinner to which
he treated them, advising them not to take too much punch,
and then went off to take some luncheon in the "Lord Forbes" '.
Afterwards 'he advised his men to go home and not wait to
see the *fun* – if fighting can be called such – and returned home
himself' to give the family his account of what had occurred.[1]

Wednesday dawned uneventfully and it was not until mid-
morning that the 'master' ventured into Longford. 'As soon
as he entered he met Charles Fox, who told him all was at an end
and that White had retired.'[2] Apparently the 'vulgar' engineer
Mullins wasn't even mentioned, but must have followed suit,
for the two Tories were to be declared elected the next day.
Troublemakers had been bound over to keep the peace on pain
of a £5000 fine and everything seemed lovely in the loyalist
garden. Even the drunken coachman who made it so difficult
for Lovell to get home that evening had become incapable in
an excellent cause! Or so defenders of the Union would have
thought. While the moral schooling of a model landlord had
its lapses, especially with Lovell as the landlord, it paid excellent
dividends on this occasion. But the time would come when
political bankruptcy threatened and the 'morality' looked seedy.

Such a schooling had apparently paid off to some extent even
in Meath, thanks to the good sense of Richard Butler. His difficulties in conveying his freeholders in and out of Trim, however,

[1] This account of the election is based upon a long letter from Mrs RLE to FE,
11 May 1831 (Edgeworth Papers).
[2] Ibid.

A corner of an Irish market

Irish peasants at work (above) *and at play*

had been considerable. Some had managed to vote as they wished – for the 'two old members', but others 'were literally dragged from their horses by the mob and forced to vote for Grattan,[1] the priests acting as the instigators to all the outrages committed'. Maria complained of how her brother and brother-in-law had both accused her of being 'blinded by prejudice' when she stated her belief 'that the priests did exert this political influence', but stoutly maintained it was based on 'undeniable facts'.[2]

Two months later her thoughts are still full of the Meath election.

> Aunt Bess[3] [she grumbled] will, I am sure, be very sorry that her county is now represented by Mr Grattan. Indeed, I am sure if she met him she'd 'take off her wig and throw it in his face', but it may be some consolation to her to know that it was only from . . . shilly-shallying and then by main force that Mr Grattan came in. Liberty and independence indeed! There never was such a terrible tyranny as that under which the poor wretched people are here [i.e. Trim]. It is literally the reign of terror: at the end of every table where the votes were to be given stood a priest, threatening every poor Catholic that came with perdition if he didn't vote for Mr Grattan and any who did not was shivering with fright as he gave his name for Mr Bligh. The Protestant farmers and shop-keepers they threatened with – 'Remember the harvest's not out' and 'No man will deal any more with you.' They seized hold of any doubtful freeholder and dragged him off to Mr Grattan's Committee and locked others up safe out of the way: who were delighted to be secure from the dread alternative of losing their souls and bodies to the Association if they voted against them, or their farms if they voted against the landlord. Of course, soul and body generally carried the day. Many respectable substantial Protestant farmers were so terrified they would have voted for the Pope if they had been told to. Several came to their landlords and begged to be disenfranchised – absolutely giving up their privilege of freemen in fear of men who call themselves patriots and friends of liberty! All this work was very pardonable in the priests when they wanted

[1] Henry Grattan, the second son of *the* Henry Grattan after whom the constitutional settlement of 1782 was named. Formerly (1826–30) M.P. for Dublin City, he sat for Meath from 1831 until 1852. He was a Repealer.

[2] ME to FE, 17 May 1831 (Edgeworth Papers). In a letter to Mrs RLE of 7 May 1831 and in one to Honora Edgeworth of 25 June 1831 ME mentions how she has been recommending novels by one G. Brittaine to 'many grand people'. The bias of these books (notably *The Election* and *Irish Priests and Irish Landlords*) was distinctly anti-Catholic. Doubtless she was temporarily very scandalised by the goings-on at Trim. (Edgeworth Papers.)

[3] Elizabeth Beaufort, the sister-in-law of Mrs RLE.

to get emancipation, but it's worse than foolish in them now, and, then people say: 'this is what you've done by emancipating the Catholics'.

Just why such a zealous guardian of the law as Maria should have felt all was fair for Emancipation is far from clear, for she seldom, if ever, argued that the end justified the means. What followed made much more sense. Indeed it showed the shrewd judgement as to character to be expected in a successful novelist. 'A great deal' of this trouble arose, she was sure, 'from the Maynooth College. The priests educated there' were 'so vulgar no gentleman can, let him wish it ever so much, keep company with them. This puts them in a class by themselves, hence they feel looked down on by the gentry and so long to pull them down to their own level and teach the people nonsense about destroying the aristocracy.'[1] Clearly the disinterested patriotism and social indignation of the priesthood should not be forgotten, but undoubtedly the social gulf between the domestically educated priesthood and the Ascendancy did exacerbate Irish problems and lend great motive force to O'Connell.

Maria meanwhile kept up her causes at Edgeworthstown, refusing to grant one lease unless the prospective tenant accepted as a condition the abandonment of the sale of spirits and striving hard to maintain the spirit of moderate reform in the midst of adversity. There was, she told Mrs Lazarus, 'an almost equal danger in granting too much or too little to the reformists'. Although party selfishness was great, her feelings about the British future were relatively optimistic. It would be secured by 'the fund of good sense and of propriety' in the 'middle ranks', 'which will resist revolution and yet require rational reform'.[2] English generosity had mitigated recent Irish distress, from which, in any case, county Longford had fortunately been free.

The rejection of the Reform Bill by the Lords shook away some of this complacency and on 4 November she penned the same lady a tale of woe.

No part of the *civilised* world, old or new, appears [she alleged] now to be quite safe for civilised people to inhabit – what with the

[1] ME to Honora Edgeworth, 12 Aug 1831 (Edgeworth Papers). For a discussion of priestly influence at Irish elections, see Whyte, 'The Influence of the Catholic Clergy on Elections in Nineteenth-century Ireland', in *EHR* LXXV (1960).
[2] ME to Mrs Lazarus, 1831 (Edgeworth Papers).

march of intellect and the march of troops. The instructors of the people do not consider sufficiently that it is not sufficient, or rather it is too much, to set the intellect marching unless they clearly know and can direct to what good purposes it is marching. To give *power* without the certain and good direction of *that power* is most danger-ous either in mechanics or education – or legislation. We in England and Ireland are now in most perilous circumstances.

Would that the Bristol mob she denounced so roundly had been nurtured on *Practical Education*! Her particular Whig friends evidently felt the Reform Bill had gone too far. If passed it would give the people more power than was good for 'the constitution' – 'more than is good for the people themselves'. Edgeworthstown had remained 'as yet perfectly quiet'. All Lovell's rent had been paid up to May 1832, and no distur-bances, tithes, cess or parliamentary reform had occurred. 'But', she concludes, 'other parts of Ireland are much disturbed and the causes lie so deep and *untouchable* that I cannot form an idea how it will end – except by general convulsion. In which case the apparent present quiet of this country only lulls us treacher-ously.' Her mind went back to 1798, for she feared there were 'secret societies all over Ireland as in the time of Lord Edward Fitzgerald'.[1] It must have been hard to feel a life's work had really been in vain.

In the event nothing so terrible came to pass. As the Rev. William Clancy of Carlow College had put it in January 1831, there would be no rebellion 'for two obvious reasons – the influence of the priesthood and the want of arms'. Despite some appearances to the contrary: 'All classes are for constitutional discussion.' The heat of these discussions was, of course, alarmingly white. Religious and social grievances were joined with political over the tithe issue, but the Edgeworths took the plunge once more for the Rule of Law. Sympathy with the

[1] ME to Mrs Lazarus, 4 Nov 1831 (Edgeworth Papers). Back in the spring Maria had felt less buoyant still. Writing to her stepmother she had commented: 'The result of all I heard at Lansdowne House convinced me that *that* party are in great doubt how the elections will turn out, but as far as I can *guess* it will be favourably for the *Bill* and the present Ministry. Even if the majority should be against them and Peel and Wellington come in it is thought by all and said *now* by the Tory party that they must and would grant some kind of reform, for instance members for Manchester and Birmingham. "But save my Boroughs Heaven" would be their first and last. And if a few rotten ones were let drop off, I am not sure whether it might not be best to let the rest alone.' ME to Mrs RLE, 30 April 1831 (Edgeworth Papers).

Anglican rector of Edgeworthstown, a Mr Keating, had not swayed anyone on the tithes issue. Egged on by a Mr Connell, who declared 'he would rather cut his hands and then his arms off than pay one sixpence, one farthing of tithe or cess', some of the people threatened the collector. Maria denounced this *and* the conduct of ministers in Parliament, whose declarations that 'tithes were extinguished' had given countenance to such junketings. The whole business struck her as futile because Parliament intended to meet the grievances at the earliest opportunity. But then she was intelligent, rational and a Protestant. So too was Lovell. While his fellow magistrates wilted before the hubbub, he had issued a warrant for the seizure of property for non-payment of cess. Four shillings and sixpence was the sum withheld. One cow therefore sufficed and, thanks to good organisation of bidders and police, with a military detachment within easy reach, a sale was effected. Upwards of a thousand of 'the boys' had assembled in vain, and the law of the land acquired an enhanced authority. Lovell was inevitably 'violently abused by the violent party'.

This had happened during May 1832.[1] In August trouble started to spread to the rent question. Once again Maria was for a tough line. She favoured distraint, convinced the tenants had the money in their pockets. Hinds (in her opinion a coward on the point) remonstrated that 'these were not times for that', but leapt into action when his mistress declared she would set him an example 'of driving'. Lord Forbes diagnosed Longford 'as in a perilous state' and had concluded that the struggles over tithe, rent and cess were not merely a matter of 'Catholic against Protestant, or Union against anti, or O'Connell against Government, but between *all* who *want to have* against all who *have*'. Maria concurred, adding: 'Observe; not merely *want* against *have*, but *want to have*, which includes many more than the . . . truly distressed classes and is much more powerful and dangerous – all who now look to revolution for plunder and to change of Government for bettering themselves.'[2] Very

---

[1] ME to M. Pakenham Edgeworth, 3 May 1832 (Edgeworth Papers).

[2] ME to FE, 24 Oct 1832 (Edgeworth Papers). W. R. Le Fanu writes of how, despite the fact that by 1829 O'Connell and his agents had managed to reconcile the local contending factions in the part of county Limerick where his family had their estates and set up a determined 'patriotic front', relations with the Catholic population had remained excellent until 1831. He went on: 'Our parish priest

probably these views were formed in part by acute anxiety about
family financial difficulties and fears as to what might happen
in the event of a serious breakdown of income through non-
payments of rent. Nevertheless her acceptance of a strong Tory's
interpretation of the fundamental issues did indicate a swing
towards the right, and conditions in county Longford had
developed in ways which made it well-nigh inevitable. Hinds
did in fact secure the immediate financial future by energetic
rent-collection. The Reform Act of 1832, however, led to
elections, the results of which were an O'Connellite triumph.[1]
The political ground of moderate Whiggery was suddenly
swept from beneath Maria's feet.[2] The sole Unionist camp of
any size was Tory, and in it most of her close friends in the
county were the leading lights.

Under the new law the county electorate was more than
doubled. What Spring-Rice termed the Irish 'Liberal party'[3]
was nowhere in the scramble for support. The race was left to
the Repealers and the Tories, both of whom made great play
with the registration provisions of the reformed system in
drawing up the electoral lists. The former operated through a
recently founded Reform Registry Political Union with its
headquarters in Longford town and three other places as 'sub-
power stations'. Most of its expenses were met from a fund of
£435. On 9 December Maria complained of 'a surplusage of
election talk'. Her sympathies were totally with the two Tory

---

also was a special friend of ours, a constant visitor to our home. In the neighbouring
parishes the same kindly relations existed between the priest and his flock and
the Protestant clergyman. But in 1831 all this was suddenly and sadly changed
when the tithe war . . . came upon us. . . . It is hard now to realise the suddenness
with which kindness and goodwill were changed to insult and hate; for a short time
we were not so badly treated as some of the neighbouring clergy, but the people
would not speak to us and scowled at us as we passed.' The Le Fanus soon learned
the lot of the Anglican parson landlord was no easy one: 'During all these troublous
times', the account continued, 'the landlords looked on with indifference and
showed little sympathy with the clergy in their difficulties. My brother used to
say: "Never mind, their time will come – rents will be attacked as tithes are now –
with the same machinery and with like success." ' He could not have been more
right. See Le Fanu, *Seventy Years of Irish Life*, pp. 42, 55, and 66.

[1] For the whole history of the Reform Act of 1832, see J. R. M. Butler, *The
Passing of the Great Reform Bill*, and Gash, *Politics in the Age of Peel*. Woodward,
Age of Reform (2nd ed.) provides a good concise account of the matter with full
details of the main provisions of the Act.

[2] See de Tocqueville, *Journeys to England and Ireland*, ed. Mayer, p. 178.

[3] MacIntyre, *The Liberator*, p. 97.

candidates – Viscount Forbes and Anthony Lefroy. The overwhelming proportion of the 'Quality' supported these two men,
although one of the Repealers was Luke White, and therefore
lacked neither wealth nor influence. For White, links with
O'Connell simply kept alive all manner of snobbish considerations. As for his running-mate, let Maria speak: 'The Catholics
have set up a horrid vulgarian called O'Rourke, from nobody
knows where – I believe furnished at the shortest notice by
O'Connell.' The actual conduct of the election was no more to
her liking: 'Horrid yells of mobs, of boys and girls and women
and priests' marred the tone. The 'voice of the country' had
changed since 1800, and 'disturbing the peace of the county'
was all the rage. Now a new turn was given to her own phrase
in *The Absentee*: 'Live with the people or be torn to pieces.'[1]

The Repealer victory had been half expected. Already on
9 December Maria had mentioned 'some fear that Lord Forbes
may be thrown out'. Until the last, however, large crumbs of
comfort had been found. 'But hopes', she had continued,
'predominate *and* figures.' Even here, though, she sounded a
note of caution. 'But there must be some *bribed to stay away*,
which I am told is *no bribery* by Act of Parliament.'[2] As it
happened, nothing of the kind took place. The poll was extremely high – no fewer than 1255 out of 1294 voters having
recorded their votes. And, ironically enough, the Repealers
had expected to do better than they did and put the blame
upon an allegedly partial revising barrister. The figures were
Luke White 649, James Halpin O'Rourke 645 (both elected),
Viscount Forbes 587, and Anthony Lefroy 582. Such proximity
between each pair of candidates suggests the wire-pullers on
both sides deserved a pat on the back. An outcome like that did
not put Maria in a mood for such things. The hills round
Edgeworthstown blazed with celebratory bonfires and in the
place itself gangs of boys went round trilling and yelling. At
5.30 p.m. on the day of the result – 22 December – she gave
full vent to her fears – at least on paper. 'I hope', she began,
'that the night will pass without any murder being committed.
We have only two policemen. I hope they will not let themselves
be seen – they cannot be felt.' What hit her hardest was the

[1] ME to FE, 9 Dec 1832 (Edgeworth Papers).
[2] Ibid.

fact that 'almost all our Catholic tenants have voted against us – they declared to me they dared not do otherwise, though they all said they wished it. James Woods is an arrant coward, so that I was not surprised at him. Gaffery was almost beat to a jelly last election for voting with his landlord. I really don't wonder at his not daring to expose himself again. But Garret Keegan has behaved infamously – telling *superfluous* lies – particularly when we meet. Now at least we know whom we cannot trust – and we have experienced the force against us. The evil will not stop at this election. It is not, as in former times, only losing an election.'[1] Here is the cry that in more modern times has led to Fascism. Happily for the Anglo-Irish there was Britain to hang on to.

The priest of Edgeworthstown, Father Gray, had been exerting himself to great effect. Meeting the agent Hinds before polling day, he boasted of how he had already secured 'the vote of every individual Catholic' in the place, bar one, and 'that he did not despair yet of that one – that of the ground keeper, Keegan'. As we have seen, Keegan went over, and Hinds believed the stories of 'mobs breaking windows' were really mere excuses to justify voting with the priests. The agent retailed a story of an alleged grave, dug opposite a tenant's door to intimidate him, that turned out on inspection to be no more than a '*trough* that a pig could have scratched up'. Maria believed the people were doing what they did for the good of Ireland, but confessed 'it is almost impossible to get at the truth'.[2] What she suspected the truth to be urged her on to action. This took the form of writing to Lord Lansdowne in an attempt to 'waken in time his fears for his Irish territories, which if there be (and what is to prevent) a dissolution of the Union will soon cease to afford him rents and presently pass into other hands'.[3] Here is someone who has ceased to pontificate on politics and is anxious to invoke aid against a real danger of possible ruin. As she had remarked, there was more to this affair than losing an election. At this time, however, she under-estimated the British determination to crush O'Connell and let local difficulties cloud her judgement.

[1] ME to FE, 22 Dec 1832 (Edgeworth Papers).
[2] ME to Mrs RLE late 1832 (Edgeworth Papers).
[3] ME to FE, 22 Dec 1832 (Edgeworth Papers).

As luck would have it, Tory persistence after the election led to the unseating of the Repealer M.P.s. Forbes and Lefroy then went off in triumph to Westminster. Not that this technical victory was more than a hollow one. The very month before it occurred, in April 1833, several notable troublemakers had been sentenced at Longford Assizes for agitating the country by 'doings and sayings'.[1] A Coercion Act in the offing had brought about 'a great change in the feelings, or, at least, in the conduct of the people in this country'.[2] Yet the fact of having to have special legislation was in itself a sufficient indication of how matters really stood. A lid on the boiling pot hid, yet did not destroy, the bubbling. Some of the old optimism must have sprung up in Maria though, for at this time she set out on what was to prove her last big journey. It was a trip to Connemara, where she sampled what fully 'Irish' Ireland was like. Unfortunately the vital 1833 money crisis with Lovell broke very soon after her return, and for the rest of the year her thoughts turned increasingly to narrowly domestic concerns.

Characteristically enough, however, she extracted material for wider intellectual interests from an involuntary concern with rent, placing her own predicament in the context of political economy. Back in 1831 the Rev. Richard Jones[3] had published a strongly anti-Ricardo essay on this very subject, and it was to him, by now Professor of Political Economy at King's College, London, that she addressed her latest thoughts. To her mind he had 'led and opened the way' to new prospects in all his writings and 'raised *political economy* not only among the sciences, but amongst the *humanities*'. But admiration had left that ever-watchful critical faculty of hers quite intact. When the worthy man had failed to be sufficiently precise for her, he had to read all about it. 'The only little alteration that occurred to me to wish in your introductory lecture is that you should give a distinguished name to *your* use of the word *capital*.' The parish pump also led her on into reading yet more literature on the Poor Law issue in Ireland. One of the latest pamphlets she summed up as containing 'much truth, much falsehood' in a

---

[1] ME to HE, 1 March 1833 (Edgeworth Papers).

[2] ME to an unknown correspondent, 5 March 1833 (Edgeworth Papers).

[3] The Rev. Richard Jones (1790–1855) was a prominent political economist of the time. He held the post at London from 1833 to 1835, and then went on to be professor at Haileybury for twenty-one years.

'well-written, but not masterly'[1] text. A description fitting the overwhelming proportion of slanted effusions on Irish issues not only then, but both earlier and later. Tied down Maria might have been in body; nothing could have completely dammed up her spirit of enquiry. Professor Jones was but one of her solaces amidst the chores of domestic and estate economy. Meanwhile, on national politics, she consoled herself with the thought that O'Connell was 'so horribly abusive that with all his abilities' he 'must disgust and defeat his own objects'.[2]

Mrs Edgeworth found comfort harder to find. She described the 1833 Coercion Act as 'a polite way of placing us under military law – which would have been ten times more useful had it been done at once without the lying assertions and disgusting debates that have degraded the House of Commons'. Nor did she regard the Act as having changed the situation in any truly material particular.

> O'Connell *and* his tail – or his 'Forty Thieves' as they are called – has done and is doing all the mischief he can to the Protestant aristocracy of this country – and I much fear will succeed in driving them out of it between the danger from armed mobs, nightly depredations and daily insults. The demolition of the Irish Church has completed their disgust and terror of all parties. If Government lay hands upon one part of the public property why not on any other? How can any gentleman be sure of his own? As to the clergy, many are already gone to Canada and . . . the Roman Catholics expect to have their church the established, or at least the principal one – and some say that Dr Doyle[3] and their priesthood openly disapprove of the Commutation of Tithes, having the latent hope (but this is only an 'on dit') that they may one day have possession of them. Some say, but this is only a rumour, that wagers are laid, that *High Mass* will be said at St Patrick's before the year '40.[4]

Her very real apprehensions would hardly have been swept away by the information, published in 1834, that one-fifth of Irish land 'was already owned outright by old Catholic families which had escaped forfeiture or by Roman Catholics who had bought land, and that nearly half of Irish land was held by Catholics on leases for lives renewable for ever, or for 99 years,

[1] ME to the Rev. Richard Jones,1 May 1833 (Edgeworth Papers).

[2] ME to an unknown correspondent, 5 March 1833 (Edgeworth Papers).

[3] James Warren Doyle (1786–1834), Catholic Bishop of Kildare and Leighlin and a prolific writer upon the state of Ireland question.

[4] Mrs RLE to M. Pakenham Edgeworth, no date, but the context suggests 1834 (Edgeworth Papers).

or for 3 lives and 31 years, while many Catholics were investing their money in fee simple estates'.[1] Like Maria before her,
Mrs Edgeworth had perhaps been too prone to forget what had
made the United Kingdom – British power. On 29 April 1834
the House of Commons rejected by 523 votes to 38 the idea of
Repeal. Only one British M.P. was among the minority. Spring-
Rice had been the principal Government spokesman against
O'Connell's motion. The 'Liberator' had met more than his
match at Westminster. And Westminster was a splendidly
backed institution on the eastern side of the Irish Sea.

At the end of 1834 internecine rows inside the Whig party
led to the dismissal of the ministry under Lord Melbourne,[2]
formed the previous July on the retirement of Lord Grey, and
its replacement by a minority administration of Tories under
Sir Robert Peel. When the Opposition made life intolerable,
Peel secured a dissolution of Parliament and went to the
country on a programme of moderate reformism advocated in
the famous Tamworth Manifesto.[3] Henceforward the Tories
were to be known officially as Conservatives, and it was to them
that Maria increasingly gave her sympathies. And this despite
her friendship with and admiration for Permanent Under-
Secretary Drummond, whose great period of office began when
Peel's bid failed and Melbourne returned to power with
O'Connellite support. Thanks to the Tory election petition,
Forbes and Lefroy were the defending candidates in county
Longford. Being in possession and having an excellent party-
machine paid handsome dividends. Luke and Colonel White,
fighting for O'Connell, failed to dislodge them. Indeed the
Conservatives actually notched up handsome majorities, and
from the outset the Repeal campaign had lacked some of the
punch mustered in 1832. Nationally O'Connell did well, and the
Whig dependence upon him for a safe majority gave the Repealers what Duncannon termed 'an almost sovereign sway'.[4]
In fact it was the working arrangement, known as the Lichfield

[1] MacIntyre, *The Liberator*, p. 104.

[2] For whom see *Melbourne*, by Lord David Cecil.

[3] On this subject Gash, *Reaction and Reconstruction in English Politics*, and Hill,
'Pitt and Peel, 1783–4; 1834–5', in *TRHS* NS XIII I (1899) are highly useful.

[4] MacIntyre, *The Liberator*, p. 140. For the direct consequences of this, see
Graham, 'The Lichfield House Compact, 1835', in *IHS* XII (1961). Duncannon
was John William Ponsonby, 1st Baron Duncannon, 1781–1847.

House Compact, drawn up between Whigs and Repealers during February 1835 that led to Peel's resignation in April. A local Repealer-setback in county Longford was not, therefore, much to crow about, and Maria watched anxiously as the tithe, Poor Law and Irish municipal questions came under official scrutiny. At home, money worries could easily have become acute had a 'No Rent' campaign got under way and the family had not regained its recently lost popularity, or managed to reassert its influence over the political actions of its tenantry. This the 1835 election result brought home in ways Maria herself found acutely painful.

With the Whig-Repealer cry of 'No Tories: no tithes' echoing round the country Maria's initial hopes of Conservative success had been very moderate. On 7 January 1835 she informed her mother, 'Mr Hinds has been here all day receiving tithe – and several have paid – and all who did pay paid without remonstrance and cordially. But there are many yet to come however. Mr Hinds has no doubt they all will come in time – I don't say due time.' Lord Forbes's illness in Dublin and doubts about the abilities of Anthony Lefroy lowered her spirits, but she did venture the remark, 'Mr White has started and is canvassing, but it is not thought that he can make anything of his opposition.' Obviously her most dear concern was as to what would happen at Edgeworthstown when the tenantry voted. Her pessimism on this point undoubtedly dampened the ardour she felt for the anti-Repeal cause. 'Our tenants', she forecast, 'will, I think, vote as before, the Protestants with us for Lord Forbes and Lefroy, the Catholics against them, or against Lefroy surely. I wish in my heart it was over, specially without making many quarts of ill-blood.'[1] Five days later, on the coach to Dublin, she fought shy of discussing politics when pressed to do so by a Catholic lawyer named Ferral. In answer to his charge that she was 'running away' from 'our' election Maria brought out the very defence so condemned in *Helen* the year before – that ladies should have nothing to do with politics.[2] The desire to keep off the controversial did not mean her powers of observation were any the less active. Certain fat Catholic priests guilty of devouring

[1] ME to Mrs RLE, 7 Jan 1835 (Edgeworth Papers).
[2] ME to HE, 12 Jan 1835 (Edgeworth Papers).

all the coach sandwiches had their misdeeds noticed by at least one recording angel. Once in the capital her caution wore off. A dense crowd round the doorway of O'Connell's committee-rooms had not prevented her from staring avidly from the coach window at the lamplight electioneering.[1] Back in county Longford polling had already started. Within a week she knew that Forbes with 797 votes and Lefroy with 549 were safely home, leaving Luke White behind with 424 votes and his brother at the bottom with a paltry 61. This over, her attention turned to county Meath, home of her relations the Butlers. There the fight was fast and furious.

Henry Grattan and Morgan O'Connell (son of the 'Liberator') were duly returned once more on 23 January. Their success had aroused much excitement in the Repeal camp; so much so that when Maria arrived to visit her sister Harriet Butler on 28 January she could remark: 'Finally we reached Trim before darkness and election mobs came on.' In her brother-in-law's opinion the young O'Connell was 'quite a gentlemanlike young man' who spoke well. And this tolerant Church of Ireland clergyman was glad to report that he 'would not cut O'Connell's own head off if he never spoke worse or did worse than he did at Trim'. 'You know, or should know,' Maria catechised her stepmother, 'that O'Connell went down to Trim and had himself proposed merely to have the advantage of speaking his speech. Mr Butler, who heard it, says it was exactly the ditto of what he spoke in Dublin. He thought him very eloquent, with a fine voice and great variety of tones, affected pronunciations (e.g. diet, dezet of Poland etc.). Richard Fitzherbert boldly attacked him and asked why he had pressed the dissolving of the Union and then changed his opinion about it. He replied that he had not changed – that he was as great an anti-Unionist as ever, but *"only is waiting his time"*.' Such trivialities were all very well in their way. Nonetheless Maria did not rest content with them. Quite suddenly the whole level of her comments shifted upwards. Mrs Edgeworth was in Britain at this time, and it was to England that Maria switched her mind. 'Upon the whole we understand, from watching the result of your English elections and our own, that the Conservatives have it. And now heaven grant the present Government, with

[1] ME to HE, 14 Jan 1835 (Edgeworth Papers).

their strengthened hands, discretion and firmness sufficient to
prevent a revolution.'[1] On the personal level in Whig politics,
Spring-Rice was again hoping for office, perhaps at the Colonial
Office, where he had lately been Secretary of State in place of
Stanley, or the much-coveted prize of the Speakership. On the
constitutional level the point as to whether the Crown should
dismiss a ministry still possessed of a Commons majority was
being vehemently discussed. Yet Maria's prime concern was
whether Ireland would be saved from revolution by Peel's
strengthened but still minority status Government. Firm and
moderate rule was now her watchword.

The aftermath of the Longford election hit her particularly
hard. Just as she had expected, many Catholic tenants had voted
differently from the family. The consequences of this Mrs
Edgeworth summarised in her *Memoir* of Maria:

> At the time of the general election in 1835, Maria was placed in a
> painful position as her brother's agent. The tenants were forced by
> the priests to vote against their landlord, and in his absence, my son-
> in-law, Captain Fox, who had been much interested for the defeated
> candidate, wished to punish the refractory tenants by forcing them
> to pay up what is called the *hanging gale*[2] of rent. Maria was
> grieved at any proceeding which would interrupt the long-continued
> friendship between these tenants and their landlord, and she was
> also anxious that there should be no misunderstanding between her
> brother and her brother-in-law.

Captain Fox wrote to Sneyd to explain his views, and having
read Sneyd's letter in reply Maria wrote 'to him of her sentiments on the occasion'.[3] The story is a moving one, and she
told it with the full force of the 'Education of the Heart'
backing up that of her considerable intellect. First she gave a
straightforward factual account of what had happened; then an
explanation of what she termed her 'opinions and feelings'.[4]

The story began somewhat trivially but soon rose to more
impressive heights!

> I was absent in Dublin having my teeth taken out and put in at the
> very time when the Longford election terminated. The evening I
> returned home, Barry, looking up from one end of the library table,

[1] ME to Mrs RLE, 28 Jan 1835 (Edgeworth Papers).
[2] The rent due the previous gale-day, which the landlord allowed the tenant to
hold.
[3] *Memoir*, III 168.
[4] ME to CSE, 12 Feb 1835 (Edgeworth Papers).

where he was sitting, to me standing at the other and said: 'Maria,
I have prepared some work for Hinds tomorrow when he is to come.
I have sent to the tenants who voted against their landlord –
Woods, Langan and Dermod – and ordered them to bring in their
rent – the hanging gale. I am determined to make an example of
them.' I am sure by his countenance and manner of speaking, as well
as by his knowledge of what I had said and done on a former election,
that he was in *doubt* at least as to my approval of this step. But as
he did not explicitly require my opinion, only announced the fact
to me, I was dead silent. I own I was surprised and sorry – sorry
particularly about Dermod because, setting aside my own opinion
of the political right or wrong which might have nothing to do with
the decision, I felt that as your agent I should never have taken
such a step without your orders and knowing your opinions by
your letter on the election (which I had not, by the by, shown to
Barry). I was the more embarrassed and anxious. Assuredly, I
neither then, or at any time, gave any sign, direct or indirect, of
approval. And so doubtful, I am sure, did Barry feel as to your
and my approval that the next morning he asked me: 'Maria, who
do you think ought to be consulted and to act for the trust estate
about these tenants and for the *other estate*?' 'You, Barry', said I,
should act as your brother Charles's representative as trustee of the
trust estate in conjunction with Sneyd as the other trustee – as to
the *other estate*, you know it is Sneyd's. He has bought it and I act
as his agent and should always refer to him. He replied something
about your being at a distance and that the two estates must follow
one rule. I spoke of Dermod, said he was your tenant and that I,
not Mr Hinds, received his rent! And I said that I could not do
anything about him and his rent without referring to you.

   That day (Mr Hinds being here), I in the study with him,
Dermod is announced before he could hobble up the backstairs.
Barry entered and said: 'Here's Dermod has brought in his rent.
But what is to be done now? Maria won't receive it, I suppose?'
Considering that it would not be kind or right to Barry to show that
there was any doubt in my mind as to what he had done, as I
was sure with the best intentions, I immediately answered: 'Yes,
Barry, I *will* receive Dermod's rent and hold it till I hear from
Sneyd. Accordingly – exit Barry – enter Dermod, hobbling and
bent . . . and followed by his young son, who presently fell to crying.
I endeavoured to keep automatically to my receiver of rents
and I fell to counting the money.

   But I have omitted to tell you two circumstances that happened
before I went to Dublin about Dermod. At the first announcement
of a contest of this election he had vehemently declared that this
time he would vote for his landlord. *They* could only cut him to
pieces, but *they* could not make him vote against his landlord again.
These words I did not hear with my own ears, but they were repeated to me at the time, about a fortnight before the election. A

few days afterwards, Dermod's son came to tell me privately that he had the night before been wakened by one tapping at the house door, who, in short, put in an anonymous letter threatening to destroy his father if he voted against his Church. The son said that he looked out 'to see did he know the man who brought the letter, but he could not know him – he fired a pistol as he passed the house and went off with him'. I showed the letter to Barry at the time and when I was afterwards speaking to him about Dermod reminded him that he was probably frightened by this letter into giving his vote against his landlord against his will. Barry told me that he did vote against his landlord – did vote I think for White, and he added that he suspected that there was some trick in that whole affair of the letter. Recollecting this, I at once spoke to Dermod about it that I might get out the truth if I could. 'Oh that letter was to serve as an excuse to you, Dermod, I suppose – now was not there some trick in that', said I to the son, 'I daresay you know who wrote it.' Old Dermod, red with indignation, declared he was ready to take his oath he knew nothing about it but just what his son told him and the son was ready to take his oath etc. So I sent for Barry that he might hear this from their own lips. He came and heard – and, I believe, remained of the same opinion still and Dermod went on paying his rent and saying that when once paid one comfort was it could not be asked for again. But he and his father before him had been paying rent to Miss Edgeworth and her father and grandfather etc., and the son went on sobbing and I counting and miscounting.

Barry very mildly, and in a most gentlemanlike manner, said it had given him great concern etc. But what he had begun he would go through with and he told Dermod that he considered he was doing him a service in protecting him against his priests, who, as he knew, had forced him to vote against his landlord. To this fact of being forced by priests to vote against his landlord against his will Dermod acceded. 'Why, there it is then and it was as much as my life was worth and my son's too to do the contrary. Count it again *dear* (to me), for I don't know is it right or wrong.' His hands trembled so between anger and pity for himself and various contending emotions that I am sure he knew no more than a fish what he was doing, and he looked to his son to *count*, who was in *no condition* either with his head upon his knees. Barry repeated that they would now be safe against the priests' oppression for that they would have it to say that their landlord had forced them to pay their rent and against another time. Dermod, throwing his old head back with a vigorous resolution, interrupted and declared that never more would he be in such a scrape, for that the very minute he got home he would burn the scrap of paper or parchment that brought all the trouble upon him (meaning the registration of his vote). I think Barry said this would do him no good and exit. The thoughts of the number of years I had received rent from that old good tenant in my father's time all worked upon me. I am ashamed to tell you my finale – that tears began to flow and though I twinkled and rubbed them out and off they did come – and Honora came in and Mr Hinds was by and it was all shameful. But I never said an *overt* word to Dermod, approving or disapproving what had been done. But told him I should let his landlord know *all about it* and I gave him a receipt in full to November 1834. But I entered his rent only in pencil in the book till I should receive your ultimatum. This I never said to Dermod, but to Barry. I gave him a glass of beer, which he drank to 'Captain Fox's good health' anyway – and his landlord's.

Then I went into the library and began to write as fast as I could to you, my dear Sneyd, and to ask your decision. Enter Mr Butler. 'So Maria, I hear you disgraced yourself with Dermod.' 'Perhaps so' (and then I spoke which I am sorry for). 'Perhaps you think so. But I think it was not easy to go through this. I could not bear to see an old tenant, a cripple too – a man from whom I had been receiving rent forty years – forced to pay up his rent in this manner. And when he had been so threatened and could not act as he wished. As to that letter being a trick on Dermod's part, I don't believe a word of it. He was willing to take his oath to the contrary and I believe him on his word without his oath.' So having uttered and repented of having uttered this, because it was a sort of reproach to Barry, I went on writing away to you and I thought Barry also intended to send a letter he was writing to you in the same packet. But when I was going to sign, seal and deliver he told me he had nothing to send. In consequence of Dermod's having actually paid his rent Barry thought, it seems, there was no occasion to appeal to you and that there was, as Butler said, no alternative now left and no use in sending Barry's letter. He destroyed it and Honora representing to me that she was sorry Barry had destroyed his letter, that he might hereafter explain and that it would be better for me to leave it to him to state the whole matter to you himself, for that I might run the hazard of creating some uneasy feelings between you and him as to his having interfered with your tenants. This fear of disagreeable feelings coming between those who have been and ought to be always united and our affection and esteem for both parties weighed with me more than all the rest and than all the political considerations put together.

A development like this had shaken the traditional Edgeworth approach to its foundations. Maria's father had always said no special favour should be shown to tenants voting in ways contrary to his own, but that was rather different from a peremptory calling in of rent long-established custom had allowed to remain in arrears. The position of Catholic tenants between the devil of the priesthood and the deep sea of landlordism was nothing short of invidious. As to the tenants' real wishes, Maria probably hit the nail on the head when declaring the truth almost impossible to come by. In some cases, no doubt, and especially with landlords in the Edgeworth class, Catholic tenants would sometimes have preferred not to vote for the Repealers. But whether or not Dermod was in this category, Barry Fox had certainly overstepped the mark. Hence all the pressure on Maria not to rock the boat and create discord in the family. One of the countless occasions in this world when those devoted to precise standards and thorough justice were called upon in the name of unity to abandon their scruples had arisen. Happily for her conscience, Maria's initial wavering was overborne by an actual request for her opinions from the misused landlord, Sneyd. She showed in the discussion of principle how very much long training by her father and deep moral conviction had overcome the temptation to compromise her beliefs in conditions of semi-panic. Affability and reasonableness were shown to be much more than weapons turned against their possessor by those of less liberal persuasion. Justice demanded not giving into others to preserve appearances. Justice demanded courage. This Maria seldom lacked.

She began her treatment of 'general principles' by ignoring the 'particular case' under review.

> I quite agree with you, as you do with my father [Sneyd was assured] that according to the British Constitution the voters at elections should be free – that the landlords should not *force* their tenants to vote with them. But a landlord must and should and even will have influence and this is one way in which property is represented and the real balance of the British Constitution is preserved. My father in fact always did use the influence of being a good kind landlord over his tenants, including the favour of leaving a hanging half year in their hands. I never knew him in any instance revenge a tenant's voting against him; but I have heard him say, and I know it was his principle, that he was not bound to show favour or affection to any tenant who voted what is called *against* his landlord.

There follows a passage proving beyond doubt the extreme scrupulousness of Maria's considered approach to the question before them.

> The calling for the *hanging gale* of rent may [she conceded] in this point of view come under his principle. As it is only the withdrawing

of a favour, it may be said to be the resumption of a landlord's right, not the infliction of an injury, or going one tittle beyond the law, nor even the putting yourself in the power of the strict law of Parliament to notice as unconstitutional. This is literally true so far, and further, I admit, for I say candidly the whole on both sides that occurs to me, I admit that I believe if my father were at this moment living and that he knew how the priests had shamefully conducted themselves at the last elections, how they had forced his tenants, and all others whom they could bully, to vote against their *own will* full as much as against their landlords, he might himself *be inclined* to depart from his principle and to use force over his tenants to balance the brutal force and violence on the other side. I say my father *might be so inclined* and his first warmth of temper and indignation doubtless would so urge him, but still 'the gold curb discretion sets on bravery' would act and run into his temper in the first instance, and his reason would rally and represent that it is never either morally lawful or politically wise to do evil that good may come out of it. Because the priests have used force and intimidation such as their situation and means put in their power, are landlords to do likewise and are the poor tenants in this world and the next to be evicted and excommunicated between them? Are we to recriminate and revenge because the priests and the people have done so, beaten or beating as brutal force decides? And if this be called sentimental and too refined morality or reasoning for common use or the exigency of these times, when it is not felt that every nice offence should bear its comment, then I ask where will the contrary course lead, putting right and wrong, and moral principle and constitutional principle out the question? Landlords, if you begin the recriminatory system on or after elections with your tenants, where will it end in Ireland?

It is argued that, by claiming this half year's rent, for instance, you defend the tenant against the power of the priests, since if the tenant can plead that his landlord has distressed him he is safe this time – and may vote with his landlord from fear of similar pressure next election. But not so. The priest will not be so foolishly and easily satisfied. He will still insist on the tenant voting with his church. And what next? The tenant is either rich enough to pay his rent and hold on in defiance of his landlord, or he is not. If he is *not*, which nine times in ten will be the case, what then? Then the landlord must drive, cavil, ruin and eject. No stopping halfway, unless to be shamed and laughed at for beginning without having well-considered the end and thus losing the natural influence of superior sense and education and prudence. Then if you go all lengths and *eject* all, the cry of *tyranny* is in the priest's favour against the landlord's and all the popular cry too against the landlord and all the Irish consequences of beating, burning, murdering etc. The honest constitutional means of resisting the horrible wrong the priests have been guilty of in the last elections is by publishing the facts, bringing them as they must now be brought in all their enormity before Parliament. As far as a very private individual can assist in bringing these truths to light and influencing public opinion by the eloquence of tongue or pen, he does right as a man and a gentleman and good member of society and wisely in the present times to stop, if possible, the power of democracy; and this, I am sure, my dear brother, is what you have done and will do – and I do not wish you to do more or less.

Now to go to particular instances and to the cases and tenants in question. Michael Langan has paid his rent, but when May comes the question remains whether he is to be called upon and forced or not to pay May 1835 as soon as due. If he can and does without force – very well. Happy for him. He may be saved from drinking by not having the money to drink. And if he does not pay, why (if the election were out of sight), I should say it is good to get rid of a drunken tenant. Ditto, I may say, about James Woods. Upon the fate of these two, who are tenants on the trust estate, *you* are, however, called on only half to decide. That is, as one *trustee* to give your opinion, and you may, if you think proper, leave it to your co-trustee to decide. As to Dermod, who is your own tenant, the case is different. If I admit that one rule should govern both estates, I must at the same time be convinced that the one rule is the wisest and best. Otherwise, it is only in fact under the plea of uniformity and strengthening the hands of one ruler and submitting to what we do not feel to be reason and giving the power of landlord out of your hands. It is for you to decide whether, next May, if Dermod brings in his May 1835 rent voluntarily, shall I take it? And if Dermod *refuses to pay*, or says he cannot pay it without ruin, is he to be driven? And are his goods, cattle etc. to be sold? and is he to be ejected? I must beg you to write me your decision. If you wish for my advice I give it at once – not to drive, to let the matter rest with him as it is. He has paid his rent a little earlier than usual and may have felt a little inconvenience and there let it be. You have not *committed* yourself by any further threat or overt act of landlord vengeance and all will heal. If, however, you should think otherwise and should feel it necessary to proceed as Barry has begun, I must at once say, my dear Sneyd, that I cannot as a woman be the driver. I must surrender Dermod into the hands of Mr Hinds and you will be so kind as to desire me to do so that I may not have the appearance of so doing in what is called a pet.

In truth it would be on *principle* and with great reluctance and sorrow that I gave up doing any, the least thing I could for you. I am particularly obliged to you for saying that in case of another election you would come over yourself. I had resolved to make this my request to you, indeed, a condition on which alone I could continue to act. I have felt a great deal of uneasiness on this occasion – more than I have ever felt, though of a very different sort than in Lovell's time – and I would not upon any account in my old days

expose myself to the same again. The uncertainty of whether I am
acting wrong or right and the fear of division and the fear, above all,
of being the cause of division between those I most wish to see
united, would be to me a sort of trial which would destroy my
happiness and health and which I know I could not stand. My
imagination, it may be said, sees all these things too strongly –
magnified. This may be so, but it is not at sixty-eight that the
habits of mind can be suddenly or absolutely changed. I know of
what I am capable and of what I am not, and I end with – I rejoice
that whenever there is another election in this county you, my dear
brother, will come over to your own estate and to represent my
father as you ought – since Lovell, alas, cannot.[1]

The unfortunate Lovell was, nevertheless, consulted by
Sneyd as to future policy in this matter and gave his opinion in
no uncertain terms. 'As to what you ask me about the tenants',
he wrote, 'I will fairly tell you what my principles on the subject
are and, as far as I have been able, how I have acted.' What
followed bore out Maria to the last letter and must have been
unpleasant reading for the precipitate and presumptuous Barry
Fox.

If we either are, or pretend to be their superiors [argued Lovell]
let us show this superiority by our behaviour towards them and
behave towards them in a manner different from that they would
behave [sic] towards us were they placed in our and we in their
situation, I mean in one word, do not show *vengeance*. There are
many small circumstances by which a landlord may mark displeasure,
by refusing small favours . . . slates or trees etc. 'No, I can't do
this for you, you disappointed me on such or such occasion.' On
the contrary, mark strong approbation to those who, in spite of
either their own impulses, or in spite of intimidation, have been
brave enough to act up to your wishes, and, above all, afford them
protection both legally and by your own personal exertions. From
the little I have been able to discover about the Irish people it
appears to me that intimidation is one of the great means by which
the political agitators work on the lower and middle classes, by
holding out those who oppose their machinations as traitors to their
country and at the same time insinuating that their landlords are
tyrants and their enemies.

Now it appears to me that the way to counteract this is to prove
to our tenantry that we are not tyrants, as we do not act from
revenge, that we are not fools, as we do not treat all alike, and that
we are not their enemies, as we protect those who have been true

[1] Ibid. J. H. Whyte, in his article 'Landlord Influence at Elections in Ireland,
1760–1885', in *EHR* LXXX (1965), offers information that shows how very common
the Edgeworth dilemma was at this and many other times in modern Irish history.

to us. But, above all, let us show that we do not act from spite, and that is a feeling which I think the lower orders of Irish understand more clearly than any other. I am convinced it was this principle of forbearance after the election before the last that influenced Gaffrey and some others to vote as they did at the last election. If we had acted harshly to them then they would have been our sworn enemies, but, independently of any interested motives, do we not owe it to ourselves to be superior to the feeling of such a paltry revenge? These are my feelings and I hope you are convinced they do not arise from the immediate cases before us, but that they have been my principles ever since I have been able to understand the Irish character. As for Langan, I know little about him, and as to James Woods, he is constitutionally a coward with a very weak intellect, but I don't consider him a traitor. I fear I have tried you by this long discussion, but you asked for my opinion and I have given it fully.

Then came by way of conclusion remarks the over-scrupulous among the liberal-minded are all too prone to make:

Perhaps I am in error. Remember it is the principle to go on, not the individual case – withdraw kindness, but do not practise revenge. However, you are on the spot and have better means of judging what should be done than I, who am at a distance.[1]

It would appear from the date of this letter – 3 May 1835 – that Sneyd had not immediately been swayed to the liberal side by Maria's immense budget of February. Instead he had bided his time until the next rents became due from the tenants concerned and then consulted the brother who for so many years had been the actual landlord. On the other hand, perhaps he had simply waited until the last minute before showing his hand, having agreed with Maria throughout, because of the embarrassment and possible political repercussions of discountenancing the steps taken by Barry Fox. After all, once the first bout of activity was over, nothing needed to be done until May. But, whichever was the case, the vital point was that Maria was backed up and remained Sneyd's representative for some years more. Two additional county elections occurred before her retirement, and these, with Sneyd's assistance, she took well in her stride.

'Driving' recalcitrant electors was, of course, a widespread practice in Ireland. Tories, and afterwards Conservatives, were usually firm believers in it, and they predominated among the

[1] Lovell Edgeworth to CSE, 3 May 1835 (Edgeworth Papers).

aristocracy and gentry of all the counties, except Kerry, at this time. Many Whigs were not exempt from toughness to their tenants in this matter, and Lord Lansdowne himself expected electoral obedience on his estates. While county Longford had a comparatively substantial population of Protestant tenants to back their 'Quality' co-religionists, numerous of the Catholic 'Quantity' were on the electoral register. One of the consequences of the Repeal agitation had been a campaign by many local landowners to replace these Catholic tenants by Protestants from outside. Both Lord Lorton and Anthony Lefroy, the Conservative M.P., evicted tenants for political waywardness, and thus supported a general reshaping of the community. They shared the opinion of their fellow Conservative landowner Denis Daly of Dunsandle, county Galway, that canvassing of tenants against the known wishes of their landlord was 'monstrously unconstitutional.'[1] Significantly enough, Lord Forbes, the other Longford county M.P., scorned such a doctrine. Perhaps, as the voting figures indicate, because all his people voted for him anyway – in itself a considerable tribute – or perhaps because he found it squared with his conscience, or paid a handsome dividend, or because of a combination of some or all of these reasons. In any case his example must have been a tower of strength to Maria and Sneyd Edgeworth and given a pleasantly bipartisan element to the cause of social and political moderation.

All the greater pity for them then that Lord Forbes's health was so poor. Illness had hampered him in the 1835 campaign, and talk was already rife in the county within a month of the polling as to who should eventually stand in his stead. Maria herself wrote to Sneyd on the subject at that time, mentioning the brother of Barry Fox. 'With respect to Charles Fox, I think he will certainly stand the first opportunity. I am not sure that it will be for his happiness to be in Parliament. But I think he will make an honest and *moderate* member and will do well in Committees, and I think you may support him fairly.' But, most important of all, 'He will not be bitter orange. He has good sense and temper – excellent.' There then emerges what is certainly the key to most of her political, social and religious thinking – the attitude that can best be termed her Colonial

---

[1] MacIntyre, *The Liberator*, p. 99.

Office mentality. 'I hate the term I have just used – *Orange'*,
she avowed, 'and Whig and Tory both I would avoid if I could,
and consider only what is right and best to be done in our times.'
Along with Spring-Rice and Lansdowne, she had disapproved
of certain aspects of the policies pursued by the Grey and Melbourne governments, particularly those relating to the Church
of Ireland or displaying democratic tendencies. She thought

> The late ultra-Reform Liberalists went far and had they continued
> in power would have overturned everything both in England and
> Ireland, would have let in upon us the ragamuffin democracy, cried
> havoc etc. I think that nothing less than the decided, perhaps
> despotic hand of the Duke of Wellington could prevent this catas-
> trophe, and the sense of Mr Peel will aid, I trust. The Duke has
> been a stander-by and has had leisure to repent the error which
> turned him out before, viz. of declaring that he could have no reform.
> Mr Peel has well guarded against this in his address on his return.
> What we must pray for is that the hands of the present government
> may be strengthened sufficiently to enable them to prevent the
> mischiefs prepared by the last administration, and that having seen
> the error, they may be wise in time. [1]

Small wonder, if Maria could have come round to this way of
thinking, that in our own day moderate Liberals afraid of
democracy or social democracy should bring themselves to
support autocratic régimes. Wellington would have been a
De Gaulle at the mildest, but more probably a Franco.

Mrs Edgeworth still suspected in March that her step-
daughter had remained altogether too liberal in the face of what
she regarded as social destruction. Maria hastened, through
her sister, to offer reassurances. Peel excited her admiration,
she said, and Stanley enjoyed her 'high opinion'. The mention
of Stanley was of especial significance, for further comments
make it abundantly clear that his course was the one of which
Maria approved most. At that juncture he was a conditional
supporter of Peel, a position Maria herself heartily shared in
view of the trends in official Irish Whig–Liberal plans. She
thought (and obviously hoped) that 'he and his Modérés'
would support 'the present Ministry if they go *straight* according to Sir Robert Peel's professions in his speech as to just
and necessary reform. And if he supports, they will stand
against the *Radicals* I trust. Otherwise there must be revolution

[1] ME to CSE, 12 Feb 1835 (Edgeworth Papers).

and an overturning of all things. . . . I don't think there will be
another dissolution of Parliament. It would be too dangerous.'[1]
A mere two days later she again states her new alignment: 'I
hope the present Ministry will stand with the assistance of
Stanley and his Modérés.' The psychological relief the Stanleyites must have provided for her should not be ignored. Any
intelligent person with liberal opinions would have found a
full-blooded individual diversion of allegiance to straight
Conservatism more difficult than a shift of support in company
with highly respected public figures of great social and political
eminence. 'Conservatism on conditions' was the theology
preached in the Stanleyite chapel of ease. Worshippers there
could feel liberally conservative and conservatively liberal. In
the words of the preface to the Anglican Prayer Book, they
could avoid the 'two extremes, of too much stiffness in refusing
and of too much easiness in admitting any variation'.

Yet though the chapel was of ease, the sentiments felt in it
were more often than not ones of unease. Maria now declared:
'I am exceedingly interested now in politics, because all our
fate and fortune and domestic life altogether hang upon this
point. Will they (the ministry) be able to prevent those who
have no property and no education from overwhelming by their
numbers those who have some property and some education?'[2]
When Peel resigned in April she described his farewell speech
as 'one of the finest most dignified' of its kind she had ever read,
and rejoiced that 'so much virtue and magnanimity' was left in
England. Lord Forbes's comment on events was scarcely likely
to disperse her heartsearchings over the future. Hard upon the
news of Peel's fall had come a note which ended, 'The British
Constitution died last night.' How changed Maria was from the
optimistic days of the letters on Emancipation to Mrs Lazarus
is clear from an apparent acceptance of the Forbesian interpretation as prima facie reasonable and from her comments on
Sir Culling Smith. This gentleman thought the constitution
'but just beginning to live'. 'He wrote me by the same post',
she explained, 'that he had sent over his bailiff to look at a
property which he is going to purchase in Galway. And that
now he thinks English capital will flow over to Ireland in

[1] ME to FE, 3 March 1835 (Edgeworth Papers).
[2] ME to FE, 5 March 1835 (Edgeworth Papers).

security. "God help your poor head" thought I.'[1] Despite the withdrawal into intellectual and estate-management activity to avoid some of the unpleasantness of the contemporary scene, she had kept her north eye open and was anyway too courageous and enquiring not to face the facts. Her interpretation of them led her into new paths and away from those of Spring-Rice. That he really agreed in many respects with Stanley and yet stayed where he was cannot have raised him in her estimation.

[1] ME to FE, 12 April 1835 (Edgeworth Papers).

3

A Bleak Outlook

CIRCUMSTANCES at Edgeworthstown did occasionally seem to offer encouragement of a tolerable future. An instance of honesty in a petty official ('wonderfully for Ireland')[1] and the permanent installation of a tactful rector as a replacement for the popular and retired Mr Keating warmed Maria's heart. An employee in the post office had actually refused to hand back a letter of hers she was in hopes of intercepting for correction. That the man might simply have wanted to be awkward with the local gentry never crossed her mind, though the fact of his being almost certainly a Protestant probably rules that possibility out. As for the new incumbent, she felt: 'It is of the utmost consequence to us to have a *mild* sensible clergyman here, as the times require great discretion and command of temper, and our Catholic priests are violent and rude.' A recent attempt to collect tithes had borne this out very well. Hinds had requested Maria to write to the local Catholic priest, Gray, for the tithes due to Keating, she 'having undertaken to collect it (compounding in short) to oblige Mr Hinds'.

This she soon came to regret, remarking, 'like the fool I was (for I should have left him to do the business), I wrote to Mr Gray and as civil a note with compliments to *Doctor* Gray as it was in my power to pen'. The man who took it returned very shaken but five minutes later. 'Oh Ma'am', he cried, 'I never saw a man in such a passion as Mr Gray when he read your note. He came out into the passage and declared he would never pay a

[1] ME to FE, 15 April 1835 (Edgeworth Papers).

farthing of the whole, ever he lived. "Tell her so. Tell her that
when on my death bed I send to Mr Keating to come to me, then
I will pay." And he scolded so, Ma'am, I was glad to break off.'
The sum under discussion was eleven shillings, and Maria
relates: 'This was said before his servants and workmen. As it
was after dinner I thought perhaps he might have taken a little
tumbler too much, but next day he met the messenger 'and
remembered it all clearly, and asked eagerly what Miss Edgeworth said when his answer was given to her.' The man,
Flower by name,

> announced that Miss Edgeworth said *nothing*. Happily it was so.
> It is quite necessary, not only to keep one's temper within con-
> junctives, but also to hold one's tongue. Nothing can come of
> nothing. The end of the matter must be that when all the rest of
> Mr Keating's tithe has been paid, which will be in a few days, for
> *all* our tenants have paid well Mr Keating's tithe, Mr Hinds must
> send again or go to Mr Gray, taking no notice of his message,
> civilly to renew the application. Mr Hinds thinks he will then pay.
> I do not. But the next step if he refuses must be to say not a word
> more about tithe, but to notice him to give up a field, which he
> holds from us, essential to his Reverend's cow and horse.

Driving an ill-mannered priest in a mild kind of way quite
appealed to the landlord in Maria. Her determination to fight
for the law by all legitimate means had not lessened one iota,
however unpromising the general outlook for her and hers
appeared to be. The plan was to 'notice' Gray 'either to quit
or pay an additional rent what he refuses as tithe – say eleven
or twelve shillings, though I would not make it exactly the
tithe. This must take effect because he cannot resist. The
Quarter Sessions will decree and oust him.' But while the law
was the law and Gray was Gray, she was

> quite of opinion that tithe ought to be abolished and that it was an
> injustice always to make Catholics pay to clergy for what they did
> not teach them and what they would not have consented to learn.
> Even in Mr Gray's answer, I think, there was great force – but
> rudeness also towards the innocent individual and the present prop-
> rietor, whom it is injustice to rob because in former time injustice
> was done in which we had neither act nor part, but took our
> property as it came to us and made our contracts with tenants
> honestly, and have a right to request that they should on their part
> fulfil those contracts, verbal or written.[1]

[1] ME to FE, 15 May 1835 (Edgeworth Papers).

Here again is an interesting revelation of the desire for a new
beginning in Ireland, based on a mutual recognition of the
difficulties certain to arise from unilateral breaches of contract,
the need to redress grievances through regular channels and
the constant readiness of the authorities so to redress them.
Given Peel and the Stanleyites, the fulfilment of the official
side of this programme was not completely out of the question
from Maria's viewpoint. Unfortunately the Irish Catholic masses
did not see things her way. In reality, as she herself often feared,
the O'Connellite lack of interest in a fundamental religious and
landholding revolution failed fully to represent the deepest
aspirations of the bulk of their rank and file. The Catholic
faith and the belief that the land had been stolen from the true
Irish people were at bottom the most potent mainsprings of Irish
national feeling. Again we are back to the old truth that Grat-
tanism had been outbidden, and beyond it neither Peel, nor
the Stanleyites, nor Maria could or would go.

As the year wore on she would appear to have stuck strongly
to her new position. After all, she could claim that the Whigs,
not she, had changed. In June she referred to Melbourne, by
then in the third month of his second ministry, as 'your Prime
Minister',[1] thus disowning him with the maximum clarity.
Amidst the quiet of high summer she lamented, 'Oh that Mr
O'Connell's heart could feel what his head might do for Ireland –
and for Ireland in ages yet unborn.'[2] And in October she is more
explicit on the point, complaining, 'As to O'Connell, I am clear
that no Ministry could buy him, because he has sold himself
to the devil of popularity and cannot get himself back again
even if he would. He must be a slave to the huzzas without
which he cannot live. He will lash himself to death with his tail.'[3]
Partisan feeling for the *status quo* apart, there was a hard core
of truth in these remarks. Mere Repeal and the achievement of
the other immediately popular demands would not have solved
Ireland's basic problems. They were matters for the head not
the heart, except in so far as human sympathy helped justify
compromise in the minds of all parties. Maria's father had seen

[1] ME to an unknown correspondent – very probably FE – 6 June 1835 (Edgeworth Papers).
[2] ME to an unknown correspondent – very probably FE – 18 Aug 1835 (Edgeworth Papers).
[3] ME to FE, 12 Oct 1835 (Edgeworth Papers).

the Union as Ireland's chance, both on account of Britain's
level of civilisation and the great strength she had for backing
it up. With such profound disagreements in her midst Ireland
did indeed require outside direction if all sections of the
population were to continue living side by side. If the 'Quality'
left Ireland, the situation would deteriorate rapidly, Repeal or
no Repeal. Hence Maria's preoccupation with ending absenteeism and pushing ahead for compromise on popular grievances.
Under her plan the 'Quality' would have continued to rule
because best fitted to do so, but at a price involving the abandonment of unfair advantages. In England the notion would
have worked without too much trouble. Divisions and resentments were nowhere nearly so marked. In Ireland it required
the backing of force. Both 'Quality' and 'Quantity' had to have
enlightenment thrust upon them before being entrusted with a
wide freedom. But even with Peel in office or Drummond running Melbourne's Irish administration on the spot, the necessary
single-mindedness was partly lacking at Westminster. Social and
party links between the 'Bitter Orange' groups in Ireland and the
Conservatives were extremely potent. Peel would have had to be
absolute dictator of his party before being able to dictate in Ireland
as Maria dreamed. He was not. On the left 'Bilious Green' elements
held Melbourne periodically in thrall, and so severely handicapped
the ever-willing Drummond. Things were a mess and no mistake, and the representation of Ireland in the United Kingdom Parliament and party politics were no small factor in making them so.

Maria could hardly have thought of O'Connell's popularity
without once more reflecting on how much he had been instrumental in reducing hers. One of her biographers commented:

> Innumerable were the improvements which were effected by Mrs
> and Miss Edgeworth for the advantage of their poorer neighbours
> in the immediate vicinity of their home. Cottagers' houses were
> rebuilt and made comfortable, schools built, and roads improved. . . .
> She endeavoured to be on the best terms with the Catholic priests
> to whom she showed constant kindness and hospitality. Her poorer
> neighbours were made sharers in all her interests or pleasures, and
> all those she employed were treated as friends rather than servants;
> all her sympathies were on behalf of Ireland. Yet she met with no
> return of affection or sympathy.[1]

[1] *Life and Letters* ed. Hare, II 262. The fate of the Le Fanus had also descended
upon the Edgeworths!

Though the last sentence was far from true before the Repeal campaign began, it had become so by 1832. In 1836 a Mrs Farrar, writing about Edgeworthstown, made the situation painfully clear:

> It was market day: so the main street was full of the lower order of Irish, with their horses and carts, asses and panniers, tables and stands full of eatables and articles of clothing. . . . But as we passed through the crowd to the schoolhouse the enmity of the Papists to Protestant landholders was but too evident. Though Mrs Edgeworth had been the Lady Bountiful of the village for many years, there were no bows for her or her friends, no making way before her, no touching of hats, no pleasant looks. A sullen expression and a dogged immovability were on every side of us.[1]

When Lord Forbes did die at the end of that year, county Longford was again plunged into electioneering. Charles Fox came forward to defend the seat for the Conservatives. Luke White once more represented the Repealers. 'A sullen expression and a dogged immovability'[2] notwithstanding, Maria went into the election with an enthusiasm born of family ties and renewed zest. She wrote to Harriet on 23 December:

> I hope I have done some little good (and no harm) by coming home, as I have secured I hope Dermod's and Kelly's votes, to whom I drove out through the snow on the ground that day, and after deep struggling internally each of them gave me their promise. Dermod was as white as a sheet and each particular bristle of his beard half an inch long seemed to feel the struggle of his mind. 'Oh Ma'am, the priest in – and I so set upon – and a lone cripple. But I will tell you what – I am much obliged to you, and my family, as you say, and myself was always so obliged to your father – the best of landlords – that I cannot, when it is put to me by yourself, I cannot refuse you. I should not die easy in my conscience if I did. So there it is – let the priests do their worst. I will vote for you. But, dear Miss Edgeworth, would you let me stay till the last day that I might get in as it were unknownst?' 'No, that is impossible, you cannot do it unknownst, and as you feel it right do it boldly.' 'Then so I will. Send a carriage of any kind for me when you will. I will go.' Now I hope he will be steady. . . . Mr Kelly's conscientious struggles you shall hear of when we meet.[3]

Vast Repealer activity whittling away the vital Forbes interest made Charles Fox's chances of winning rather slender.

---

[1] Ibid. Mrs Farrar was an American visitor of the Edgeworths.
[2] Ibid.
[3] ME to HE, 23 Dec 1836 (Edgeworth Papers).

Moreover the challengers had been busy with registration business, an item they had rather let slide – to their cost – prior to the last contest. Maria recognised the trends, commenting, 'Upon the whole this day, the prospect has a little brightened for Charles Fox, but I cannot say I think there is much chance of success.'[1] And so it turned out, for White was elected on 30 December by 619 to 526 and 'two to three thousand pounds'[2] of Fox money appeared to have gone well and truly down the drain. The Repealers had leapt ahead on the fourth and last day of polling. Writing to Miss Ruxton the day after, our heroine expressed gratitude for Fox's 'noble stand', declaring:

> The Conservative interest in Ireland *must*, or at least ought to feel deeply obliged to him. The gentlemen of the Conservative side did not act zealously together. If they had, if Sir George Fetherston had not sacrificed to an eighteen years old pique the interests of this county, and, if this county, his own principles too in politics, Charles Fox would have been at this moment our member.

Considerable consolation was to be had, nonetheless, because:

> We have had the pleasure of seeing among our own tenantry and many of the yeomanry of this county strong instances of virtue and zealous attachment – especially in Mr Hinds we have seen the warmest friendship and gratitude, and a degree of courage *military and civil* beyond anything I could have imagined in him, or could really have believed, unless it had been brought out by these trials in action. The fatigue he has gone through with his slight pale frame is quite astonishing. I am sure he had not three hours sleep any night these four nights. He was up and out in his carriage driving to tenants and voters at four o'clock in these freezing cold mornings. Even Medy the housemaid said to me yesterday, 'I wish you to send Mr Hinds.' It is surprising how much all the servants admire this sort of zealous attachment and duty doing. Cassidy has shown great attachment and it is really pleasant to feel that those who are to remain and live with us are good and grateful.[3]

Nor had encouragement stopped there. 'Our own tenants', continued Maria, 'all behaved well, except two or three who shall be nameless. I will have nothing to do with vengeances, simply with rewards – more effective I think.'[4] For her the

---

[1] Ibid.   [2] ME to Sophy Ruxton, 31 Dec 1836 (Edgeworth Papers).
[3] Ibid.   [4] Ibid.

application of Bacon's maxim that 'Boldness, boldness, boldness' should be 'the one two three in public life' had yielded some results in the quarter where she was most concerned. Loyalty had to begin at home. What was even better, she had managed it without reducing 'public life' to 'public roguery', contrary to her expectations of the 1820s.[1] Personal independence of her father and wider experience had taught her the two were not automatically synonymous. The Repealers had again been foolish enough to confuse them and give the Conservatives another chance to petition. The 'popular' side in Longford politics seemed to have an unfortunate knack of missing the happy medium of activity – enough to achieve victory and yet keep the seat. Violence 'on the part of the priests' had again 'been beyond description or belief'[2] and the Conservatives soon set about collecting subscriptions to finance a petition. If it succeeded, the Foxes would not have spent their funds in vain. Enough of the Repealer votes would have been found invalid to put the Conservatives into the majority and seat their candidate.

Before the process got under way, Maria and the Butlers went west for a visit to the Moores of Moore Hall in county Mayo. This family was Catholic and of a pleasingly tolerant disposition, fitting in well with the Edgeworth ideal of a happy and prosperous Ireland. Its land policy was at once progressive and kindly, its awareness of social responsibilities well developed. The friendship had sprung up but lately after an introduction by their mutual friend Mr Strickland of Lough Glynn in county Roscommon. George Moore, the head of the house, was of a scholarly turn of mind. Indeed it was after reading an article he had written for the *British Review* on the Treaty of Limerick that Maria had asked to meet him. Dean Butler was 'much edified' by the company at Moore Hall. It must certainly have made a highly pleasant change from the militant priesthood of his own county. 'He had always sought the society of open-minded Catholics, and his talks with the Moores, and particularly with George Moore, recalled to him the theory which he had held in his youth, namely that a reformation not *from* nor *in*, but of the Roman Catholic Church in Ireland might be pos-

---

[1] See ME to FE, 8 May 1824 (Edgeworth Papers).
[2] ME to Sophy Ruxton, 31 Dec 1836 (Edgeworth Papers).

sible.' His view that moderate Catholics would ultimately slip
into a virtual Protestantism was undoubtedly shared by the
Papal authorities and Irish Catholic militants, but in the cosy
atmosphere of Moore Hall everyone was able to agree that
the 'strange fashion that had grown up' of late 'of baiting all
parties into consistency by ever recurring to first principles
and rejecting compromise and common sense' was to be
utterly 'deplored'.[1] The older people were also at one on
politics, but George Henry Moore, the heir to Moore Hall,
was farther to the left, had upheld O'Connell in school debates
at Oscott, and later became the leader of the Irish Independent
Brigade of the 1850s. As we shall see, however, he was not a
Repealer and remained like his father in the Whig fold, though
on its leftmost extremity. The religious factor stood in the way
of the older man's deserting to the Stanleyites or Peel, but his
general opinions accorded quite well with theirs and enabled
him to accept Maria's political diagnosis and suggestions as to
the curing of Ireland's ills.[2]

With a possible unseating of Luke White in prospect, 'the
good people in Edgeworthstown' were 'in transports of joy'.
Reading newspaper reports to the effect that White would not
be defending himself against the petition, men such as the
stalwart Cassidy 'seemed to take it for granted that Charles
Fox was seated'. Maria was more cautious, remarking to Mrs
Edgeworth, 'I fear that there will be a dissolution of Parliament
very soon and all to be done over again, and that may be the
reason why Mr White does not think it worthwhile to go to the
expense of defending himself. They say that the Catholic party
will have nothing to do with him next time.'[3] In fact White did
fight back and the Repealers did run him again in August 1837,
when another general election took place following the death
of William IV. Of particular significance at this period was the
seemingly greater sensitiveness of Maria to the dangers she

[1] Hone, '*The Moores of Moore Hall*, pp. 74–80.
[2] Ibid. p. 54.
[3] ME to Mrs RLE, 21 Feb 1837 (Edgeworth Papers). Charles Fox was the
third of the four sons of Richard Fox and Lady Anne Fox (*née* Maxwell) of Fox
Hall, county Longford. He lived from 1791 to 1862. His brother Barry – the second
son – had married Sophia Edgeworth, half-sister to ME, in 1824. His dates were
1789 to 1863. Richard Fox – the father – was the only son of one Francis Fox and
Mary Edgeworth, sister of RLE. Both Barry and Charles had independent means
due to inheriting under the will of their grandfather Lord Farnham.

felt were springing from increased Catholic power. The fact that she used the word Catholic as a synonym of Repealer in a political context was, although not new, indicative of O'Connell's failure to broaden his appeal in any significant way. But more than the straightforward pursuit of 'Patriot' politics was worrying her. In April 1837 she harped back once more to the alleged evils of Maynooth, writing of 'the dangerous spirit and tendency of Catholicism' and stressing the sinister quality of 'those closed doors' and 'this concealment', which told against Maynooth more 'than anything that could be seen or said'.[1] Closeness to Thomas Drummond had not brought her to approve of the Lichfield House Compact, and weakness in governmental circles heightened her fears still more. The likelihood of Peel returning to office, with or without a dissolution, gave her a great fillip. Actual correspondence with him encouraged her still further in the belief that he would do 'some good for real goodness sake – to make up his political soul'.[2] Meanwhile Melbourne was still prime minister and the Catholics uncontained. Their combination of authoritarian secretiveness and flagrant intimidation in private and public struck her as a foul menace to all that was valued by the liberals of the whole United Kingdom.

On 5 May 1837 Charles Fox was declared to be the rightfully elected member for county Longford. Maria was temporarily elated. The affair would prove 'so useful in the consequences'. 'The striking off of those bad votes' struck her as being 'in itself an indemnity for the past and a security for the future'. Then followed a diatribe on her current King Charles's Head: 'This committee have had an opportunity of seeing something of the Irish priests themselves and of tracing their influence upon others. They must have been shocked at the violence and the perjury, and between times they must have been relieved and amused by Paddy's blunders both wilful and involuntary.' Yet good would come out of evil, for

> The labour they have gone through has had this excellent result that Parliament must, in consequence of their report and representations make some reform in the mode of registering votes in this

[1] ME to an unknown correspondent, 15 April 1837, and ME to Mrs RLE, 24 April 1837 (Edgeworth Papers).
[2] Ibid.

country. One distinct declaration of what constitutes a good vote would do away at once with the necessity for all the registering barristers' varying opinions and would prevent the cheating at elections and the squabbling, and undue returns and subsequent petitions.

Such a panacea was not to be produced in her lifetime. Still, she lived in hopes, and in Edgeworthstown the downfall of White had an instantaneous and, to her, a beneficial effect. Better than that, the whole neighbourhood was more salubrious 'in the immediately altered tone of the people, their being relieved from the dread of the priests and the beatings'. 'As they say', Fanny was informed, 'we have been worried between and betwixt our priests and our landlords – and they are rejoiced when the pressure on one side is taken off.'[1]

Had it been possible for Maria to have been made a peeress in her own right, the motto 'Prudence in joy and sorrow' would have been most appropriate for the accompanying coat of arms. The realisation that another election was in the offing led her to counsel caution in the Conservative rank and file. 'We requested our well-wishers not to make arches, illuminations, or triumphing on Charles Fox's being seated, because it would only irritate the defeated and it is much more dignified, as well as more provident, to take it easy – in the placid security of being and having been in the right.' Conservative 'virtue' had now apparently taken on the quality of divine truth. So great was the satisfaction at having been 'in the right' that some secret conclave with W. E. Gladstone might well have been suspected, except that that gentleman never visited Edgeworthstown at that or any other time, nor treated the Edgeworth family to any of his tortuous letters, nor received any from them. Imagine, though, the mood of wet-blanketry wafting out of the 'big house'. When the ebullient Cassidy first found voice on the topic of victory, insisting in 'a rich brogue', 'Then Ma'am, we'll have Mr Charles chaired through the town, so we will,' he was met with a response such as 'to moderate his joy'. His rejoinder revealed defeat and disappointment alike – it was a simple 'Oh well'. But, as Maria remarked, 'As Charles is in London, there was time for reflection.'[2]

[1] ME to FE, 9 May 1837 (Edgeworth Papers).
[2] Ibid.

Although the next general election was imminent, not all her reflections were concentrated on practical politics. For one thing, there was Harriet Martineau's new book on America to worry about. It was tantalising, because as Mrs Lazarus was told, while all the facts produced told heavily against 'a democratic form of government and against the spirit of democracy', Miss Martineau's opinion 'theory, argument, soul and body' was powerfully in favour of 'absolute democracy'. Women were to form part of her electorate. 'Does majority of numbers include majority of sense, judgment, moral feeling etc?' the unoffending American lady was indignantly asked.[1] Nearer home the problems of tempered oligarchy were at that moment probably more pressing. For all her zest in wishing Charles Fox success and a firm continuance in his 'taste for independence', Maria opined on the anniversary of the Fall of the Bastille that the election was 'a plague . . . to everybody who has anything to do with it'.

As a prominent sufferer from numerous pressures, some much less welcome than others, Lady Forbes, widow of the former M.P., doubtless subscribed to this sentiment. Quite understandably she declared her non-intervention, for, as she rightly remarked, there was no call now actively to campaign. The Conservatives had had reason to regret the falling away of the Forbesian electoral 'clan' at the by-election of 1836. Nevertheless, had she changed her mind, there would have been the Repealers' reaction to consider. Well before any indication of her intentions had been made: 'The priests of Longford and Newtown Forbes sent her word, that is, said to a person whom they knew would repeat it to her, that "if she took the part they supposed she would (the part of Charles Fox in short) *they* would report her to the Government and bid her remember that she was now a servant of Government (Lady of the Bedchamber)'. To this she answered: "I am not a servant of the Government's, I am a servant of the Queen's. I fear no reports. I shall act as I think right" and she intends to go to Carlow during the election.' Maria was moved to pity by the lady's plight: 'Now! she is . . . an unprotected widow in that half-burned-down castle – in the midst of the people who have twice

[1] ME to Mrs Lazarus, 11 July 1837 (Edgeworth Papers). The book referred to was *Society in America*. For Harriet Martineau, see below, p. 104 n 2.

fired at her steward – and surrounded by intriguing priests and party spirit which has neither reason nor feeling.'[1] Certainly there was cause for alarm, and the idea of leaving Castle Forbes a good one. The election became even more disorderly than usual, and 'exclusive dealing'[2] cropped up on quite a widespread scale. Charles Fox and his senior partner, Anthony Lefroy, both lost their seats, and the White brothers avenged the humiliation of 1835, Luke getting 671 votes and Henry 667. The Conservative figures – 561 for Lefroy and 556 for Fox – showed once more how crucial the Forbes interest had been and just why the priests were at such pains in their concerted efforts to ensure the by-election defections were sustained.

Some considerable time passed between this election of August 1837 and Maria's next significant pronouncement upon politics and social policy. Only in February 1839 did she again take the plunge, speculating to Fanny as to whether Thomas Drummond would continue his work in Ireland for much longer. The life of the Melbourne ministry was constantly threatened, and upon it Drummond's position largely depended. His departure would have been unwelcome to her, despite the obvious and strong desire she had that the Government should not 'hold together another season'.[3] Under his surveillance Catholic Emancipation had at last become something of a reality. Positions of trust within the gift of official patronage were no longer exclusively doled out to Protestants. Yet satisfactory administration struck her as inadequate in itself if accompanied by flirtation with or dependence upon O'Connell.

It is, nonetheless, curious that no letter or memorandum has survived in the Edgeworth papers in which her direct views on the tithe and Poor Law legislation of 1838 can be found. Perhaps the apparent silence denotes a reluctant approval. As we saw, she did not share the idea, widespread among the 'Quality' and interested British opinion, that the campaign to abolish the payment of tithes to the clergy of the established Church of Ireland was 'an insidious politico-religious con-spiracy on the part of the Catholic population, organised by O'Connell and his henchmen, against the revenues and hence

[1] ME to FE, 14 July 1837 (Edgeworth Papers).
[2] MacIntyre, *The Liberator*, p. 126.
[3] ME to FE, 16 Feb 1839.

against the existence'[1] of that Church. It was the non-payment
while the amounts were legally due that stuck in her gizzard.
She undoubtedly approved mightily of the government assistance afforded the clergy back in 1832 and regarded the 1832
Tithe Act, enforcing a permanent composition throughout the
country, as a step in the right direction. Her passion for law and
order had divided her even at that stage from the bulk of Irish
Whigs, but the British Whigs had kept her temporarily satisfied. That the 1838 Act converted tithe composition into a rent-
charge 'at seventy-five per cent of the composition' without
diverting any possible surplus to narrowly Catholic education
cannot have been displeasing to her. But the Government's
initial plan to use surpluses for 'secular purposes' might well
have made her uneasy.[2] As to the Poor Law Act, though Spring-
Rice disapproved of compulsory relief, no indication exists
as to whether she agreed with him. What is almost certain,
however, is that in her heart of hearts she would have favoured
carefully administered outdoor relief as part of the scheme,
provided it was practical and not open to abuse. Certainly she
disapproved of excessive bureaucratic rigidity and inhumanity.
Common sense alone had made her favour some national system
of relief. Even the 'Quality' at its best could not cope entirely
with the problem on an *ad hoc* basis. Nevertheless, the recom-
mendations of the Nicholls Report of the year before had had her
uneasy approval. Despite the appalling revelations made before
Lord Grey's 1833 commission, its report had not favoured the
introduction of the Poor Law into Ireland. The Government
had therefore set it aside, and shortly after Mr (later Sir George)
Nicholls of the English Poor Law Commission had been
deputed to take the enquiry further. Working fast and furiously
he had found his predecessors' work accurate enough and had
gone on to recommend the extension of the principles of the
English Poor Law to Ireland. Under such a scheme workhouses
would be instituted, where 'relief and employment should be
afforded to the poor, infirm and able-bodied'.[3] The whole

---

[1] MacIntyre, *The Liberator*, p. 167. For the whole background to Anglican
problems in public questions just then, see Chadwick, *The Victorian Church*, part I.
Ball, *The Reformed Church of Ireland*, and Godkin, *Ireland and her Churches*, are
also useful.
[2] *Two Centuries of Irish History*, ed. Bryce, pp. 362–3.
[3] Ibid. p. 366.

country would be divided into unions and the system strictly administered by local boards of guardians. Overall control would lie with a specially constituted authority in Dublin. Lord Melbourne built his Bill around these features, omitting a law of settlement, limiting the elected members of the boards to a maximum of one-third, prohibiting membership to all ministers of religion, and laying down that the Dublin Commissioners should be chosen from the English Poor Law Commission. Following an amendment passed in the House of Lords at the instance of the Duke of Wellington, the cost of maintaining the paupers was not to fall on the union at large, but on the parishes within it from which the paupers came. O'Connell's efforts to have the proposed system humanised and Sharman Crawford's moves to include a law of settlement and provide for some outdoor relief came to naught. As passed in July 1838 the Bill was close to what Nicholls had recommended.

So while there is nothing from Maria on the Poor Law Act itself, her comments on the Nicholls Report may be taken as giving a good lead as to her opinion of it. The Rev. Professor Jones, translated two years previously to Haileybury, was her chosen confidant on the subject.

> Write straight [she begged] and tell me how you like Mr Nicholls's late Report on poor laws for Ireland. I hope you will not tell me I am wrong in admiring or rather esteeming it as I do. I was much averse, for the reasons which your works (much more than Miss Martineau's) furnished me, to *any* poor law for Ireland. On the principle of non-interference of legislative enactions between land-lord and tenant, and industry and its wages, and idleness and its punishment, and overpopulation and its consequences, I deprecated the measure altogether. But Mr Nicholls's Report has brought me to the belief, I was going to say conviction, that the workhouse system which he proposes, guarded by the destitution test, may be *safely* tried in Ireland and that the probability of its advantages to this country far outweigh the expense of the experiment. It is not in human power to do the work of Time and to carry any country suddenly through what Nicholls well calls the transition state with its necessary attendant evils, but whatever *can* be done by legislative aid in the circumstances this measure will, I trust, effect. In short Mr N. seems to me to have solved the problem of doing with the least chance of mischief the greatest chance of good by a poor law to Ireland.[1]

[1] ME to the Rev. Richard Jones, 2 April 1837 (Edgeworth Papers).

Not even the combined forces of Malthus[1] (for whom she had 'a most sincere regard and admiration'), Martineau[2] and the much-esteemed Jones could keep Maria on the straight and narrow path of orthodox 'political economy'. Her sense of the national welfare, community interest, public safety and sheer charity lured her away from the altars of *laisser faire*. Eminently practical, she was very well aware of how aid and relief were liable to be abused in Ireland. None of Paddy's little ways, above all his weakness for the Life of Riley had escaped her eagle eye. She had long been vehemently opposed to the mere doling out of benefits as kindnesses to tenants without exacting a price, however small it might be. Nevertheless actual starvation was actual starvation, and actual suffering was actual suffering. It would have been downright stupid as well as heartless to have expected self-help under such chronic circumstances, and political economy scarcely sported the spiritual riches desirable in a social gospel.

Maria had a social gospel. The landlord's estate was a moral school for his people. The water of Professor Jones mixed ill with the wine of a highly developed sense of social responsibility. Hence she was bound to accept Nicholls's line once she had thought the matter through, using graphic evidence of what was going on in Ireland beyond her day-to-day experience. Her way of going on meant the poverty problem was not one the inhabitants of Edgeworthstown found pressing hard upon them. Co-operation and paternalism on the spot made acceptance of an abstract approach to a matter like the Poor Law easier to take up. Reality was bound to make a person of Maria's outlook drop it as quickly as her desire to be in the intellectual mainstream would allow. Nicholls struck her as having solved the problem

---

[1] Thomas Robert Malthus (1766–1834), author of the famous *Essay on Population* and in 1805 a professor at Haileybury College. He was an Anglican clergyman, one time fellow of Jesus College, Cambridge, and from 1819 an F.R.S. In 1815 he published *The Nature and Progress of Rent*, a document containing doctrines that later economists came to accept. As a supporter of the Factory Acts and national education he also attracted much attention and had a profound influence upon the development of political economy. His pronouncements upon the Poor Law question therefore carried considerable weight.

[2] Harriet Martineau (1802–76). *Illustrations of Political Economy* (1832–4) and *Poor Law and Paupers Illustrated* (1833) were the two works of hers that ME had found relevant to the social problems of 1837–8, although, of course, the general implications of *Society in America* (1837) had preoccupied her a great deal.

of how to aid without demoralising – hence he got her good will. Even so, from what we know of her character it is hard not to conclude that if some organisational means could have been found for a watertight system of outdoor relief as a supplement to the main scheme she would have pressed for its adoption. As things *were*, the size of the problem throughout most of Ireland, the nature of the peasantry and the lack of both time and inclination for prolonged service among a landlord class, lacking an adequate administrative machine and often heavily burdened with financial embarrassments, really meant that any workable plan had to be based upon concentration points such as the workhouses. By writing of Nicholls having a solution, Maria probably meant no more than that he was proposing the best course possible in the circumstances. Such things are often taken for ideal answers in the short run, but she was too fly to do that. Her letter to Jones reveals a lively realisation of the immensity of her country's ills. Everything could not be put right at once, therefore any substantial improvement should be gratefully received. She subscribed to the inevitability of gradualness in the revolution she wanted for Ireland – evolution into being a second England.

Autumn 1839 saw the Whigs still jogging along in office. The near-static condition of Irish politics in the late thirties, with O'Connell's wilder men severely hampered by the Lichfield House Compact and something of the zest gone out of the Repeal movement through delay and Whig patronage, tended to put a moratorium upon agitated discussion. Maria was not affected by it, and on 6 September reported back to Mrs Edgeworth a long conversation she had had with one Hugh Tuite, soon to be a successful Whig candidate in county West Meath. They had, as she put it, talked much 'about grand things – the state of all Ireland'. The gentleman somewhat unexpectedly satisfied her stringent Stanleyite tests:

> I was surprised and glad to find him so far from a Radical and so *really liberal* and properly *conservative*. He spoke of O'Connell and his doings with excellent judgment. He sees that he has neither principle nor discretion, even as to his own views or interests. He considers O'Connell's power and influence as certainly declining fast and forever in Ireland. I doubted, because his Catholic rents are still as great as ever and I looked upon this as a measure of his popularity and power. Hugh sensibly and conclusively answered:

'The *amount* may not be diminished, but before you can decide that this is proof of his *power* not being diminished you must inquire from whom, from what class of persons, the rent is raised. I can tell you it is raised from the lowest and most ignorant and lawless and that the middle class of Catholic farmers or shopkeepers pay not one farthing now to O'Connell and are not his followers, but his opposers and enemies. They have lost all confidence in him. Now the mob will be led by this upper and better-informed class immediately, viz. contact with them and all their interests (unless there should be a revolution).' Hugh Tuite added that *he* measured the decline of O'Connell's power by the number of his own plans and engines of power which he had formed and framed and given up – and had been no doubt compelled to give up. He named five, I think, including the 'Precursor Society'. He conceives that O'Connell has no real thought of dissolving the Union, but only uses the cry to increase his popularity, as he always must have some means of *agitation* to keep himself afloat and in apparent advance towards a public object. In *short* (after being so long), I was quite pleased with Hugh Tuite's sensible views of what should be in this country, whether he be mistaken or not as to the fact of O'Connell's decreasing popularity, this conviction remains in my mind in favour of Hugh.[1]

Wishes had certainly fathered some of Tuite's thoughts, and Maria had shown that long strain, political and financial, had not lessened her critical powers, even when she was hearing what was music to her ears. Nevertheless the next general election was to prove the first fundamental setback the 'Liberator' underwent at the polls. It was therefore true to argue that the Repeal movement had to a serious extent suffered political decapitation. This meant, of course, that the influence of the 'Patriot' cause at Westminster would be severely curtailed and the chances for any ministry to pursue a firm yet reforming line much increased in scope. Mischievous though the Lichfield House Compact might have been to her mind, in some important respects, there was no doubt it had run O'Connell temporarily aground with the electorate. Whether the unenfranchised mob could win back the initiative for him depended upon the depth of his constitutionalism – how much in fact he shared a passion for one of the Edgeworths' favourite gods – the Rule of Law.

[1] ME to Mrs RLE, 6 Sept 1839 (Edgeworth Papers). An interesting work in comparisons concerned in part with this stage of the story is Thompson, *Ireland in 1839 and 1869*.

Not surprisingly, this god had dominated the latter portions of the conversation with Tuite. It was almost impossible not to discuss law and order in any serious consideration of Irish affairs. Just prior to Hinds quitting the agentship that same year, he had himself become a landlord in county West Meath. Almost before he had had time to get his affairs straight a large quantity of his hay was maliciously burnt. When in due course the matter came up before the West Meath Assizes, several of the Grand Jury were dead against granting him compensation. They claimed he was merely 'an imprudent parvenu and an oppressive landlord and that he had brought all that had happened upon himself by shutting up passes, filling up a well and sweeping ejectments'. Fortunately for Hinds he had found a stalwart champion in Tuite, who argued his case 'upon the broad lines of justice'. 'Mr Hinds had done nothing contrary to law – he had a right in law to do what he pleased with his own property and if imprudent, still the people who burned his hay etc. had acted contrary to law and the *law* gave Mr Hinds the right of being remunerated for his losses occasioned by public outrage. He gained his point and was right, and the cess was laid on and paid.' Maria's attitude here was probably a trifle casuistical, but the story revealed the state of demoralisation to which some at least of the Irish aristocracy and gentry had been reduced. Knowing just what she and those who thought like her were up against, an overstress on the technicalities of the law was one of the few weapons at her command for bringing back public figures to a full sense of responsibility.

Just how threatening the situation for Hinds had been is clear from what Tuite and his friend Lyons passed on to her. She had previously doubted the authenticity of the stories supposed to prove real danger and thought 'the people only wanted to frighten him'. 'All that story of a man waiting with a pistol in his hand at a gate, waiting to shoot him as he returned from church in broad day' had struck her as 'so glaringly absurd' that she had dismissed it as poppycock. On being consulted by Hinds as to whether 'he should cut and run or stand firm', she had lightheartedly insisted he 'stand firm', both 'because this was his public duty to his country and for his private interest and honour'. 'Whether my advice really did influence him or not', she wrote, 'I cannot be certain, but I know he has declared that it did and that it was the preponderating weight when he was undecided and decided him. I should be very sorry to have led him into danger and I understand that he is still in danger.' The basis for supposing this was the word of a Catholic priest, in fact none other than the local bishop, Cantwell. He had imprudently informed Lyons's wife that had he not used all his 'skill' as well as all his 'power' after a priest, one Fitzgerald, had 'called' Hinds – that is 'denounced him and pointed him out to the vengeance of the people' – the unfortunate man 'would not have been alive two months afterwards'. So tender and affectionate a person as Maria was naturally shocked at such news, but prudence rapidly reasserted its customary role. Instead of changing her advice, which her first impulses tempted her to do, she had determined to recommend a conciliatory policy once the 'hubbub' had subsided. The peaceable should be rewarded by reopening the well 'at whatever personal inconvenience' and by 'either opening the old passes or providing new and equally convenient' ones. When this 'humane and respectable' agent finally left Edgeworthstown he carried wise advice with him. Advice, however, given without giving an inch on matters of principle. Only after the 'hubbub' subsided were concessions to be made.[1]

News of chronic 'hubbub' came to Edgeworthstown at the very end of 1839 and in the spring of 1840. First there was the 'horrible murder of that poor inoffensive, not wise but good-natured Lord Norbury' spoiling Maria's peace of mind and arousing her fears for the Irish future. As she told Mrs Moore, the event was immediately followed 'by evils aggravating the crime if possible, making the consequences every hour worse and worse for the country'. 'A gentleman' present at Charleville Court during the unfortunate lord's last dinner reported him as saying with perfect sincerity: 'I shall never be happy living in a fine house by myself till I see all my tenants living in comfortable houses.' Norbury had lingered for some time after being shot, and when Lord Charleville attempted to approach the house by carriage in the belief that nothing final had occurred, a crowd greeted him with the cry 'He's dead. He's dead', uttered in such a way as to baffle Charleville as to whether it was pleased or sorry. Nevertheless the catcalls, groans and hissing

[1] ME to Mrs RLE, 6 Sept 1839 (Edgeworth Papers).

raised behind the carriage as it passed on could have left him in no doubt as to how *he* was regarded. Shoetracks revealed the probable murderer as a member of 'the lower class'. Indeed the only man Norbury could have deeply offended had been ejected with his family two years before after dismissal as a servant. The actual ejectment was said by some to have taken place with Norbury standing at the cottage, 'pistol in hand', while his agent forcibly took possession. Such a proceeding Maria deemed violently out of character, yet did not deny its possibility. As to the consequences for the tenantry, she approved strongly. The misfortune had soured but not brutalised the victim's family. Like the Edgeworths in 1835 it took non-co-operation from the tenants (in this instance a failure to furnish easily available information about the crime) as a cue, not for a bout of revengeful bullying, but withdrawal of a privilege. They were denied the much-coveted pleasure of carrying Norbury's coffin at the funeral.[1]

The springtime disaster was also a murder, this time of a Mr West, brother of an Irish Whig M.P. The circumstances were even more horrific than in the Norbury case. 'The only assigned cause' was that the victim 'had ejected or served an ejectment upon some tenants on an estate to which he was agent'. When returning home one evening 'on a jaunting car, driving it himself', two armed men rushed up, fired at him and scored a hit. Two tenants who were riding beside the car engaging him in conversation rode off post haste. 'The murderers went up to West to see if he was dead and observing signs of life' one of them reloaded his 'piece' and 'fired it at his ear'. 'Somehow it swerved' and the bullet merely grazed the back of his head. Thinking their mission accomplished the murderers made off, but West, though unable to walk, crawled into a ditch. There he lay for some hours quite undisturbed, until about midnight when the police turned up in search of him. Unfortunately he mistook them for the murderers and made not a sound. The upshot was that when he was ultimately located the cold and wet had done exactly what the murderers had failed to do – doomed him to die. Two days later he died from the effects of exposure.[2] How could Maria have failed to reflect on how wise

[1] Hone, *The Moores of Moore Hall*, pp. 121–5.
[2] ME to HE, 3 April 1840 (Edgeworth Papers).

and self-preserving, as well as idealistic, her 1835 refusal to be a driver had been and how near to death her friend Hinds had doubtless come through taking her well-meant advice?

To cap all this came the death of Thomas Drummond, reported in the newspapers of 17 April 1840. The removal of so just and liberal an administrator from a scene as troubled as the Irish was a blow indeed. Hard work and over-anxiety had aggravated what was anyway poor health, and through his going the Whig Government faced an even bleaker outlook. Although the Municipal Bill had passed its second reading in the Commons, right-wing troublemakers promised renewed resistance in the Lords. And in the background the agrarian war went on unabated in many regions, little heeded by the O'Connellite M.P.s, yet so fundamental to the current Irish situation and in some ways the true essence of Irish national feeling among the Catholic masses of the countryside. Maria's respect for Drummond had remained very high to the last. She commented to Fanny:

> From all I read of his evidence before Parliament I formed a very high estimate of his integrity and zeal in doing his duties and of his sincere wish to do good in and to this country. Also I formed a higher opinion of his abilities as a man of business from that evidence than people in general here have held or professed to hold. Party indeed sways so much that not only we cannot depend upon the impartiality or clearness of the judgments, but scarcely upon opinions being sincerely what the persons believe who pronounce them. Probably often put forward to serve party purpose to run down a party opponent and the abler and the higher character, and the more feared and respected the individual, the more virulent the abuse. Now that Mr Drummond, for instance, is no more, I am sure there are many opposed to him in politics who must feel that they have not done him justice. I don't think I am at this moment biased much by private feeling for the kindness he has shown.[1]

Nor was she, for the conclusions given here accord absolutely with the basic ideal of non-party conservative liberalism preached by Maria throughout her time in commenting on the deeper aspects of Irish problems and public life in civilised states. Only the conviction that Melbourne supped too often with the devil without a long spoon had turned her towards the Stanleyites, just as in the beginning her Whiggery had largely been based

[1] ME to FE, 18 April 1840.

on the belief that it was *the* means for achieving equality before the law and a balance between the deplorable factions in Irish public life. Party had not come easily to her, and Drummond would almost certainly have held virtually the same place in her estimation had she never clapped eyes on him.

4

O'Connell Contained

BACK in the years before O'Connell rose to real fame, a wishful-thinking reviewer in the *Methodist Magazine* had insisted that if payment of the priesthood were to accompany Catholic Emancipation, Ireland would turn to Methodism within a matter of a few years. In fact this prophecy had never been put to the test, but there developed from 1838 a powerful movement advocating something valued highly by the overwhelming majority of Methodists – that something was temperance and its chief advocate was Father Theobald Mathew,[1] a trainee of

[1] See J. F. Maguire, *Father Mathew*. The ecumenical contacts fostered by Mathew's movement are made clear by Harriet Edgeworth in a letter to her brother M. Pakenham Edgeworth, then in India, dated 27 March 1841 (Edgeworth Papers). 'I saw yesterday one of the most remarkable men of this or any other age, I think – Father Mathew. He came into this town on Thursday last. We were on the church tower to see the procession. He was unluckily in a hack chaise. If he had rid [*sic*] like his attendant priest it would have been fine. The band, not being, I suppose, up to the 'Conquering Hero', played gaily the 'Troubadours', expecting, I suppose, that everybody would think only of the words 'welcome thee home'. All the cabins and houses were decorated with laurel. . . . Men marched two and two as before in silence till his carriage came under a triumphal arch when they gave one grand shout and another when he reached the chapel. He gave the pledge to 20,000 yesterday, but though he has been preaching and giving it from 10 to 2½, he was so kind as to come up to see us, and very glad I was to be acquainted with him – a low man in height with a very fine head – handsome nose, good mouth, blue eyes, dark brown hair and sallow complexion, with a very grave benevolent sweet expression, a southern brogue, but an air of natural dignity, perfect ease, perfect simplicity, no assumption of greatness, no affectation of humility. . . . His manners and all he said expressed: "I thought it was my duty and I did it." I said, "I think you must be the happiest man in the world." He said he had been happy in his attempts to do good. At going he took both my hands and pressing them affectionately said, "When you see your own family, remember me most gratefully

Maria's pet aversion – Maynooth. While corresponding with the Editor of the *Westminster Review* during 1840 Maria had suggested an article be written on Mathew and his doings. The idea caught on straightway, and she was deputed to find someone to do it. With her brother-in-law Dean Butler in mind she wrote off to her sister Harriet,[1] though more knowledgeable on the subject herself than she was willing to admit. There were temperance activities going on full blast in county Longford under her very nose, and she was well aware of its ins and outs. Even in the letter to Harriet she describes one interesting occurrence: 'By the by, we met, as we were coming from Pakenham Hall[2] the other day, a procession of Teetotallers – with their medals and blue ribbons and flags flying, and music, and a tail of ragamuffins after them admiring – all sober and proud of themselves looking. I fancy this processing and notoriety form an essential part of the charm.' Characteristically for the author of *Practical Education*, she comments, 'But how is it that the poor people find time?' and adds, perhaps with a note of slight irritation, 'What they save from whiskey to be sure they can spend in this sort of entertainment. Mr Farrall, who was here last week, told us that he knows Father Mathews [*sic*] has received twenty thousand pounds and he should think a million has passed through his *hands cleanly*.'[3] As always she had rather hoped temperance would lead to saving for a rainy day, not another kind of spending spree.

August 1840 saw the Irish Municipal Reform Bill finally pass into law. Spring-Rice, whose distaste for a popular style franchise in local government was particularly marked, had retired the year before and entered the peerage as Lord Monteagle. Late in 1840 Maria was in London once again.

---

and kindly to them." Maria and my mother had asked him to Edgeworthstown. I then took the liberty to say to him, "What first made you think of giving the pledge?" "It was the Quakers in Cork were always asking me to do something about the people and temperance societies, and one day Mr Oldham, a member of the Established Church too – he is at a temperance meeting, said to me, 'You are the man, Father Mathew – if you'll undertake it, it will succeed.' And then I thought of making them pledge by promise. Before that they used only to write down their names." '

1 ME to HE, 1840 (Edgeworth Papers).

2 The home of Lord Longford and the Pakenham family, friends and relations of the Edgeworths. It was situated in the northern extremity of county West Meath.   3 ME to HE, 1840 (Edgeworth Papers).

Almost inevitably the two met and talked, though not as of old, for a curious chill in the relationship had developed on her side for reasons, as she put it, 'best known to herself'. Describing their meeting to Harriet in a letter of 30 December, Maria declared that from the first he had been determined to try for a thaw and had sought to break the ice first by enquiring after Fanny, and then by switching to Father Mathew, whose church-building projects had attracted his attention. Then for the first time we get something about the Irish Poor Law Act. The impression given by Maria is one of suspended judgement backed by a powerful feeling that the system will probably not be enough. In other words the concern for the possibility of outdoor relief, suspected to have been strong in 1838, was in fact a preoccupation two years later. She summed it all up:

> With courage that would have surprised you, but which, thank Heaven, never fails me when I have an object in view, I spoke to my Lord Monteagle much more and roundly and with less deference to his knowledge than I should (with good reason) to Mr Butler, and in short, Dr Hawtrey nodding approbation: '*All will depend* on how you follow up this test of destitution. When your workhouses have shown all they can do – viz. to *number* and provide for the absolutely helpless – all that in Ireland will ever go into them – then it remains to supply employment and wages for the able-bodied and willing to work, and this can be done in some measure by Government lending money and trying again with more precautions what was tried with Mr Nimmo and others. He pressed me to name the employments, making roads and footpaths and draining bogs etc. "good, good" '[1]

Talk of Father Mathew proved more popular generally, however, and on 10 January 1841 she sent back to Ireland for her temperance medal, so keen was everyone to see it: 'So many wonder why I did not bring it with me.'[2]

Shortly afterwards Harriet was sent an account of what must have been an extremely lengthy conversation with a civil servant named Scott. His anecdotes of leading statesmen and politicians of his time had quite rightly impressed Maria as being both authentic and significant. The already strong admiration she felt for most of these men had clearly been heightened. Any lingering elements of her earlier tendency to regard high politics as a species of roguery were by this time

[1] ME to HE, 30 Dec 1840 (Edgeworth Papers).
[2] ME to HE, 10 Jan 1841 (Edgeworth Papers).

tenuous, to say the least. 'He began', she said 'with Canning, whom he never saw, but who was his father's friend and procured him this situation.' This had not marred his judgement over the points he covered, for 'he spoke of him as a person universally respected by all those who were *under* him and none were *above* him in their estimation either for talents or kindness of nature and manner. He always remembering to help and push or lift forward each in his turn, and if obliged to miss a turn or disappoint or refuse, as oft a Minister must, never once offending' – an assessment of one aspect of the late prime minister's career few fair commentators could query. His failure to rebut charges about 'sincerity, or perfect integrity, or wholeness according to the primitive meaning of the word' struck Maria quite forcibly. She was by no means in a mood for willingly suspending her disbelief. While prepared to accept Canning's popularity with his underlings, her comment on the great man's character was 'no remarks'; and though not challenging the view that Lord Aberdeen[1] was slow but sure, she found the characterisation of Lord Dudley[2] as 'con amore for quickness and decision' quite amazing.

The judgement on Palmerston, however, she swallowed whole. It was convincing in itself and anyway echoed the general appraisal. 'Lord Palmerston' had the role of 'the dominating star', but young Scott was no worshipper at his shrine. 'Bright', reported Maria, 'he acknowledges him to be. The cleverest of them all as to absolute ability, but insufferably unfeeling and disliked by all under him.' 'Unbearable discord' was making each and every of his assistants cry out 'against him as loud as they dare and cursing deep'. Chapter and verse were at Scott's hand.[3]

> He is so reckless of the feelings and time of his Clerks and Messengers that he will send for a Messenger, say go to Constantinople immediately and bid the Clerks get ready despatches and take a pen to make out the minute of their orders for despatches. But

[1] George Hamilton Gordon, 4th Earl of Aberdeen (1784–1860), had been Foreign Secretary under Wellington, and subsequently, as a Peelite, presided over the coalition of 1852–5.

[2] John William Ward, 1st Earl of Dudley (1781–1833). He served as Foreign Secretary 1827–8, and from 1832 was placed under restraint.

[3] ME to HE, 19 Jan 1841 (Edgeworth Papers). The source of all this information the civil servant Scott, was the son of Sir Walter.

keeping them all – pens up, mouths open, ears cocked waiting – he will lay down his pen and turn to the box of arrears of letters and set about looking them over and minuting for them, regardless of both Clerks in the office and messengers in the antechamber cooling or kicking their poor heels – and when, at length, reminded of the Messenger in waiting – 'Oh, too late for today – let him be here tomorrow' – and tomorrow – and tomorrow – and tomorrow – fresh kicking heels, if not cooling temper the Messenger is doomed to endure. And this sometimes for ten days consecutively.

Accurate enough, no doubt, but almost certainly a necessary concomitant to the formulation of foreign policy based on an intense intellectual analysis. Immediate availability of minions in the event of hitting upon the correct line of action was, is and almost certainly will continue to be an imperative feature of executive government. An excellent minister always tries to avoid working against the clock, but also holds everything in readiness for when his mind is made up. Nevertheless to Scott it was the underlings' outlook which counted and, according to that, 'The Duke' – that is Wellington – was an altogether preferable being. He declared him 'One by himself and superior – alone – of the fewest words, but these few always straight to the point and doing the business to be done at once. In writing minutes or directions of any kind, short and full and clear – clear as any dunce could wish and such in so simple a form that almost anyone would think: "I could have written that" till he tried.' Maria had found all this credible, yet raised an eyebrow on being told of how the clerks 'found the Duke very kind and considerate in manner'. Even so, widespread testimony on other matters does suggest Scott was not dallying with fancy and that the brisk 'no nonsense' soldier had a highly benevolent side.

With O'Connellite politics a waning force in ordinary electoral politics and local Conservatism unable to displace the brothers White from their hold upon county Longford, Maria must have found the 1841 general election an oddly mixed affair. On 31 May she was busy telling Harriet Butler about Charles Fox's description of the anti-Conservative operations beginning in anticipation of a contest in Armagh. 'The enemy' was allegedly discounting bills for some voters, and bribery 'in all forms' was being practised. Rumour had it that one of the Whites had declined to stand for Longford and that, Sir

Percy Nugent having done likewise, there was a place going for what she pessimistically termed 'a new radical member'.[1] Nothing on the actual contest in July appears in the correspondence, not even a mention of Peel's triumphant return to office with a firm majority, and her information about candidates proved false. Henry White had shifted his ground considerably since the end of the thirties and become what amounted to a Whig-Liberal. Luke, though a Protestant and large local landowner, stuck to the 'Liberator'. Both secured 621 votes as against the 482 given to Anthony Lefroy. After the contest was over, when the left-wing was congratulating itself upon having maintained the supremacy of its particular brand of a 'popular front', Luke White found himself unseated upon petition in April 1842 and replaced by the assiduous Lefroy. Certainly this belated victory for the new Government must have given pleasure at Edgeworthstown House. There are no indications then or later of anyone there having regretted their Stanleyite tendencies and having allowed Henry White's change of heart to lure them away from supporting Peel's Longford county cohorts. O'Connell's recourse to more sustained extra-parliamentary strategies did not in actual fact lead to increased risks of fundamental change. On the contrary, in opposition the Conservative party had frequently been able to secure important moderating amendments to Whig-Liberal proposals made possible by the Lichfield House Compact. Now, as the Government, it could shape any legislative proposals in these less vital categories as it chose and face O'Connell with a choice between armed insurrection doomed to bloody failure and a fully apparent political fiasco. For the moment the fundamental change of power structure in the Commons appeared to presage not only a loss of face for O'Connell on the spot, but a possible weakening of his hold upon the Irish Catholic masses. While these things never really came about, the extra parliamentary agitation did have the effect of creating much more solidarity between Conservative and Whig unionists. Persons like Maria were persuaded that the Trojan-horse danger among the latter had been reduced to minimal proportions. 'Society' and its formidable array of services and hangers-on were fully mobilised to face the new threat. At

[1] ME to HE, 13 May 1841 (Edgeworth Papers).

that stage of Irish history such a development (London and the armed forces being 'staunch') was sufficient to guarantee safety for the owner-occupying classes – at least for the foreseeable future. Hence Maria's preoccupation during the next few years with the more mundane, albeit fundamental, problems of Irish life, such as famine and poverty. With the *pays légal* in the unionist bag, there was a real chance to turn to the hard facts of ordinary existence.

When the newly widowed Mrs George Moore produced a *Life of Christ* for the young with the express permission of her Catholic bishop, Maria saw it as an encouraging sign of things at last going the way she wanted. Rome's notorious hostility to the use of the open Bible had always been a major stumbling-block between Catholics and Protestants, and the book was based upon the order of events to be found in the Gospels, unadorned by 'note or comment'. Coupled with the new Catholic line of allowing readings from the Scriptures provided no interpretation was attempted, such a thing could in her eyes serve as a commendable concomitant to the new-found political stiffening among the Whigs. She was to be severely disappointed for her friend's book was soon to become well-nigh forgotten and the cause of toleration to remain in its customary state of chronic weakness. Be it Father Mathew himself, any preacher seeking to quieten sectarian strife had set himself an impossible task.[1]

Lovell died in England during 1842, and while over there Maria wrote to her liberal Catholic friend about the plight of the Irish countryside. This, rather than religion, was to be the thing to bring Irishmen of all classes and opinions temporarily into a mood of co-operation, though not until it was too late to yield really satisfactory results. And these unattained, the former bitternesses returned, augmented and deepened by fresh suffering.

I hope and trust [she told Mrs Moore] that all pleas of necessity are now generally attended to by Irish landlords – and that the examination which the parliamentary commissioners are to make into the state of landlord and tenant in Ireland will bring out facts proving to public satisfaction, perhaps *surprise*, in England. I find many in London of great wit and means of information

[1] Hone, *The Moores of Moore Hall*, p. 111.

talking of Irish affairs with great fluency, but *amazing* and *deplorable ignorance*. All luckily agree on one point and I hope you will agree with them and with me that the Catholic clergy should be paid by the state handsomely and respectably, and not be, as now, forced to wring from the hands of the poor parishioners their due in vile shillings and sixpences.[1]

But so 'English' an easing of peasant burdens was totally unacceptable then, as both earlier and later, to the Catholic clergy. A body of men anxious to preserve its hold over an agitated, agitating anti-British population was just not willing to risk loss of authority by taking the money from Dublin Castle. So while her preoccupation with Ireland's agricultural crisis had immense relevance to the immediate needs of her people, the constant nagging away about the chances of killing the sectarian-nationalistic and poverty birds with one stone had virtually no prospect of entering into the realm of practical politics.

Just prior to crossing from Dublin, Maria had written of how the Edgeworth lands were 'let low, scarcely any above thirty shillings per acre, except immediately near the town' and of how they had 'had no difficulty in getting the rents paid, except that' they 'were obliged in humanity to give weeks or months longer than usual'.[2] By the time she returned home things would appear to have deteriorated somewhat further. At any rate this is the impression left by a letter penned to Mrs Francis Beaufort on 27 October 1842: 'There is much difficulty this season for the poor tenants to make up their rents; cattle, oats, butter, potatoes, all things have so sunk in price. In these circumstances it is not only humane, but absolutely necessary, that landlords should give more time than usual. Some cannot pay till after certain fairs in the beginning of November.' It would appear these delays were keeping her at Edgeworthstown against her wishes, but far from bearing any grudge she accepted it as akin to a duty. 'Indeed', she explained, 'they have shown so much consideration for me, and striven so to make up the money that they might not *detain* me, that I should be a brute and a tyrant if I did not do all I could on my part to accommodate them.'[3] The idea of her even approaching the

---

[1] Ibid. p. 128. [2] Ibid. [3] *Memoir*, III 214.

role of a 'brute' or a 'tyrant' is far-fetched, but the sincerity
with which she wrote is plain enough.

Over in Mayo the poorest parishioners of Ballybonane
parish on the Moore estates had been given five pounds as
direct relief by young George Henry in July, it having been
'at last proved' that they were in distress. 'Weak and panting'[1]
at their priest's door, they had stood in need of immediate
sustenance. At Edgeworthstown matters had not reached such
a pass. In fact it was one of the current ironies that the lot of
the very poorest there had been slightly improved through
price falls affecting basic commodities. The more the cattlemen
and graziers lost, the more the near-submerged liked it. The
more farmers generally felt the pinch, the more they had to eat.
A visitor to Maria's little domain at this time found things very
much more cheerful than had the disappointed Mrs Farrar
six years before. It was hardly surprising that O'Connell's
threat as a bogyman had ceased to dominate Maria's mind.

The visitor was Mrs Anne Hall, who pronounced most
favourably upon the neatness, niceness and prettiness of
Edgeworthstown – a place having a marked 'aspect of comfort
cheerfulness, good order, prosperity and their concomitant
contentment'. 'There was no mistaking the fact that we were
in the neighbourhood of a resident Irish family with minds
to devise and hands to effect improvements everywhere within
reach of their control.' Overall the village struck her as 'almost
public property'. Much practical good to Ireland had sprung
from this example of model landlordism alone, and, much more
than that, great benefit for the whole civilised world. By her
policies Maria had, in the opinion of Mrs Hall, redeemed the
character of Ireland 'and so largely promoted the truest welfare
of human kind'.[2] Nor was this the only bouquet bestowed
upon Maria that year. She also received honorary membership
of the Royal Irish Academy. Recognition must have made up
just a little for the frustration of many of her wider political,
social and economic hopes.

The prospect for these had been going from bad to worse.
While the Government could be relied upon to stand firm and

[1] Hone, *The Moores of Moore Hall*, p. 126.
[2] Mrs Anne Maria Hall (*née* Fielding), *Sketches of Irish Character*, p. 186,
quoted in Clarke, *Maria Edgeworth*, p. 171.

the *pays légal* continued to shy away from the Repeal agitation,
support for O'Connell's cause had become better organised
among the Catholic masses and much more widespread among
the Catholic clergy. By the end of 1842 every single priest in the
dioceses of Ardagh and West Meath had adhered to Repeal,
and no priests anywhere had actually come out with a condemnation of what was afoot. To some extent the process went on
without much hullabaloo because of the leader's prolonged ab-
sences during the parliamentary session and his work as Lord
Mayor of Dublin. But the latter ceased in November 1842 and a
great public campaign was put under way to exploit the progress
recently made by the Repeal missionaries. Monster meetings
on the Hill of Tara and at Mullaghmast provoked the Government into taking security measures. The expiring Whig
Arms Act of 1838 was replaced by a much more stringent
affair, strong official eulogies of the Union and its maintenance
poured forth, and during the spring months as many as 35,000
troops arrived from Britain. As an added sign of meaning
business, Lord fFrench, O'Connell and thirty other Repealer
magistrates were removed from the bench. Meanwhile
O'Connell had in February got a motion in favour of his policy
through at a meeting of the Dublin Corporation and was busy
planning to call together 300 patriotic representatives – the
exact membership of Grattan's Parliament – into deliberative
conclave and stepping up his rousing tours. Everything was
order itself, but Peel was quite ready in the event of a shift to
violence.

After seeing what she termed the 'vast loyal crowds' shep-
herded by 'loyal policemen' at the opening of Parliament at
the beginning of February,[1] a return to Ireland could have
proved a thoroughly nasty political experience. But as usual
there were powerful exceptions to the national trend, and the
popular manifestations at Trim on St Patrick's Day 1843
proved most cheering.[2] Father Mathew's strictures against
sectarian strife appeared to have gone right home in that
district at least. It was in an elated mood, therefore, that she
wrote off to Miss Ruxton on 20 March:

On Friday last, being St Patrick's Day, there were great doings here,

[1] *Annual Register*, 1843, p. 10.
[2] Inglis-Jones, *The Great Maria*, p. 253.

and not drunken doings, not drowning the shamrock in whiskey, but honouring the shamrock with temperance rejoicings and music, that maketh the heart glad without making the head giddy or raising the hand against the law or fellow-creatures. Leave was asked by the Temperance Band and company to come onto [the Butlers' lawn] to play a tune or two, as they were pleased to express it, for Miss Edgeworth. The gates were thrown open, and in came the band, a brass band, with glittering horns etc., preceded by priest Halligan, whom you may recollect, in a blue and white scarf floating graceful, and a standard flag in his hand. A numerous crowd of men, women and children came floating after, kept in order by some Temperance Society staff officers with blue ensigns.

As she was to tell Fanny a month later, Halligan,[1] 'mounted upon as fine a black horse as ever you saw – with body clothes and all elegant and ears and all decorated', had been followed by another attendant priest – 'very generously dressed in black and a touch of the blue ribbon and well-mounted too, but on a younger horse that could not stand still while the band played, and played exceedingly well' while a great crowd surged round in the village street. Maria had been quite ill and though merely convalescing was allowed to view the joyous morning scene from her bedroom window. Throwing it open, she 'thanked them as loud as' she 'could and curtseyed as low as' her 'littleness and weakness would allow, and was bowed to as low as saddle-bow' by the mounted priests and ordinarily by the pedestrian musicians and their audience in turn. Harriet Butler stood 'on the steps, welcoming and sympathising with these poor people', and her husband went one better and did the very thing Maria valued perhaps most of all at Irish social gatherings. 'And delightful it was', she enthused, 'to see Mr Butler, bareheaded, shaking hands with the priests, who almost threw themselves from their horses to give him their hands.' He spoke kindly 'to all without Catholic and Protestant distinctions' and encouraged 'this harmless mirth – this most innocent enjoyment'.[2]

'Innocent enjoyment' was not, however, to be the keynote of that year, or indeed of its immediate successors. Mirth, harmful or otherwise, was also to be at a very low premium. By the second week in May the Repealer campaign had done

---

[1] *Memoir*, III 217.
[2] ME to FE, 29 April 1843 (Edgeworth Papers).

much to undermine the renewed confidence Maria had so cherished since the Conservative takeover. Edgeworthstown had, as usual, been slow to fall in with the national trend, but now the rot set in and as a result of priestly goading and encouragement the peasantry once more adopted the less friendly manners of the mid-thirties. She became severely depressed, over-pessimistic and quite blind to the many weaknesses of O'Connell's position. Neither the hopeless Repealer position in terms of real force, nor the essential constitutionalism of the 'Liberator's' politics formed part of her calculations. Consequently the slow inflow of rents on the family estates struck her as a sign of impending doom. An understandable mistake, particularly in view of her bad health, old age, heavy responsibilities and acutely taxed sense of duty. 'At the rate O'Connell is going on, the rents will not come in at all. Suppose the Repeal were to end in holding Parliaments alternate years in Dublin and London. But first O'Connell should be put down or put up, i.e. put up on the gallows and hanged.'[1] Draconian stuff, yet there is her usual recipe – let the rule of law be made to prevail before the reforming concession is made. Just how the courts could have sent her pet aversion to his death is far from clear. Nevertheless there is no lack of clarity about her depth of feeling. Perhaps feebleness of body was in itself both a cause and a consequence of feebleness of nerves. Whatever the explanation, we see here for the first time in her signs of an attitude of mind habitual among the more Conservative of the Protestant Anglo-Irish. Of such material are the potentials of autocracy made and, with certain more modern accretions, Fascism too.

Along with her anger and fear went a certain intellectual desperation. Her own reason had weakened in face of a threat, yet she still lamented that others had first abandoned the dictates of what she and many of her like regarded as common sense.

Alas [she commented], very sensible people seeming to turn fools when party spirit gets into them. 'The Day after the Repeal in Ireland.' I wish somebody would write 'The Day after the Repeal in Ireland', just showing the difficulties and what is to be done. Taxes and no money, Protection wanted – French threatening and no fleet, or in peace no commerce with England on the old terms.

[1] ME to Francis Edgeworth, 9 May 1843 (Edgeworth Papers).

The Catholic Junta ruling as the Orange one did. Then good morning to the Protestants. Poor Edgeworthstown – all the Edgeworths willy nilly must bid them farewell, and fare well you will not, that's certain. 'Where's that good angel that used to be with beef and blankets for us all in the illness? The Lord love and pity her – and those were good times. Long as she had it, we had it and more than she had. We got the life out of her. Though she looked so blooming last time I seed her in the white turbot with her son master Francis crossing my hall. I wish then he were the master still. But the Repeal has done for us all!'[1]

Beneath the literary form is a cry from the heart. She is sorry for herself, but very much sorrier for Ireland. And was she not right in some senses and would not Ireland have suffered much more than she actually did at that time and in the crisis of the famine without the British administration and the good elements of the aristocracy, gentry and Protestant clergy? Did they not blunt the full, terrible effects of the population explosion and insanely uneconomic agrarian customs and methods? What could O'Connell have done to set things right? Bad, thoroughly bad, though the land-system run by the Anglo-Irish was, there were compensating factors too often forgotten in the general enthusiasm for political freedom and the rights of 'nations' struggling to be free.

Proof of Maria's seemingly endless perseverance with and affection for the Edgeworth tenantry came up at the end of July. She explained in a letter of the twenty-third:

I have had a loss of twenty-two pounds odd lately and am threatened with an additional loss of sixteen pounds. All for one and the same folly. And 'Served me right' must be my own verdict upon myself. It is a long story. The short of it is that I went security like a fool for young Newcarron (my mother knows who he is), a tenant's son, who had obliged us by voting at one election for Charles Fox and having his windows broken in consequence etc. At the father's request I got a coach agent's place for the son with Mr Dummond. Mr Dummond giving it upon condition that I would sign a written security for him against all deficiencies on account of embezzlements etc. So after going mighty well for three or four years, he turns out an errant rogue.

The old father had taken the matter badly and had tried to make restitution. But ten pounds had proved his ceiling. Thus our heroine was left sad, sorry and poorer.[2]

[1] Ibid.

[2] ME to an unknown correspondent, 23 July 1843 (Edgeworth Papers).

But not so sad, or so sorry, or so poor as to prevent her crossing yet again to England that autumn for a visit to Fanny at Hamstead Hall, followed by quite a prolonged stay in London, where her keen sense of humour came back into something approaching its own. One old man of her acquaintance afforded her great amusement with his 'odd, ignorant, inconsistent, benevolent, intolerant, liberal, almost radical opinions all mixed up together, frying and hissing within him and boiling over sometimes'. Apparently he conceived of Ireland

as still a dreadfully persecuted country, treated quite as a conquered country – shockingly. Therefore [as she sarcastically remarked] he cannot but wish for the Repeal of the Union to set Ireland free at last. It is so horribly unjust, he says, that Ireland should be oppressed by the English debt.[1] But then I tell him England does not tax us and opens her markets to us. But still, says he, she is insulted as a conquered country – has no Parliament of her own. It was taken from her by the Union. There must be a Repeal of that Union (stamping about on the hearth and the tear full in his eye about nothing). Then your Irish tenants are so cruelly oppressed by your Irish landlords. There must be a redress of grievances and fixity of tenure. 'Stay till you hear more – A Commission is now appointed in Parliament and you will find that our tenants' rights are respected and that they may have fixity of tenure without more ado. If you mean that their farms will be relet to them and improvements allowed; if you mean by fixity of tenure that all the tenants should remain in fixed possession of the landlords' property, the landlords must leave Ireland, because they cannot live upon nothing. Both Catholic and Protestant landlords must go.'[2]

Note the extraordinary mixture of romantic optimism and exaggerated fear for the landlord position. Great though the prejudice and sheer ignorance of the old man must certainly have been, Maria's own picture of the Irish agrarian scene was ridiculously weighted in favour of her class. The idea that tenants' rights had been or were going to be universally respected in Ireland was simply an unadulterated fantasy. Nor did her allegation as to *de facto* fixity of tenure derive from a realistic appreciation of how things were actually working in the country at the time. Then, too, that particular way of regarding the term was highly personalised and would not

[1] On this subject, see Murray, *A History of the Commercial and Financial Relations between England and Ireland.*
[2] ME to Mrs RLE, after 5 Nov 1843 (Edgeworth Papers).

have been accepted as useful by advocates of reform. Nevertheless she seemed to get away with it on this occasion and carried the war into her companion's camp by introducing the religious question.

Mr Moilliet, for such was his name, reacted strongly to mention of the word 'Catholic'. It provoked 'quite a new train of ideas' in his mind.

> Observe [she gloated], the Catholics are his great plague at Geneva, where they are now all at sixes and sevens. He can't abide a Catholic priest, he turns short round and throws his hands out as if pushing the idea of a Catholic priest from him with abhorrence. But the seven million of Catholic poor Irish, he thinks, should have perfect toleration and emancipation. I tell him they have – only none can be Archbishop of Canterbury or York and cannot be Generalissimo of the armies.[1]

Fair game for mockery though her subject was, and understandable though a tendency to defend a system the fundamentals of which she wished vehemently to maintain is to any just observer, there is no denying that here once more are distinct indications of a judgement impaired. Age, fear and ill-health were taking their toll. And, more probably than not, a simple patriotism, albeit inextricably interwoven with class interest and pride, had obtruded itself without her fully realising it into what was a wrangle with an ill-informed 'foreigner'. Still, it is fair to say her efforts did a little to alleviate his condition.

Towards the end of the same month of November Maria's political morale got a boost from a meeting with the 2nd Lord Dudley and Ward. According to an account sent off to Miss O'Beirne from North Audley Street on the twenty-third, she was in fine form and prepared to contemplate the Repeal campaign in a light reminiscent of 1842. 'I think you need not be alarmed for your friends in Ireland' is certainly a different tune from that sung in the spring. It would, nonetheless, be wrong to suppose the new hope had sprung entirely from talking with Dudley. As she was quick to point out, 'If I had thought there was any danger, I should not have run away from' Ireland, 'little as I could do by staying.'[2] About six weeks before, on 8 October, the projected climax to O'Connell's

[1] Ibid.
[2] ME to Miss O'Beirne, 23 Nov 1843 (Edgeworth Papers).

Repeal campaign at Clontarf had been stymied by government intervention. The 'Liberator' had had to bow before the veto on the meeting and lost considerable face. Less than a week later he had been arrested and charged with sedition and conspiracy. The actual trial was not to come on before the following year, but meanwhile it was undeniable the great man had for the time being shot his bolt. All Repeal activities now had about them an air of anticlimax. The extra-parliamentary campaign, like the parliamentary one, appeared to have run onto a sandbank.

Never mind about the fires [Maria confided], they are only bravado, bullying fires. They would not blaze if they were meant to burn for mischief. They will merely burn out. You see, no consequences have followed from the blaze. The military preparations are such now in Ireland as to prevent the necessity, I trust, for their being used. O'Connell will fall into discredit when his head is not on the block, or a Parliament in College Green next spring. There is no getting out of that promise to his own party. Accustomed to eating his own words and dextrous as he is at swallowing false prophecies, this will choke him at the Corn Exchange I guess. Meanwhile I hope he may not play his old game of conquering by delay and slipping through the fingers of his awkward imbecile prosecutors. I beg pardon for the word imbecile, but I cannot retract or scratch it out. I am not clear but that Sir Robert Peel wishes that this trial may fail in order that he may go to Parliament for a more stringent law and say: 'You see – the present law of the land in Ireland is insufficient'.[1]

There is no mistaking the message here – let us hit this man while he is down and hit him so hard that his getting up again will be out of the question. Eager for a return of politics within the bounds she held consonant with her favourite brand of liberal principles, Maria thirsted for the agitators' blood. They were destroying the chance of reforming Ireland from the top and therefore were by definition a bad thing. The situation invited a blow from the strong arm of the law, a strong arm likely to do better with an extra knuckleduster meaningfully attached. Here is the mentality which has lain behind the attitudes of countless anti-leftists during the twentieth century – many of them as passionately devoted to the ideas associated with championship of the Rule of Law as she always was, but gradually accepting that their countries' legal

[1] Ibid.

systems shall act as direct upholders of their party view and cease to serve as highminded ringmasters. Assuredly Maria wanted O'Connell's trial fairly conducted. Yet 'fair' to her was unconsciously beginning to mean something new – 'fair' had started to denote 'against O'Connell' and that was a dangerous thought. Whatever mental reservations she might have had in favour of 'safeguards', such politics amounted in practice to Orangeism, albeit Orangeism confined to the lay sphere. In the great battle for the Union, Whiggery had become severely handicapped. In order to preserve its customary sphere of operation it was obliged to modify many a basic principle for consumption by the 'loyal'.

On 3 December Maria dined at Dr Lushington's[1] and talked at length with the famous Sydney Smith.[2] Although vehemently denying any capacity for Boswellising this clerical wit and Whig, she certainly got very near to doing so in her lengthy account for sister Harriet. He had 'talked much of churches, Catholic and Protestant, and applied' to Maria 'for information as to the state of the Catholic priests' – 'in my opinion', as she put it. 'My opinion I told him', she wrote, adding with characteristic modesty, 'though I could be worth little or nothing on the question to him.' She had told him 'the facts which had actually come within' her 'own knowledge' in her 'own neighbourhood and county, or others within' her 'reach and means of verification'. And they were to the effect that these men had been, 'before they took to politics, excellent parish priests'. But she had found that 'willingly and truly', though the tale had been told, 'these facts did not accord at all with his preconceived notion of their oppressed, depressed state, diabolically treated by the Protestant Church, Protestant landlords and a Protestant and Tory government'.

He had 'civilly waived aside' her 'evidence and looked: "You may go down off the table, where I only set you up when I thought you were on my side." "Six millions, O'Connell says seven, trampled on still by one – notwithstanding this talk of

---

[1] Stephen Lushington (1782–1873), a prominent legal luminary of the then high court of Admiralty and since 1838 a Privy Councillor.

[2] Sydney Smith (1771–1845) was a frequenter of Holland House, a canon of St Paul's with a penchant towards Paley's theology and a former fellow of New College, Oxford. In 1807 he had published the *Plymley Letters* in defence of Catholic Emancipation.

emancipation. There must be a *reformation*, redress of grievances." ("Reformation! Of what, or of whom?" I simply asked.
"Redress of grievances? What and which be they?")' Smith
thought the 'Catholics should have an established Church'.
When Maria pointed out that 'an' would soon turn into 'the',
he had shown no distaste. On the contrary their majority status
struck him as justifying any such change: 'Well, where would
be the harm or the injustice, seeing they are the majority?' 'I did
not ask: "What constitutes the majority?" ' she explained. 'I
was afraid of setting the Abbé Siéyès[1] and Sydney Smith at it
lest the whole French Revolution should come upon my head.
I saw I need not, must not go to spiritual considerations either,
so keeping to temporalities, I merely begged his Reverence
would consider that we poor Protestants had bodies to be saved
and did not like, only one million as we are, to be trampled
upon by seven and to have our Church pulled down about our
ears and to have our clergy buried under the rubbish – and their
church lands and our estates taken from us. He scoffed at such
suppositions. But I appealed to his own knowledge of history
regarding the encroaching and predominantly predatory nature
and art of Catholics etc.'[2] The 'Thus far and no further' school
of thought in Irish Whiggery, so like that in numerous other
moderate liberal groups, had most probably seldom had its
case so frankly put. 'Our fellow citizens of the other camp can
have as much liberty as does not conflict with the maintenance
of our hold upon the major resources and institutions of the
country.' That and just that was the purport of Maria's remarks.

Smith's actual reply was that 'without looking to remote
consequences', the government should 'do what justice and
humanity' required. According to the account, he then

> showed he was utterly mistaken and misinformed as to the present
> state of the priesthood in Ireland and the revenue of the Catholic
> Church. 'What so unjust and unjustifiable as their church paying
> tithes to another in which they don't believe. Ireland never will,
> never can, never ought to be quiet under such a grievance.' He
> seemed convinced that the Irish priests have not enough to keep
> body and soul together. He would not listen (except with civil sneer)
> to any of my poor little *facts*. But Dr Holland put him down with

[1] A prominent French revolutionary and author of *Qu'est-ce que le Tiers État?*
Born 1748, died 1836.
[2] ME to HE, 3 Dec 1843 (Edgeworth Papers).

Lord Lansdowne's name and authority, added to his own observations in going through Ireland lately. Lord Lansdowne says that the average salary of the Irish priests is 290 pounds per annum and the average of the Protestant [clergymen] 120 or 130 pounds. Sydney Smith was staggered by this and said he must enquire further. Meanwhile, he asked me whether the Catholic priests are a moral, sober, well-conducted people. To moral and sober I gave good and I trust true testimony – as clergy – formerly, ere they took to politics, zealous and excellent parish priests. But further – as to well-conducted in politics and elections and so forth, and Repeal agitations –

So the talk had turned full circle with no one's views substantially changed. The story of the raucous and uncouth bishop served to relieve the tension and 'The Smith of Smiths' regaled the company with an account of a conversation held 'in former days'. It had been with Bishop Doyle, and had begun: 'My Lord (propitiously and propitiatingly), don't you think it would be a good thing if your clergy were paid by the state?' Back came the assurance 'that it would never do' – such an offer could never be accepted. 'But suppose there were lodged in the bank for all your clergy at an average 100 or 150 pounds a year and suppose five per cent for arrears was allowed?' 'Ah, Mr Smith, you have *a way of putting things*' was the honest bishop's reply, and with that the good Sydney switched to the subject of O'Connell.

On this he made what was for him the unusual admission of scarcely knowing what to make of it. Dr Holland, another guest, insisted lying and cowardice to be the 'Liberator's' stock in trade, and Smith seemed 'perfectly aware' of his being right, but still argued in favour of the alleged villain. 'Has not he a real enthusiasm for his religion and his country?' he asked, and turning to Maria sought her opinion. 'I could only say', she explained, 'I believe him to be a sincere bigoted Catholic – yet I *could* not say enthusiastic, for I *took* a distinction between bigotry bred in a man and enthusiasm natural and genuine. However, let that be between God and him and his conscience. One has no right to judge and no means of ascertaining. But by his works you may judge of his patriotism or his selfishness.' Holland followed up with a full account of O'Connell's 'history' – 'Catholic *rents*, debts paid, college fines, money in the Funds for him, wrested and wrenched from the hands of poor not vile peasants'. 'Staggered more and more', Smith then recollected a lie, 'uncourteous, absolute, unblushing and base, which O'Connell had uttered and published of his revered self'. Apparently he had said that when 'asked *whether*' he would swear that he believed the Thirty-nine Articles Smith had answered, 'Certainly, I only wish there were three or five hundred more!' Maria felt convinced that this 'lie against himself struck Sydney Smith more than all the rest and that he seemed right glad to repudiate him'. Maybe – but the great wit definitely had not lingered on the point and, as remarked on by Maria herself, had soon gone on to discuss Macaulay – 'Macaulay bursts like a beer barrel and it comes all over you'.[1] It would have taken much more than one 'cure' to have unnerved the Whiggish, self-assured and capriciously tolerant parson wit.

For Maria *the* great event of January 1844 was the opening of O'Connell's trial. Being in London, she was obliged to follow the proceedings through the newspapers and content herself with a mind's eye picture of the scene. Here her novelist's powers turned up trumps once more. Coupled with what were by then vehement feelings against the accused, they created vicarious pleasure and excitement of no mean order. Nor was she wrong to give the affair the bulk of her attention. The 'Liberator' was not facing his ordeal unaided. On the contrary, the flower of the Irish Bar was his for the asking at every turn, and a good time was squeezed out of what initially appeared a most unpromising situation. As a misdemeanour the crime of conspiracy could be tried by a special jury. Before a start could be made with the real business, a great tussle took place over the composition of a special jurors list, the striking of the panel and the selection of an actual jury from it. The upshot was total exclusion of every single Catholic in a case where all four of the judges appointed to try it were Protestants. The next year the Lord Chief Justice of England commented: 'If such a practice should be allowed to pass without a remedy, trial by jury will be a mockery, a delusion, and a snare.'[2] The eleven-count indictment was of inordinate length and likewise provoked condemnation for its confused nature from the same august quarter. How, it was asked, could the accused really understand

[1] Ibid.
[2] *Two Centuries of Irish History*, ed. Bryce, p. 390.

what exactly it was he had to answer? Maria, however, was much too Irish and much too *engagée* to feel such misgivings. Like O'Connell himself she seems to have revelled in the fight, though not blind for all that to what the prosecution's success or failure would involve. There was, of course, her conviction that failure might well provoke extra repressive legislation to provide a certain element of 'Heads we win, tails O'Connell loses' and take some importance from the precise nature of the outcome. Nevertheless, 'English' *par excellence* though she was in Ireland, the old old Hibernian Eve was bursting out in her by the standards of 'English' England. 'I am very interested in O'Connell's trial', Mrs Edgeworth was informed. 'I think the Attorney-General's opening speech excellent – the cross-examinings of the traversers[1] on O'Connell's side very provoking and often injudicious for their own purposes and terribly long – just speaking against time and Justice. The Mullaghmast history and the use O'Connell made of it were really wicked. The manner in which he turns all that off in jest and ridicule is terribly clever – one of the greatest proofs he has given of his oratorical powers adapted to all occasions.'[2]

The immediate upshot of the affair was that the jury pronounced against O'Connell and his companions on five counts and declared them guilty of separate and distinct conspiracies on two others. Technical factors had disposed of the remaining counts and the judgement against all the accused was general: 'that the party for his offences aforesaid shall be fined and imprisoned'. At that time a criminal appeal proper was unknown to English law, but a new trial could be moved for in respect of points of law. During the trial Pennefather, the presiding judge, had spoken of the counsel for the traversers as 'the gentlemen on the other side'. Nevertheless, although not unanimous, the Court of Queen's Bench refused to grant a motion based on a protest about these words, and O'Connell found himself called up for judgement on 30 May, having also failed to sustain a motion in arrest of it put forward on the ground that certain counts of the indictment were bad in law. However, his resources were not at an end. One of the defence counsel was convinced he had found a substantial defect on the

---

[1] Traversers: those being prosecuted.
[2] ME to Mrs RLE, 25 Jan 1844 (Edgeworth-Beaufort Papers).

face of the record of the trial. In the event of his being right a writ of error might well do the trick, so a motion in arrest of judgment was again made – this time in the Dublin Court of Queen's Bench – with the idea of laying the foundation for a writ of error in the House of Lords. On 4 September that body swept away the whole result of the previous proceedings, but such was the then practice that the exonerated men had already been imprisoned and it was only three days later that they secured release – release welcomed by scenes of 'indescribable rejoicing'.[1]

Many things, good, bad and indifferent, had happened to Maria and, indeed, to Ireland during the course of these complicated and exciting junketings. The bustle of London life struck her as far too much of a good thing, despite its intellectual and social compensations. It was all very fine to observe the Queen opening Parliament – 'It was more a girl's well-read lesson than a Queen pronouncing her Speech';[2] all very well to discuss the merits of different schools with numerous parents and reach the interesting conclusion that 'Rugby is now the best school in England';[3] and all very well to exhaust her mental energy in thinking up and sorting out the 'worshippers of Bentham' – 'Cobbett, Burdett, O'Connell up to Romilly, Ricardo, Shelburne, Lansdowne and Grenville, Priestley and Brougham'[4] – and in throwing herself wholeheartedly into the usual intellectual pursuits. Harriet Martineau took pride of place in a letter to the Rev. Professor Jones written on 4 May. The comments upon 'Miss Martineau's system' of 'anti-charity principles' go far towards confirming the speculations as to what Maria's inner yearnings about Poor Law schemes

---

[1] *Two Centuries of Irish History*, ed. Bryce, pp. 390–1.
[2] Inglis-Jones, *The Great Maria*, p. 254.
[3] ME to HE, 25 Jan 1844 (Edgeworth Papers).
[4] Jeremy Bentham (1748–1832), the famous jurist and political philosopher. William Cobbett (1762–1835), essayist, Radical politician and agriculturalist. Sir Francis Burdett (1770–1844), initially a strong Radical, but from 1837 until his death Conservative M.P. for North Wiltshire. Sir Samuel Romilly (1757–1818), law reformer and admirer of Rousseau – a Radical and for some years an M.P. in that interest. William Petty (1737–1805), 1st Marquess of Lansdowne and 2nd Earl of Shelburne, succeeded Lord Rockingham as First Lord of the Treasury in 1782, but fell from power the next year. Created Marquess of Lansdowne 1784. George Nugent-Temple-Grenville (1753–1813), 1st Marquess of Buckingham and at one time Lord-Lieutenant of Ireland. Joseph Priestley (1733–1805), a theologian and scientist. ME to HE, 25 Jan 1844 (Edgeworth Papers).

might be. The good lady's 'reasoning' appeared 'unanswerable'.
That she admitted freely.

> But if we attempt to *carry it out* – to carry it through into practice,
> it must appear either impolitic or it must create more evil to society
> than it could produce good. In the first place – to leave all misery
> consequent upon improvidence and ignorance, to say nothing of
> imprudence and vice to their own *reward* (anglice *punishment*) and
> to refuse any relief by charity to those who are perishing and
> perhaps before the eyes of the anti-charitable-ist in the death
> struggle, would require a heart of iron: a nature in which the natural
> instinct of sympathy or pity have been expelled or destroyed. Now
> by whatever means this be done, whether by selfishness confessed,
> or by reasoning assuming to be philosophical, that *result* would be
> more dangerous, more injurious to society (supposing that the thing
> were possible) than any imaginable good which could be effected
> by refraining from charitable aid to our fellow creatures. The
> extinction of pity and sympathy – instincts implanted in our nature
> by our Creator so we may presume, without talking high *a priori*
> sentimental cant, for wise and good purpose – could not be effected
> without violent change and danger to the whole fabric of society.
> Take away horror of seeing human beings perish – without offering
> aid – by famine even without supposing the sight of blood. You
> diminish, you destroy the horror of murder, the dread of being
> *the cause of death* proximate or remote. You raise, you educate a
> race of political philosophical thugs.
>
> There are whole bands of the *selfish* well-prepared for this
> education and quite ready to seize philosophical reasoning as a
> pretext – a master – a safeguard from public execration. Therefore
> it is that I say Miss Martineau's anti-charity system cannot be
> carried the whole length to which her reasoning would lead and
> urges. It cannot be carried into effect without proving the truth of
> the ancient maxim that the extreme of justice is injustice. Or, in
> more accurate statement, that finite eyes cannot see where the
> boundary of justice lies and consequently must and should admit
> that compensation called mercy.

As usual Maria has equated virtue with good sense. It was
both morally desirable and practically necessary to be com-
passionate and pitying to the less and least fortunate of mankind.
What true religion demanded was no more than what a well-
run society required. And Jones himself had, she claimed, come
practically to the same conclusion in his own writings. Living
as she did in a country where the superficial hold of civilisation
was evident enough, she knew full well the narrow distance
between herself and the horrible potential of a Martineau-style
world. 'You have continually occurred to me in all these poor

law discussions', she confided, 'and I have repeatedly wished that the landlords of Ireland would read your' views 'on Cottier rent and could be convinced of their true interests by your reasoning – which would be a better cure for many of our evils than can possibly be any legislative interference. I wish you would write again on this subject.'[1] *Avec moi le déluge* must have been a thought constantly in her mind. As a wise member of a foolish and short-sighted upper class she can be seen in yet another classic tragic role. Wisdom told her that the mentality of a group or groups is what lies at the bottom of the virtues and vices of a society. Good legislation can go only part way towards the remedying of ills, if those ills form part of deeply ingrained modes of thought and action among those with the bulk of power and initiative. Because of their 'loyalty' and status as property-holders and voters, the landlords of Ireland would not be abandoned by the British authorities. Because of this, these same landlords would persist wantonly in the follies of blind selfishness and unilateral gain from a vastly unjust series of practices in the Irish agricultural system. Such oppression usually sprang less from the letter of the law than from the particular ways in which it was constantly abused by these men. New laws might meet every single abuse, but without a change of heart fresh injustices would appear, or the laws suffer distortion and even open evasion. Consideration for the underdog was at a low ebb in the Irish Ascendancy, but Maria saw that only through mutual sympathy could a happier state of affairs evolve in her unhappy country.

Yet health was vital and at her age a constant source of worry. By the summer a severe bout of erysipelas had driven her to bed once more, and existence became something of a burden. In a letter of 12 July to the Rev. Professor Jones she told him sadly that 'if I come to England next year, or if ever I come to England again' she would gladly visit his family. Though 'at death's door' the previous month 'for three weeks', she had been 'so well treated by physicians and dear good friends', including her sister Harriet Butler, from whose house at Trim the letter came, that her health had become 'better than ever'. For all her seventy-six years she was feeling: 'quite as happy as ever I was in my life' and 'not in the least tired of

---

[1] ME to the Rev. Richard Jones, 4 May 1844 (Edgeworth Papers).

existence, but very much obliged to the old and new friends who all contribute so much to make it (despite of all the infirmities of age) so delightful to me'. Of her intellectual friends in England she considered Jones possessed 'the greatest and deepest power of thought' and urged him to visit her and her family in Ireland. He would, she claimed, find 'ample food for speculation on all the subjects most interesting' to him and 'to humanity'. A bold statement, yet probably true enough. Meanwhile her convalescence was hastened on by looking at a Bill for 'the letting of Field gardens' devised by the versatile professor. He would doubtless have echoed her conclusion that 'It appears wondrous difficult to guard all the provisions and objects of an Act of Plt. so as to make it fulfil the purposes even of its framer and to defy a lawyer to drive a coach and horses through it.'[1]

On the surface Ireland appeared to be faring better. From the Devon Commission, set up the year before to enquire into the alleged malpractices into the land-system, had come some quite encouraging signs. Though the moderate efforts made to implement reform achieved but little, the admission by Peel that the Ascendancy stood in need of restraint did something to lower the political temperature, and the tenantry felt officialdom was no longer ranging itself unreservedly upon the side of its 'oppressors'. At the same time no resentment was aroused among the masses by any move to restrain the local passion for sub-division. Mass overpopulation and uneconomic units at the bottom of agrarian society were not only beyond the reach of government control and rectification, but way outside the sphere of function authority arrogated to itself at that time. Marginal matters, such as elementary education grants, were dealt with generously, and an Act was passed allowing Catholics to hold property and accept bequests for charitable and religious purposes. More conciliatory noises began to emanate from vice-regal lodge and the idea of an increased grant for Maynooth College met with widespread support. An attempt, a very mild attempt, was being made to kill Repeal by a smattering of kindness.

Maria's recovery was slow, but by mid-November her indefatigable interest in public affairs had fully reasserted

[1] ME to the Rev. Richard Jones, 12 July 1844 (Edgeworth Papers).

itself. She wrote to Mrs Edgeworth about a pamphlet upon Irish affairs due to be sent to Sydney Smith. He too was presently engaged on a work on the same topic. 'I think it sensible and impartial' was her considered verdict. And added what was both interestingly profound in itself and a sound indication of a return of calmer judgement with better health. 'Sensible and impartial so far as impartiality *can* be with the main principle all must agree as self-evident – that to preserve a wish in Ireland for the Union with England, the interests of the two countries must be in fact and fairly united.' Back again with renewed vigour is the notion of administrative and political adjustment as well as religious toleration.

> Some of the facts [she pointed out], such as that only six hundred pounds is bestowed per annum on the encouragement of arts and sciences by the English in Ireland, are striking and shameful – and the bringing of such facts before the public eye is likely to be of great use; and the less objurgation the better. All said about extending the absentee tax to those who reside on the continent is also just and well put. I wish you could tell me whether what this author states respecting Church lands is true: that the Rent charge is still *paid* by the tenants, not by the landlords. As to the main point which [was being advocated] respecting the Repeal or non-Repeal of the Corn Laws, it is so complicated and difficult a subject that I am not among the fools who rush in where the wise fear to tread.

The old and well-tried critical faculty of former years is still hers, and the frequent use of the word 'flippant' in attempts by the pamphleteer to discredit those, such as Lord Spencer,[1] with whom he is in disagreement has not passed unnoticed. But though quick to spot blemishes, she is keen to give credit where credit is due. The statement 'There is now no such thing as a home market. Steam has annihilated it. Markets thousands of miles distant are for certainty and facility almost on a par with the nearest' struck her as tellingly accurate and consequently earned her warm approval. 'This is very true and the truth is placed in a clear and almost new light.' And then again what was said of ways 'of employing the people in drainage and

---

[1] John Charles Spencer (1782–1845), Viscount Althorp and 2nd Earl Spencer. He was Chancellor of the Exchequer for a time under Earl Grey and had become a strong enemy of O'Connell's. From 1834 until 1841 he had given himself up to private pursuits, but during the second Peel ministry became a strong advocate of Corn Law repeal from the Whig front bench in the House of Lords. His temporary withdrawal from public life had begun when he succeeded to his earldom.

public works and employing the people in Poor Houses' she deemed 'excellent'. Some of the facts alone were to her mind of a very high significance. Among these were the statistics of Anglo-Irish trade and 'the great augmentation of the tonnage of shipping, particularly steam vessels, in the port of Dublin – now the second port in this respect in the British Empire, equal to Liverpool, Bristol and Hull put together. If this be true, it is most encouraging to Ireland and all we need ask is that things be well done.' Here is hope on the old lines once more. And with this fresh bout of optimism came a burst of humour. 'Can it possibly be true', she asked, 'that a great Law Lord seriously proposed looking out for a good quiet cat to whom to give an Irish bishopric just fallen in? "Ben trovato" at any rate.'[1]

A trifle over three weeks earlier one of her heroes had undergone a terrible humiliation. It came as a most unpleasant surprise. Describing her reactions in a letter to her sister Fanny Wilson of 25 October, she left no doubt as to her horror.

> We never heard of the dreadful catastrophe you mention of Father Mathew. We are all in amazement and dismay. Since I began this note Mrs Edgeworth and I have been to Longford and have paid various visits and of everybody who could be supposed to have heard we asked: 'Have you heard of Father Mathew lately – and what?' Mrs Curtis, wife of the head of constabulary, was the only person who had heard anything, and her information was from the 'Packet' newspaper – that a man had arrested him for a debt for the price of medals – had just kneeled to him to take the pledge from him – then started up and arrested him – then kneeled again and begged his pardon. So strange a story makes me almost hope there is no truth in it. Oh, my dear Fanny. I cannot tell you how we are grieved by even suspicion lighting on such a man. So much good as he has done![2]

But there was 'truth in it' well enough. Far from being in possession of the vast sums alleged by his numerous enemies Mathew was at that time in debt to the tune of £7000 and had long faced financial difficulties. Indeed, the more successful his mission in the temperance field had been, the greater his pecuniary embarrassments had become. While true that pledge-takers numbered many thousands, even hundreds of thousands, the contention that all purchased medals and so

---

[1] ME to HE, 15 Nov 1844 (Edgeworth Papers).
[2] ME to FE, 25 Oct 1844 (Edgeworth Papers).

lined his pockets with gold and silver was very wide of the
mark. Most of the masses who flocked to his blue banners
lived on the verge of destitution and had to content themselves
with the fact of abstinence alone. A medal for them was an
unattainable luxury. And as ill-luck would have it the arrest
was made for the balance of an account due to a medal manufacturer. The scene was just as the *Packet* described – 'the
bailiff to whom the duty was entrusted knelt down among the
crowd, asked Mathew's blessing, and then quietly showed
him the writ! It may be mentioned, as an instance of Father
Mathew's presence of mind, that he did not falter even for an
instant, but continued to administer the pledge, as if nothing
had happened. This self-possession was fortunate for the bailiff
whom not even he could have saved, had that treachery been
made known at the moment.'[1]

Whatever apologists may say, Mathew, like O'Connell, was
certainly imprudent in money matters and, while absolutely
honest, did allow enthusiasm for his cause to lead him into
spending more than he should have, given the resources actual
and potential at his command. Maria kept a keen look-out for
news and reported to Fanny on 31 October: 'I see in today's
papers a statement about Father Mathew which acquits him
of all but imprudence in spending money before he had it on
works of public utility. But the want of prudence and forecast
and punctuality are absolutely to be deplored as public mis-
fortunes in such a man – destroying such a vast power of doing
good. Many of the poor people in our neighbourhood have
lately broken their pledges – Garret Keegan – Gahan's brother
and others. Alas! Alas!'[2] But, as usual, she did not leave the
matter there and wallow in despair. Fanny was being told on 2
December of how, on seeing the still sober and righteous
Gahan standing 'with one hand upon his hip and the other on
his mouth' and regarding 'his work before he quitted it in
inexpressible admiration', she had rushed down from her
'dressing table throne and begged a bottle of raspberry vinegar
from' the female servant, who had 'made a good quantity with
her own hands last autumn for Frances to give to the tenants
instead of whiskey'. 'Gahan, thank heaven and himself', she

[1] Maguire, *Father Mathew*, p. 309.
[2] ME to FE, 31 Oct 1844 (Edgeworth Papers).

rejoiced, 'is one of the pledge takers.'[1] And he would continue faithful if she had anything to do with it. Clearly heaven had a place in her view of things, but a highly matter-of-fact deistic belief in human factors never tempted her into trusting that all could safely be left to providence. There was nothing like making sure. A sentiment shared by influential members of Father Mathew's following, who the previous month had taken steps to divert some money from the craze of raising monuments in his honour and so ensure his present and future solvency.

[1] ME to FE, 2 Dec 1844 (Edgeworth Papers).

5

Good Works *versus* Self-help

THE year 1845 was to go down in Irish history as a year of
disaster and the harbinger of yet more disaster. It marked the
beginning of the great famine – a calamity not fully over at the
time of Maria's death in 1849. Quite rightly this half-decade is
commonly regarded as 'a major dividing-line in the history of
modern Ireland'.[1] After it, political, social and economic
developments showed distinctly new tendencies – though, of
course, the basic point to note is the unceremonious rapidity
with which profound changes rampaged through the land,
reordering in a matter of months things many had expected
to see altered over a generation at the least. Often the very
suddenness of the breaks has hidden many very important
elements of continuity, but there can be no doubt of the 'indelible
mark on the popular memory'[2] the shocks left behind. This, as
much as the population decline, the widespread transfer of
property and the reshaping of agriculture, must be carefully
borne in mind when considering Ireland during the next
seventy-odd years.

Famine in itself was no new thing: 1817, 1822 and periods in
the 1830s were times of acute hardship. Nevertheless 'The
Great Hunger' is a highly apposite title for the new outbreaks.
For extent and intensity the earlier calamities were child's
play compared with what succeeded them. A small, densely
populated country of 8,000,000 inhabitants was without any real

[1] Beckett, *The Making of Modern Ireland, 1603–1923*, p. 336.
[2] Ibid.

warning plunged into overall and repeated potato-crop failures. No less than about half the population depended 'for its subsistence upon the potato'[1] and were sometimes living at a density of 400 persons to the square mile in purely rural regions. Moreover the national population-density average for arable areas was no less than 335 per square mile. As the Irish population had rocketed over the previous years 'the margin of safety, always precarious, had grown narrower',[2] yet no provision had been made to meet the onset of a general calamity. When the first serious signs of potato blight were observed in September 1845, opinion as to their significance was far from united. Britain had survived its outbreaks of August without undue difficulty, and some saw no reason to suppose Ireland would necessarily be any harder hit. There was a pessimist school, but reports of good crops in many places seemed to belie its woeful forecasts. Only when many apparently good yields putrefied after digging was it proved right. And, even then, such truly sound specimens as there were seemed to augur well for the future.

In January, however, the world was oblivious of this particular aspect of impending doom. Maria had been busily perusing Dean Stanley's[3] study of Thomas Arnold.[4] Her main conclusion, as she informed Fanny in a note on the twenty-eighth, was that Arnold's main actions were in accord with his declared principles. Admission of consistency was not, of course, the same thing as acceptance of the doctrines behind these principles. She found the 'notion of a Church without Churchmen and liberality for Catholics at first and horror of them at last and toleration of all save those' Arnold could not tolerate utterly 'unintelligible';

---

[1] Ibid.

[2] Ibid. p. 337. Connell, *The Population of Ireland*; Edwards and Williams, *The Great Famine*; McDowell, *The Irish Administration*; O'Brien, *The Great Famine*; O'Rourke, *The History of the Great Irish Famine of 1847*; Trench, *Realities of Irish Life*; Trevelyan, *The Irish Crisis*; and Woodham-Smith, *The Great Hunger*, plus the relevant learned articles listed in the bibliography, are invaluable for studying the whole question of famine in Ireland.

[3] Arthur Penrhyn Stanley (1815–81), Dean of Westminster and the son of Edward Stanley (1779–1849), Bishop of Norwich. Involved in numerous ecclesiastical controversies in the course of his life, he was a Broad Churchman and hence a highly sympathetic biographer for Dr Arnold. At one time he was a fellow of University College, Oxford.

[4] Thomas Arnold (1795–1842), best known as headmaster of Rugby, but a former fellow of Oriel College, Oxford, and an advocate of Catholic Emancipation.

though it is only fair to add that his attitudes towards pupils had her unfeigned admiration: 'There is something truly noble in his never being either displeased or mortified by his school pupils not obtaining College honors. When their character and principles were good he was satisfied.'[1]

By the spring her attention had passed back to Ireland and the perpetual cat-and-dog relations there between Catholic and Protestant. Once more it was an Anglican clergyman – this time Sydney Smith – who provided the basic reading-matter round which she wove her thoughts. The last work published before his death that February was a pamphlet entitled *A Fragment on the Irish Roman Catholic Church*. It was destined to run into six editions in a very short time, and Maria's interest must have been shared by numerous others of the serious-minded and socially concerned. In a letter to her sister Fanny on 16 April she gave an admirably balanced assessment of its worth, displaying an indulgence towards error and sheer ignorance only to the extent of recognising its value as amusement. 'I think pretty much as you do, my dear, about the pamphlet – only I *think better*. I mean I think more highly of the wit and humour than you seem to do – and I think this playful jocular mode of dealing with the subject, though it is *unbecoming*, will have great effect.' Smith was, she thought, 'prepared for all the abuse' which he would meet with, and 'the very circumstances of illness in which it was written' would 'prove the earnestness of the benevolent intention to do good'. Humour would lower the temperature of sectarian strife. 'I have no doubts that it will do good when people laugh – they don't face one another quite so bitterly. His way of parleying with O'Connell is admirable.' In matter, as opposed to manner, she found him badly wanting. 'About the Catholics and Chapels I reject all the exaggerations and ignorance . . . They are, however, so absurd that they will do no mischief. People will vent their abuse upon his ignorance and his sense will remain and operate.'[2]

With the central core of his argument, nevertheless, she found herself in substantial agreement as to principle, only doubting the feasibility of its successful transference into

---

[1] ME to FE, 28 Jan 1845 (Edgeworth Papers).
[2] ME to FE, 16 April 1845 (Edgeworth Papers).

practice. State payment of the Irish Catholic clergy, as we have already seen, was no new panacea in 1845. Indeed, it was a well-worn topic of conversation and correspondence between Smith and Maria. He had long ago gleaned that she did not consider it a hobby-horse worth grooming. Yet groom it he did and for years, stubbornly ignoring what a man of his intelligence and perception should straightway have grasped. A whole clutch of reasons militated against his idea, and the spirit of patience running through Maria's comments does her great credit. Charity served to maintain her intellectual honesty in mint condition. Undoubted intelligence gave it punch and sustained effect. Her opinions were invariably well-grounded, and seldom wavered unless in face of further relevant evidence. Hence almost a fortnight before she had told her brother-in-law the Rev. Richard Butler of Trim of how 'In the main point of paying the Catholic priests he [i.e. Smith] is right, if he could do it and if they would take payment, and if he could prevent them afterwards from taking their dues from their parishioners – that is taking double payment.'[1] Fanny got almost exactly the same on the point. 'In the main he is right about the payment of the Catholic clergy – if it *can* be done, it will be done now. The matter is so boldly brought to issue. But where is the money to come from? The Catholic priests are better paid as to actual income now than the Court could pay them, though that income is raised, as Sydney says, in an unfit manner.' Naming as authority Francis Beaufort, her stepmother's brother, whose means of knowing these things she considered better than hers, she claimed to have 'instances and proofs that the *manner* of raising the Catholic priests' incomes – the disputes about *dues* and *sacraments* – are really horrible. There is no exaggeration in the pamphlet on these points.'[2]

Really severe criticism of Smith, however, was reserved for her brother-in-law. 'He does not seem to be aware of what it is wonderful that so clever a man should not have been aware, that the priests love power as other men do – as well as money – and that their love of power over their flocks cannot easily be bought up or bought off. Methinks I see you throwing the pamphlet from you even at the first page! You see, he would not

[1] ME to the Rev. Richard Butler, 3 April 1845 (Edgeworth Papers).
[2] ME to FE, 16 April 1845 (Edgeworth Papers).

believe the true information we gave him as to the incomes of
the Catholic priests. As to the manner of raising it, though his
description is exaggerated, it may have much truth in it.'[1]
This year, 1845, was to see the extension of the Maynooth
grant in face of bitter and substantial opposition in Parliament
and numerous other places in many parts of the United Kingdom.
The Conservative Government found aid at the centre in-
finitely easier than salary payments at the periphery. Smith's
idea was never to be applied and the 'horrible' disputes went
on unabated.

True to form Smith had indulged in some hair-raising stories
about the 'hovels' of Catholic chapels, compared with the fine
and virtually 'empty' Protestant churches.[2] Maria took it all in
good part, contenting herself with the remark, 'Sydney Smith
should have travelled through Ireland and should have seen
the chapels and Roman Catholic cathedrals now built or
building.'[3] With him dead there would have been little point
in recriminations. Still, there was a widow waiting to receive
comment, and writing to her had taxed Maria's diplomatic
skill to the utmost. Avoiding falsehood or the infliction of
needless pain had proved very difficult. Had the dead author
looked further on the non-ecclesiastical side there would have
been plenty upon which he could have feasted his zest for ex-
posing the 'horrible' without having recourse to evidence of
doubtful validity. That very month found Maria regaling
Fanny with news of how the 'Molly McGuires etc. in the county
of Roscommon' had thought up an 'ingenious mode of sowing
the land with *needles* to prevent cattle grazing on it and the
taking of it over their heads'.[4] The mind boggles at the thought
of what a witty Whig cleric would have made of this had he
opted to feast his imagination. It would have been veritable
ambrosia for the sensationalist. Thanks to Lord Macaulay, a
manuscript devoted to the history of English 'misrule' in
Ireland, left unpublished by Smith at his death, has remained in
total obscurity. After all, what could the widow do when so
brilliant and responsible a person advised oblivion? If he

[1] ME to the Rev. Richard Butler, 3 April 1845 (Edgeworth Papers).
[2] ME to FE, 16 April 1845.
[3] ME to the Rev. Richard Butler, 3 April 1845 (Edgeworth Papers).
[4] ME to FE, 21 April 1845 (Edgeworth Papers).

considered it would recreate bitterness about remedied grievances then who was she to contradict? At least one bombshell
on the Irish 'troubles' has therefore never burst.

On the main political front the impending creation of the
Queen's Colleges – a major blow against nationalism on both
lay and clerical fronts – and a lull in the Repealer onslaught
seemed to offer some hope to those moderates favouring the
Union. Around Edgeworthstown that spring 'the people' were
'all busy making the most of this fine weather and blessing God
for it, and not troubling themselves about O'Connell, or any
of his nonsense or wickedness'.[1] Diminution of a threat had
not undermined Maria's convictions as to the true significance of
Daniel O'Connell and his party. One false move on the part of
authority and the whole country might easily blaze up. Anyone
so experienced in Irish affairs could not relax easily, whatever
the state of his or her intellect. For a shrewd judge like her,
readiness was a number one priority. She knew the sickly state
of liberalism in Ireland and feared for it always. Although
prepared to make the most of fine political weather, she realised
sharp rain, if not thunder and lightning, were bound to come
again. Recurrence of trouble was endemic in such a social,
economic and political climate. The most she allowed herself
at this time was qualified optimism.

> There is a great national difference between agitation and activity
> and the country people here at least seem to feel and understand
> this. It comes home not only to their business and bosoms, but to
> their pocket. And I shrewdly suspect they will not much longer
> pay O'Connell's rent. His prestige is gone, I fear. But he is much
> depressed. He can have no moral courage because he has no
> morality and I am assured by those who have had opportunities of
> seeing and no temptation to falsify or set down aught in malice –
> I have been assured by some of his own religion and of his own
> party that he has no physical courage. White feathers throughout
> and no religious will and support.[2]

This is not mere wishful thinking. O'Connell's stock had certainly fallen, and while small extremist elements deserted him
to form what in the next year was to be a distinct Young Ireland
movement, the Catholic masses generally were gradually

---

[1] ME to an unknown correspondent, April 1845 (Edgeworth Papers).
[2] Ibid.

cooling down into a state of semi-demoralisation about Repeal
and semi-hope about the material prospects of their community.

Before six months were out the semi-demoralisation in
politics became as nothing in comparison with the immense
demoralisation about the chances of actual physical survival.
Maria's tone to Fanny on 9 September was quite optimistic.
'Thank you for the caution about the potatoes. Francis says his
are good and so, he hears, are all the potatoes in this neighbourhood. The north country man, Dr Montgomery, who was here
yesterday says the potato crops were all good in his part of the
country – Belfast.'[1] By 14 October things had changed. 'The
disease in the potatoes', she lamented, 'is appearing, alas,
among our conacre potatoes. All the poor labourers are complaining.'[2] And on 9 November Fanny was sent news of large-
scale disaster: 'We are laying out all the money we can . . . to
provide meal *against* the famine. I this moment asked Francis
what I might say to you on the present state of potatoes. "May
I say that the potatoes are getting better, or that they are not
worse?" Answer: "No, I do not think that you may say any
such thing." "What then may I say?" "That nothing can be
worse than the potatoes are in our neighbourhood." (Universal
Dismay, this fair day.)' Characteristically, Maria found some
slight ray of hope to pass on. The family had not yet begun to
make the impressive self-sacrifices so readily undertaken later
on, and she was at pains to emphasise that some supplies were
still left. 'Nevertheless, I must add', she wrote (and here her
passion for the balanced picture can be seen at its best), 'that
nothing can be better than the potatoes we have every day at
dinner – one dish boiled, another dish mashed.'[3]

The gradual impact of the famine in many parts of the country
meant that very frequently the junction of political and social
with economic grievances was effected well before serious
demoralisation on all fronts set in. More often than not the
upshot was violence. Not violence of a kind directed by some
nationalistic organisation based on Dublin or the towns, but
sporadic vendettas long associated with local Ribbonist or

[1] ME to FE, 9 Sept 1845 (Edgeworth Papers).
[2] ME to FE, 14 Oct 1845 (Edgeworth Papers).
[3] ME to FE, 9 Nov 1845 (Edgeworth Papers).

Whitefoot groups. Not surprisingly Maria received her budget of cases and passed it on rapidly along the gentry grape vine.

> I have just heard [she told Fanny] of another dreadful murder in Tipperary in noon day, and people all at work or idle within view. This system of picking out landlords for vengeance is worse than open rebellion – much more difficult for civil or military force to deal with – when the mass of the people are leagued with the party or interests of the assassins, so that no information before or after the fact, nor assistance against the assassins at the moment can be obtained. It appears to be the system of the leagued people to show that no landlord's or agent's life, let him be ever so good, can be safe unless he gives up possession of his land, either for the present rent, whatever it may be, or in short to give up rents altogether. It would soon come to *that* if the first demand were granted.[1]

Circumstances were rapidly to crush the 'leagued people' as effectively as they would have liked to crush the landlords. But this argument about the peasants imposing rents on the landowners and their principal lessees was to appear again as a feature of Irish agrarian strife not so long after Maria's death and to remain one of the principal foci of mutual misunderstanding between landlords with a concept of rights revolving around Irish glosses on the English law of real property and a peasantry wedded to the notion that the land was theirs by right. 'We'll live content and pay no rent in dear old Donegal' was no superficial ditty. It was at once a threat, a *cri de cœur* and a profound aspiration. With such a mentality Maria had no real contact. She was for justice in the system as it stood, not for a new system, and thought along lines of Ireland being West Britain. Yet, even if she had entertained any sympathy for the aims of the 'leagued people', their methods would still have appalled her. Reform by due process of Parliament and the law courts was perhaps the most deep-seated of all her political principles – next, of course, to her passion for justice under the rule of the best educated.

One of the most remarkable of the many remarkable things about her was the way she demonstrated over and over again how someone in the role of a virtual frontierswoman could really comprehend the nature of her local situation, operate

[1] Ibid.

successfully in it and remain in the van of intellectual enquiry. She fitted without difficulty into a world which had left the afflictions raging in Ireland a long way behind. Naturally other instances, such as Field-Marshal Smuts, come to mind when this sort of spiritual dilemma for the cultured segments of ruling-class groups in new-frontier societies is under discussion. Maria's achievement is nonetheless remarkable for that, and foremost among the qualities helping her not merely to survive but triumph as an agent of high civilisation was the keen sense of humour so evident in her novels. Despite the famine and despite the terrorists, she felt inclined to spend time spelling out for Fanny a joke about the Catholic priesthood. A Catholic priest – an acquaintance of a friend – was invited to dine at a 'gentleman's house'. The meal turned out to be a grand affair. 'The lady of the house asked the priest if he would take a glass of wine. "To please you Ma'am then I will, for to say the truth these grapes (holding up a glass) is no more than a daisy to a bullock." '[1] This was no heartless jest – no fiddling as Rome burned; just a business-as-usual comment upon something that had long troubled as well as amused her – the failure of the Irish Catholic clergy taken generally to provide that level of social example she deemed necessary in those entrusted with the exercise of power. The important thing is that amusement as well as the concern could go on at such a time without any element of callousness. Nothing could have been more genuine than the moves she made to try and alleviate the suffering round about her. Although convinced that very little could be done to avert a vast tragedy – the potato crop being ruined, the people so helpless, and the essential supply of water so seldom near the cottages – she nevertheless set to and left nothing untried. Mrs Moore of Moore Hall was full of worthy but impractical suggestions. She thought a mill should be set up to which the people might come for supplies. Reflection nevertheless convinced her the cost of carrying grain away would almost certainly prove prohibitive and aroused doubts as to whether the idea would catch on. Her interest was also aroused by the notion canvassed by a chemist, Dr Leibig, that the peasantry should use sulphuric acid as a means of saving their potatoes. Maria poured scorn on the whole plan and felt

[1] ME to FE, 16 Dec 1845 (Edgeworth Papers).

'dealings with sulphuric acid, chemist not attending, in remote cottages' would very likely end in disaster.[1]

Throughout that sad and trying time Maria remained convinced that mere giving would do untold harm. Hard practical experience had steeled her against giving way to undiscriminating and uncontrolled sentimentality. She therefore insisted the people do something before being given relief supplies; and this accorded well with official government policy. Once it was clear the crisis had reached staggering proportions, Peel had acted quickly, boldly and to no small effect. Though aware he would be open to the charge of seizing upon circumstances to undermine the corn laws, £100,000 worth of maize was bought in United States markets for shipment to Cork – and bought on his own responsibility. The plan was that a relief commission, set up by the Government at the same time – November 1845 – should organise local committees of the Ascendancy classes to raise money, distribute the food, and see to its sale at non-profit-making prices. The Board of Works was to initiate schemes of road construction and so provide employment for the growing numbers of workless. It was hoped the wages paid would enable most of those without cash to buy whatever immediate food supplies they required. Some of the relief workers inveighed against the official horror of giving too much aid, but Charles Trevelyan, Assistant-Secretary to the Treasury, and the director-general of operations, certainly stuck to the principle of self-help, far more because of abstract devotion to 'political economy' than an old Irish hand like Maria. Taken as a whole, however, his work went rather well up to the summer of 1846 and even the Repealer *Freeman's Journal* paid tribute to Peel for his 'foresight, promptness and determination'. Looking back on these months from 1847 it declared: 'No man died of famine during his administration, and it is a boast of which he might well be proud.'[2] Maria would have said 'Amen' to this about counties Longford, Meath and West Meath, where, as she told the Rev. Professor Jones, there had been no prolonged distress.[3] Down in Kerry, O'Connell's tenants had fared badly, and if the situation could

---

[1] Hone, *The Moores of Moore Hall*, p. 128.
[2] Beckett, *The Making of Modern Ireland*, p. 338.
[3] ME to the Rev. Richard Jones, 8 Nov 1845 (Edgeworth Papers).

have been said to hold any compensations for our heroine they surely must have arisen from the feeble response the famine had evoked from the 'Liberator'. Taken unawares, he had been totally outclassed by Peel in coping with his starving supporters.

Spring 1846 found Maria contemplating a visit to London six months hence. As she remarked that summer, travel had become much easier and faster with the coming of the railway. 'Per railroad and plus steam 'tis but eight and forty hours from London to poor little Edgeworthstown.'[1] More pressing matters, however, arose out of her opinions on Father Mathew and his temperance movement. During the first week in April, in a letter to a friend named Ralston, she had, so she thought, cast some doubt on the priest's integrity. Subsequent information had restored her high opinion of him, and a request from Bishop Stanley of Norwich,[2] to whom the Ralston letter had been shown, that it should be published therefore threw her into a considerable tizzy. Anxious to preserve 'the joint weight and respectability of the name' left by her father, she refused point blank.[3] Such facts as there were in the letter the bishop was welcome to, but that was all. Not that Stanley had wanted to discredit Mathew. On the contrary, he was probably very eager to publicise what was in fact the real nub of the matter – that the priest's movement was apolitical. This Maria had cottoned onto, writing to Harriet on 19 April: 'I have some notion that he [i.e. Stanley] might wish to have an Irish correspondent's name to support the opinion that there is no *political union* underneath this teetotallism.' Doubtless the bishop thought that the temperance cause – and he was the one prelate of that decade openly identified with it – would suffer if it could be said that its Irish side was O'Connellism in disguise. The 'respectable' segments of British society were anyway inclined to be suspicious of teetotallers, and their image would hardly have been improved by association with a 'disreputable' set-up like the Repeal party. Yet although she had said what Stanley wanted said in her letter, she was nevertheless most unwilling to go beyond allowing quotation of fact alone. 'I am sure I *hope* and, so far as I can judge *believe*, that there is not any' political

---

[1] ME to the Rev. Richard Jones, 24 June 1846 (Edgeworth Papers).
[2] See p. 142 n 3.
[3] ME to HE, 19 April 1846 (Edgeworth Papers).

union. 'But my belief is not so firm as to make me ensure it. I haven't facts enough to judge. Nor, even if I could
make up my mind on sufficient proofs, should I even then
wish to write myself down an insurer of this or that political
fact for any party. It is against my principles and my father's
advice to meddle with politics in any way, or to lend my name
etc.'[1]

Meddling or no meddling though, she was ready enough
with strong verbal support for George Henry Moore after his
defeat in a by-election in county Mayo. Severe famine had not
knocked the stuffing out of the Repeal party there. Its candidate,
Joe MacDonnell, well known as 'a twenty tumbler man', had
carried almost all before him, and at Ballyglass Moore had
actually been attacked by an O'Connellite mob. Maria congrat-
ulated his mother upon the 'very handsome, conciliatory and
truly patriotic and Christian-like speech and conduct' with
which he had met such behaviour. He has sought 'to make
peace upon earth and goodwill' in face of 'party spirit and
factious acts'. But then his liberally inclined unionism was to
her above party in the doctrinal sense and accorded well with
the Edgeworth notion of making England in Ireland. 'We feel
for you and *with* you,' she wrote. 'We rejoice that you see
in the poor people as well as in the gentlemen in your county
the attachment to your son and the signs of approbation of his
conduct which he deserves. A good sign of the times for Ireland
and in time of need.'[2] The old optimism and yearning for
apolitical politics were as vehement as ever. They seemed to
flourish on hardship and setbacks. Seldom can 'challenge and
response' have been better exemplified! Her friends were not
made of such stern stuff. Moore himself had lost votes for
refusing to give up support of Peel's new coercion measures.
He felt them to be absolutely essential for the present, though
convinced Repeal would come in due time. Like Lord George
Browne, who claimed he owed his life to clerical intervention
with the election mobs, he believed Ireland needed reconquering
then and there if law and order according to British wishes were
to reign supreme. His mother was doubtful as to whether
England was going 'to be always satisfied to hold Ireland at

[1] Ibid.
[2] Hone, *The Moores of Moore Hall*, pp. 134–6.

such expense'.[1] So, either from Repealer persistence or British desperation and fatigue, they thought there would be no hope for a stable future under the existing system. It could not be liberalised by oases of sympathetic landlords of the Edgeworth-Moore type and would therefore be superseded.

Peel's Coercion Bill never became law. What Wellington termed a 'blackguard combination' of Whigs, Radicals, Repealers and rebel Conservatives in the House of Commons threw it out – and with the bath-water went the baby. Peel resigned, never to hold office again, and was replaced by a minority Whig Government under Lord John Russell. His last great achievement had been the repeal of the Corn Laws and the new administration naturally upheld a policy the left-wing groupings had in fact advocated openly some time before he had committed himself. So straight after having been ejected from the premiership by the Whigs, Peel and his loyal followers felt obliged to uphold them against the Conservative protectionist rebels under Lord George Bentinck and Benjamin Disraeli. In the midst of famine the Conservative rebels had foolishly indulged their spite against Peel and blocked legislation their traditions and, in the opinion of many, common sense cried out for – even Russell found himself obliged to invoke coercion the next year. Understandable though rebel anger might have been against a leader whose performances over Catholic Emancipation, Maynooth and the Corn Laws seemed to amount to sustained treachery, it was nothing short of foolish from their viewpoint to install a Whig administration and bring on what soon amounted to fairly active co-operation between men so lately at loggerheads as the Peelites and the left-wing groupings. Whether Peel would have continued to keep his Irish copybook clean is impossible to tell. That Russell tackled the subsequent stages of the Irish famine less skilfully than he had the first is nonetheless not open to contradiction.

At first Russell appeared to have quite a rosy prospect in store for him. The weather in May and June had been good and the potato crop in Ireland was doing well. Then in August the worst happened. The blight struck for a second time. Unfortunately government policy was not modified to meet the new

[1] Ibid.

and more serious contingencies. 'The government was prepared
to promote public works, to help with the organisation of
relief committees, and to make some financial contribution;
but its basic thesis was that Irish poverty must be supported by
Irish property.'[1] So great was the official passion for conforming
to the precepts of 'political economy' that much of Russell's
activity came to naught. As no public money could be spent on
projects likely to benefit private citizens, land reclamation and
drainage were just ruled out. Peel's methods for keeping prices
down were abandoned, yet relief committees were told they
should not sell provisions below local prices for fear of damaging
the economic position of professional commercial men. Political
instability at Westminster and crass ignorance in official circles
made for doing much less than was called for. As most of rural
Ireland had a subsistence economy and the peasants were not
really helped by money wages when there was no proper
system of retail shops in which to spend them, it was sheer
folly to expect things to right themselves without the aid of
exceptional distribution-methods launched under central direction. Then, too, many landlords proved both unable and
unwilling to fulfil the role Russell had cast for them. Many
others failed in one respect or the other. Had it not been for
private charity, such as that set on foot in Dublin and London in
November by the Quakers, the fate of the Irish masses over
the terrible winter months of 1846-7 might well have beggared
description.

Sheer pressure of events persuaded the Government that they
must undertake the work of seeing the people were fed. New
measures at the beginning of 1847 still retained the principle of
local responsibility – 'The provision and distribution of food
was to be a charge upon the rates; though the Government
would, where necessary, advance funds to start the new scheme,
these advances were to be repaid, and running costs met, by the
ratepayers'[2] – and could not be brought into operation over-
night, but by August 1847 some 3,000,000 individuals and
more were being fed each day at public expense. Many of the
poorer areas soon went bankrupt, and in practice the central
Government had therefore to foot the bill in many of the

---

[1] Beckett, *The Making of Modern Ireland*, p. 339.
[2] Ibid. p. 341.

hardest hit places. Workhouses proved quite inadequate for taking in the masses of fresh paupers, so the 'workhouse test' went by the board and even outdoor relief was introduced as a temporary measure. But like many 'temporary' measures it lasted for quite some time – right through to the late autumn of 1849 in fact, when Maria had been six months dead. Not a large acreage had been sown with potatoes for 1847, but the success of the crop did much to restore faith in the traditional fare. Nevertheless its small size did little to alleviate general conditions. Then there were vast outbreaks of typhus and relapsing fever, and nothing a specially constituted Board of Health could do approached bringing the situation to rights. Founded in 1846, it set up a 'national system of temporary fever hospitals'.[1] Once more, however, it was the case of too little and too late. And when full-scale famine followed the potato blight of 1848, the menace of disease remained as great as ever. Indeed, never again in Maria's lifetime did the Irish masses enjoy either the amount of food or the level of health of the years immediately before the famine.

Her main correspondence upon the famine began with the full impact of disaster reaching her immediate neighbourhood at the beginning of 1847. On 9 February she wrote telling Harriet of how the then vicar of Edgeworthstown – a Mr Powell – had persuaded her ('much against the grain') 'to beg some relief for the poor from the Quaker Association in Dublin'. She had accordingly penned a letter to a Mr Harvey – 'the only person I know on the committee' – and 'prayed some assistance . . . to get us over the next two months'. Mrs Edgeworth had been making strong representations to her about the plight of the men and boys taken on for draining work, who could not possibly '*stand* the work in the wet for want of strong shoes'. 'So in for a penny, in for a pound; ask for a lamb, ask for a sheep', the Friends had been asked 'for as many pairs of brogues as they could afford, or as much leather and soles, which would be better still, as this would enable . . . sundry starving shoemakers' to be set to work. The response came by return of post, promising £30 for food and £10 'for women's work', offering 'a soup boiler for eighty gallons' (in case she didn't possess one of sufficient size), and informing her the 'shoe petition'

[1] Ibid. p. 343.

would be put before the clothing committee.[1] Optimism must
have radiated from the great house, for almost a fortnight
later she was describing how the peasants were sticking to their
usual routine. Longford had not been hit anything like so hard
as areas in the south and west. Energy and determination to
strive for recovery had therefore remained at a relatively high
level. 'The people are now beginning to sow', she reported,
'and I hope they will accordingly reap in due course. Mr Hinds
has laid down a good rule – not to give seed to any tenants but
those who can produce the receipt for the last half year's rent.'[2]
Adversity for the masses had not caused even as liberal a
régime as the Edgeworths' to abandon the usual caution in
dealing with tenants. The economy of the Leinster midlands
was much more money-based than that of the more primitive
counties. Still, to demand a clean slate before affording the
means of providing for survival was quite a hard doctrine in
its way, though a characteristic piece of useful help was thrown
in for the 'deserving'. Barry Fox had 'been exceedingly kind
in staying' at Edgeworthstown and 'looking after blunders in
draining'.[3]

It was to Fanny that she first announced the arrival of leather
supplies. The Quaker clothing committee had come up trumps
and given generously.

The *skins* are come – huge skins of leather for brogues, forty or
fifty pair. The shoemakers may shake their elbows and the naked
footed draining workmen rejoice. To the smell of the leather to
which you say 'Faugh' I say delicious. There is a parcel of clothes –
large as *the tea table* – packed in brown linen now lying in your
mother's dressing room delightfully encumbering the passage. It
is full of fifty garments and two additional pieces of flannel thrown
in by these excellent Quakers to make Friend Maria E. amends for
having delayed the clothing a few days. The parcels cannot be
unpacked till tomorrow – too late today – *so* I may take the rational
recreation of writing to you. The contents of parcel and leather were
to have been divided between your mother and Miss Powell, but
Miss P., who is at this moment come in to see the joyful sight, has,
most judiciously in my opinion, advised that my mother should
have all (including all the trouble) as she knows best all the people
and their wants. What a mercy it is in the midst of these disturbed
times that, instead of quarrelsome power loving ladies and gentlemen, such as fell to quarrelling on Longford Committee, we have

[1] *Memoir*, III 250.   [2] *Memoir*, III 251.   [3] Clarke, *Maria Edgeworth*, p. 188.

Powells – especially for your mother, who has such constant business with them about the poor.

Understandably enough, the Quakers had 'sent down a very
reasonable list of requisitions with this bountiful supply of
clothes, begging that the Committee', which was to dispose of
them should 'go to the houses of the poor and actually *see* before
they distribute and give to the most destitute and deserving'.
They had also 'sent down a *warning* printed advertisement to
Pawnbrokers not to take any of the goods in pawn and the made-
up clothes' had all been 'stamped *in conformity*'. A request had
also been enclosed to the effect that 'the brogues should be
marked before' being given. 'They particularly desire', she
stressed, 'that we should take every means in our power to
prevent the clothes being pawned and we will, of course, do
all we can. But that all is very little and whether there be any
legal power over the pawnbrokers I cannot say.' Perhaps
Fanny's husband, Lestock Wilson, could help on the point. If so,
he would be saving her 'a hunt in the Dining room closet and a
rummage through a folio *Pawnbrokers' Act* of Parliament. You
comprehend that *our* Committee is composed of us six – viz.
Mr, Mrs, and Miss Powell, Mrs E. Mrs Francis E. and Maria
E. In short your mother is the Committee – God help her!'[1]

She was too modest here and scarcely did herself justice.
To the hated O'Connell, however, she was determined to do
justice. Maria was undeviating in her desire to be fair to all
except herself – the devil himself was never denied his due,
not even her pet political devil.

In this day's 'Evening Mail' [she went on] there is a sensible
speech of O'Connell's. I see that the people in Parliament as well
as out are attacking Lord John about the seed business. Perhaps
it will come to 'Non sara'. There is a monstrous waste of public
money now going on – salaries of two, three and four hundred
pounds per annum to *Overseers* or Inspectors of Drainage etc.
About half a million as Mr Blackhall[2] has calculated is at this instant
job-job-job-jobbing among these people, who do no earthly good
to anybody or anything in Ireland. I don't swear to Mr Blackhall's

[1] ME to FE, 9 March 1847 (Edgeworth-Beaufort Papers).
[2] The newspaper referred to was the *Dublin Evening Mail*. Mr Blackhall was
S. W. Blackhall, who in the coming August was elected as M.P. for county
Longford as a Liberal 'favourable to the consideration of the Repeal question', the
extension of the franchise and a Tenant Right Bill. The long and short of it was
that he was more of a reformer than a Repealer!

calculation, as I have no means of verifying, but I know that we have seen half a dozen in this county and Mr Tuite says twelve hundred pounds per annum is now to be spent in this manner in Westmeath. Calculate what this money will do in buying seed or tilling the land. Is not Sir. J. Burgoyne a jobber.[1]

The old dangers her father and she had found so disgusting in pre-Union Ireland seemed to be growing up again. Strict 'political economy' was leading to waste and was anyway beside the point. If the localities were going to have to pay, then they should be enriched to help towards the cost. After all, while the landowners might gain from seed sown and land tilled, they had to find the bulk of local finance and in the long run their default would mean the expenditure of another kind of public money – that from central government funds. Why not let the country produce wealth instead of merely absorbing it? Maria had never been a rigid *laisser faire* devotee. Practical experience and a tender conscience together had preserved her empirical approach. Hence she had seen at once what needed to be done and been ready to voice her criticisms when it was not undertaken. Admittedly there were signs of official repentance in the face of failure, and she was ready to recognise a change for the better, however belatedly made and however difficult it was going to be to put matters straight. 'I am glad to see', she remarked, 'that the Government (Mr Labouchere at least)[2] now determine to turn the people from cutting down and breaking up roads to cultivating their gardens and tilling their fields "as far as this can be done with *safety* to the public". So there is a Government confession of the mistakes of their own doings. It is now dangerous even to undo, but it is idle to talk of past mistakes. The present so presses and the future to be immediately provided for under the penalty of worse famine, worse disease, destitution and death next year.'

The same spirit of justice and a keen awareness of Ireland's real and urgent needs brought her to approving of O'Connell, yet kept her from unconstructive carping and harping on the immediate past. Her anti-party convictions stood up well to the

[1] Sir John Fox Burgoyne (1782–1871), an engineer officer with wide war experience, who served as chairman of the Irish public works board from 1831 until 1845 and then went off to be Inspector-General of Fortifications until 1868.

[2] Henry Labouchere, 1st Baron Taunton (1798–1869), currently President of the Board of Trade.

situation, and indeed one could say that only in crisis was her
type of politics likely to get a proper hearing and massive
support. When men and women were fighting for their lives
and property, lesser matters, albeit ancient quarrels deep and
widespread, tended, to pass into oblivion. Like Liberal Unionism, Gaullism and other constitutional forms of national-interest
grouping, the Peelite or Stanleyite ideal to which Maria
subscribed really found its moment when 'unofficial' partisan
spirits were laid low. As circumstances forced a fumbling
Government to come to grips with the situation she was ready
with support. Not surprisingly on this occasion, it was accompanied by a streak of pessimism. Her next words were something of a lament:

> It is said that numbers who have been employed in public works
> and numbers who have been unemployed at home are so much
> weakened that they cannot, really cannot, work without being
> supplied with food. *Spite* of all soup shops and Charity it is come to
> this. *Spite of all*, I say. I could not venture to say in *consequence* of
> the gratis feeding, because there must be an exception to the
> general rule 'If thou dost not work, thou shalt not eat', for here it
> has been: 'Even if thou dost work, thou shalt not eat.' Here is a
> calamity – National calamity by the hand of God, inflicted no doubt
> for wise purpose, but which all the wisdom of men cannot avert or
> remedy completely. The vast numbers that have died it is dreadful
> to hear of (not in our county).

So caution with tenants and careful insuring of the Edgeworth
financial future was one thing, a refusal to notice and attend
to the general catastrophe quite another. Maria would not have
denied practical *ad hoc* aid to debtor tenants and certainly spared
herself no personal sacrifice in the crisis. Yet only by husbanding
estate resources would the future of everyone be guaranteed.
Aid had to come from the continuing creation of agricultural
wealth in Ireland supplemented by outside help. She saw no
sense in extending family resources to breaking-point when the
combined effects of charity and government help for its starving
subjects could bridge the gap in her neighbourhood. Thus hard-
headed farming and national concern could be reconciled,
especially as the situation appeared to show signs of having
been successfully got under control.

> There are some circumstances that look a little better in this
> neighbourhood. There are more potatoes now appearing than we

had any idea existed. Harriet Butler tells my mother that several of the little farmers *built* up their potatoes to prevent themselves from eating them during these winter months of distress and now they are coming out for sale and for planting. In the market at Trim last market day potatoes were sold at eightpence a stone – in this market for sevenpence – and at Tullamore for eightpence, as Mary Anne Fox said in a letter received today. The usual price at this time of year being from threepence to fourpence. We find that the people are as eager and as forward in tilling their ground as ever at this time of year, and though many are much in want of *seed*, many more have seed oats than we knew of or imagined. My informants as to the present are Mr Powell and Mr McNally, who have both good means of information and habits of observation.

With all the hardship and the none too comfortable life most of the local people led during normal times in this comparatively prosperous part of Ireland, it was a great tribute to their inherent desire to work that these things should have been so. It was an even greater tribute to them that Maria should find one theft of food so important as to be worth commenting upon at some length.

I am sorry to tell you [she wrote to Fanny] that in spite of all the good your mother does and the gratitude of the people, there are some, or one at least, vile, base enough to steal from her. A sack of oats was stolen out of the stable a few nights ago. Gahan had been sowing oats and put the remaining sack into the stable at night. In the morning – gone. The window which had been shut was open, but that was only a sham. The sack could not have been got through that window, nor could it have been hauled over the yard walls. It must have been carried out at doors and gates. The theft must have been committed by some habitué and the keys must have been taken from Gahan's house where they are kept. The thief was cute enough to empty the oats from the sack in which they were marked *FBE.* and to leave that in the manger. I suspect Murtagh junior and I understand that the suspicion of the country is against him. He is going off to America next week. You know he was the person who committed some years ago that audacious theft during the time we were at church and Edward driving us there. Broke into Edward's box in his servant's bedchamber and took thereout fifteen shillings. Edward pursued him closely, found him in a public house drinking silver and he and his family were so frightened that the money was immediately repaid Edward and *no more about it. But* he cannot be detected now. 'No one can swear to their own oats.'[1]

So, given that her hunch was right, it took a criminal to steal food at Edgeworthstown in the midst of severe famine. The

[1] ME to FE, 9 March 1847 (Edgeworth-Beaufort Papers).

cynical might say that blaming a man about to leave for
America was most convenient for the inhabitants generally. But
cynical views of Edgeworthstown were not often right.

And virtue had its reward. In mid March £5 arrived from
the Birmingham Relief Committee for 'the starving Irish'.
Maria was delighted: 'How good people are!'[1] she exclaimed;
and so they were, for her requests to friends in the United
States brought handsome responses all round. 'The ladies of
America and especially those of New York had been asked for
barley seed as well as cash. To be of real use the seed had to
arrive by May, but the ladies got to work with a will and the
"real Argosie" '[2] was soon afloat. A group of her admirers in
Boston sent over 150 barrels of flour addressed to 'Miss Edgeworth for her poor'. Both when the seed and the flour arrived
in Ireland the porters employed to bring them ashore from the
ships refused payment. Each eventually got a woollen comforter
knitted with her own hands as a sign of appreciation. A remarkable piece of labour for a woman of her age already loaded
with duties, but perhaps outshone by another of her activities.
Helen had come out in 1834, and since then she had attempted
to write precious little for publication. Now, to raise money
for the starving, she wrote a story in the hope of selling it to
Messrs Chambers for publication in their *Miscellany*.[3]

Nor did any useful morsel in the newspapers escape her
attention. 'Having seen in the newspapers that the Australians
had sent a considerable sum for the relief of the distressed Irish,
and that they had directed it to the use of His Grace the Archbishop of Dublin, meaning Dr Murray',[4] the Catholic prelate,
she wrote off to 'our' Archbishop Whately,[5] his Church of

---

[1] *Memoir*, III 251. Flanagan, *Irish Novelists*, p. 105.

[2] *Memoir*, III 252.

[3] It was in fact *Orlandino* and appeared in Chambers's 'Library for Young
People' in 1848. A second edition appeared in 1853. Meanwhile an American
edition had appeared in 1848 and a French one in 1849. Devoted to the subject
of temperance, the book had as an illustration both sides of Father Mathew's
temperance medal.

[4] Daniel Murray (1768–1852). He had been appointed in 1823.

[5] Richard Whately (1787–1863), a former fellow of Oriel College, Oxford, and
Drummond Professor of Political Economy at Oxford for three years before taking
up his position in Dublin in 1831. He had presided over the commission on the
Irish poor, 1833–6, and pushed hard for interdenominational co-operation in
education. His financial contribution towards famine relief in 1847 was most
substantial.

Ireland opposite number, 'playing upon this graceless proceeding towards him, and to the best of' her 'capacity, without flattery'. She described what followed in her characteristically lively style:

> I did what I could to make my letter honestly pleasing to His Grace, and I received back the most prompt, polite and to the point reply, assuring me that the Australians were not so graceless in their doings as in their words; that they had made a remittance of a considerable sum to him; and that if I apply to the Central Relief Committee, in whose hands he placed it, he has no doubt my application will be attended to. This was nuts and apples to me – better at present, rice and oatmeal, and I have accordingly written to 'My Lords and Gentlemen'. The Archbishop, civilly, to show how valuable he deemed my application! has sent me a corrected copy of his speech, with good new notes and preface. He says it is impossible to conceive how ignorant the English are of Ireland, and how positive in their ignorance.[1]

For most people, making a successful contact with such a man and securing what amounted to a promise of support for the Edgeworthstown cause would have been enough – at least for the time being. But Maria was not like most people, and, before any material response could have come from 'My Lords and Gentlemen', she had got the vicar to send a list of local subscriptions amounting to some hundred guineas up to Dublin Castle in order to take advantage of the Government's offer 'to give as much as any parish subscribed towards its own relief'. The money duly turned up and so that we 'may encourage them (i.e. the local people) to cook at home and not be mere craving beggars' it was spent on 'bread and rice and meal – not all in soup'.[2]

Irish administrative machinery had proved pathetically inadequate in coping with the famine. It was no less a failure in recording its immediate effects. Maria simply could not tell Lady Beaufort just how many persons had died by the beginning of May 1847 and, what is more, believed no one could 'form a just estimate'. 'In different districts the estimates and assertions' were 'widely different and the priests' were keeping 'no registry'.[3] During a visit on the seventh Mr Tuite had complained of the contradictory statements made by Irish Members

---

[1] *Memoir*, III 252–3.
[2] Ibid.
[3] *Memoir*, III 253–4.

in the House of Commons. They were in his opinion bound to
have a bad effect and diminish what little credit the Irishmen
still had with the English. According to police reports some
250,000 souls had perished up to the end of March and Tuite
'thought a third more deaths than usual had been in his neighbourhood'[1] of county Longford. Mrs Edgeworth and the vicar
on the other hand maintained that 'the increase of deaths above
ordinary times' had not 'been as great as one third'[2] on *their*
home ground, but as the days went by their comparative good
fortune came to be threatened. 'The fever, or whatever it is'
had been 'dreadful about Armagh' and 'many gentlemen' had
caught it.[3] The danger might well spread, and then so con-
scientious a family as the Edgeworths would stand to face
grave risks. Maria recounted to Harriet the story of one victim
who had 'exerted himself much for the poor' and died as a
result. While engaged upon distributing meal he had come
across 'a poor girl so weak she could not hold her apron
stretched out for it'. Feeling pity he had gone and 'held it for
her'. 'She was in the fever. He went home, felt ill, had the
fever and died.'[4]

One very important death took place on 15 May. Convinced
that his end was near, O'Connell had set off for Italy with the
express intention of spending his last days in Rome. Fate had
cheated him, and he breathed his last before quitting Genoa.
The time was one of great heart-searching in his movement,
for although he had condemned Russell's policies as inappropr-
iate and inadequate, no final breach with the Whigs had taken
place. Such an equivocal position had exacerbated still further
the differences between the Young Ireland ginger group of
intransigent nationalists and the Repeal party proper.[5] In
January the extremists had gone so far as to set up a separate
organisation called the Irish Confederation and to secure
Smith O'Brien, a Protestant landlord and Member of Parliament, as its leader. For a short time, with the famine so severe
and a strong mood of national solidarity affecting the vast
majority of political elements, it looked as though the split

[1] Ibid.   [2] Ibid.
[3] Ibid.   [4] Ibid.
[5] Duffy, *Young Ireland* and *Four Years of Irish History*, and Nowlan, *The
Politics of Repeal*, are most instructive on this topic.

in the 'Green' party might not get out of hand. An all-party gathering in Dublin during the same month made a united call for changed government measures in Ireland. But in a country like Ireland such a thing was almost bound to prove a flash in the pan. Very soon the old animosities burst out afresh. Despite some talks between O'Connell's son John and the Young Ireland devotees, the split widened, with the leftmost of the latter going off to worship at the altars of Wolfe Tone and the cult of violent revolution. Meanwhile the sufferings of the masses went on unabated, and party politics must have seemed an utter irrelevancy to most men and women of all classes. And indeed the maintenance of the Repeal movement on a national scale with a steady flow of 'rent' became a thing of the past. Certainly Maria remained preoccupied with the practical aspects of the awful calamity that had come upon her people. The garden alone provided her with genuine solace. At the approach of midsummer we find her writing to the Rev. Professor Jones: 'This minute, after having in the last year gone through as much misfortune in this family as could well be, and now, and for months, public distress, famine and fever surround us, yet and nevertheless I find myself taking pleasure in the roses you gave me and grieving for a fern that has been killed by the frost.' She still had hope of recovery, but couched her thoughts in cautious language. 'Our harvests promise well, even the potatoes. But we must not brag or hope too soon, for we are not yet come to the season when the blight, or blast, or whatever it should be called, seized the potatoes and parsnips last year.'[1]

The picture of a disaster, however great, can so easily be overdrawn. Edgeworthstown had got off more lightly than many areas, not only because of devoted leadership, but because of important acts of foresight taken after the first bout of trouble by many of the peasants themselves. Jones was given a full report of their virtue, for which, of course, the 'moral training' on that particular estate was doubtless in part responsible. 'Many more potatoes had been stored by small farmers and even by cottiers than had been known or supposed to exist last year. These people had built them up, *walled* them up

---

[1] ME to the Rev. Richard Jones, 14 June 1847 (Edgeworth Papers).

literally from themselves and their families, and have this year *planted* them.' Laudable though this had undoubtedly been in the circumstances, Maria was nonetheless anxious to see new basic diets introduced. 'The great good arising from the change of national food for this country' would, she was certain, remain when the famine was over. 'The potato for many reasons is not fit to be the staple food of a country – not storable – not employing industry or labour sufficient in its cultivation for the moral purpose – and it brings in the lowest price, affording nothing to fall back upon in case of failure. I have letters of Ricardo's in which all the *requisites* for a safe national food are ably stated and the potato is lowest in his scale.' Apparently the storage achievement of the tenants had struck her as no more than something resulting from a degree of skill unlikely to be widespread, 'yet and nevertheless' she did not aim like 'some Political Economists' to secure the total abandonment of the vegetable. 'I do not', she declared, 'consider it as an evil in itself, but a good that has been abused. The introduction of other food and vegetables requiring more care and cultivation etc. will be an improvement no doubt. But each good has its price and none need be sacrificed for nothing.'

Turning to the question of outside help, she dilated on the subject of waste and maladministration.

> The quantity of provisions, corn and so on that have been sent over to Ireland to be locked up in stores till certain time, or certain prices prevailed and the quantity that have been wasted and spoiled of these stores, when opened, is lamentable! Also the quantity of money that has been wasted and is now wasting in paying officers, watching officials, hundreds per annum to oversee draining and other works, of which they (the overseers) are perfectly ignorant, is also lamentable. It is surprising how clearly, how acutely the common people and the very lowest Irish labourer sees these blunders and calculates the sums wasted. 'Sure!' said our under gardener, who by the way cannot *write*. 'Sure, the half of the fifteen hundred a year that's spent in this country on them Englishmen teaching us how to drain, which we know well enough, or I'd learn it without 'em, would have bought meal enough to have fed all them that has died of hunger and *is* perishing still.'

Barry Fox must have been guiding his hand on drainage questions, yet, whether or no the man knew his business, there can be little doubt that he had a point. If the 'experts' were not exactly teaching their grandmother how to suck eggs, they were trying to show 'Paddy' things that were often not among the most pressing matters to hand. Obviously the future had to be planned for, but starving men don't make the most adept pupils for agricultural improvers.

It would be wrong to assume from this that Maria had become wholly critical of Britain's part in tackling the second bout of the famine. She was the first to admit that the 'very great sympathy that has been felt in England for our Irish distress and the munificent assistance your country has afforded us have been strongly felt and, I trust, will be gratefully remembered long in Ireland, and will increase good feeling and cement real Union between the countries.' Turning to the political aspect of the situation, she told Jones how 'happy' it had been for Ireland that 'the great agitator did not die' there, and that he was dead. 'But his prestige had gone before him. Confidence cannot last where truth is not in the man.' About this dead man there was no good to be said. Just as national solidarity feelings had passed away quickly amongst the politicians, so they were transient even in the mind of a woman believing *par excellence* in national solidarity. O'Connell's death and the relief work done for the masses struck her as offering a chance for the politics she really craved for – those of a contented people following an enlightened ruling class along the road to Englishness.

> The cry against Irish landlords, which has been unjust, will [she insisted] be completely put down by the humanity and most active exertions of the landed proprietors during the distress in Ireland. It is not fair to argue either as to good or bad from a few instances, but it is fair to take them into account. I could name at least ten or twelve great landed proprietors who have this season and last year lost their lives from overexertion and from fever caught in attending their tenants and the poor. And Protestant clergymen in great numbers have so zealously exerted themselves that they have won the affections of the *poor* Catholics and even their priests, convinced that they have not used any undue means of *conversion*, are much conciliated. This is a *good* which will survive the evil.[1]

There was something in this and certainly some 'good' did survive the 'evil'. Even so the deep desire for the land and the ingrained sense of distinct national identity with which it was inevitably linked were not going to be washed away in a sea of vague good feeling built upon instances of kindnesses done

[1] Ibid.

by individuals, however numerous both the individuals and the kindnesses. It was a vain hope to suppose that the new-found sympathies would linger once the usual realities of Irish life were restored. The politicians were already leading the way back to normal, the priests would soon fall in line, and the Catholic masses would not need much working up against those who were, after all, their natural opponents in a classic social, economic and political struggle.

Maybe prejudice sustained Maria's optimism. It certainly aided hard experiences in maintaining her suspicion of undiluted unilateral welfare measures. The Quakers and their like were all very well, but presently 'the great difficulty' would come. She asked the long-suffering Jones:

> How shall we get the people who have been fed gratis to believe that the government and their landlords are not bound to feed them always? They evidently have formed this idea. It was impolitic in the past circumstances to adhere strictly to the wholesome maxim: 'They who do not work shall not eat.' There were such numbers who had no *work* – who could not work from extenuation, disease etc. Humanity could not leave these to perish from hunger – or if humanity had been out of the question fear could not have ventured it. The character of Paddy knows well how to take advantage of his own misfortunes and of all fears and blunders.

Now that the situation was easing, old ideas were reasserting themselves in her mind. If she was reverting to a tougher approach, the recrudescence of partisan spirits amongst those less committed to the ideal of national unity was hardly surprising. And the attempt to count the cost and look to the future – in itself a somewhat premature move to make – involved her in the very confusion between immediate needs and coming developments which she had condemned in the Government. Of course her opinion that 'A greater blunder than granting outdoor relief to the poor of Ireland could not, I think, be committed by any legislator in the present circumstances' must be judged with especial stress upon the last four words. As pointed out above, it was the practical difficulties surrounding outdoor relief, not the thing in itself which appalled her so. Whether or not a famine was on, Maria's attitudes comprised a mixture of the 'political economic' with the humane, and this bid to tighten up, undoubtedly brought on by the extent of the breakdown in normal conditions, represented a mood of uncertainty. Her own words prove it to have been so: 'Am I foolish in saying or in thinking this?' she asked. 'Please to tell me what I ought to think and why.'[1] The weeks passed. June was soon over. July flitted by and August came on without mishap. 'Potatoes are coming again! Potatoes are coming again!' was her cry to friend Jones.[2] They were not the only thing on the way – a general election was planned for the middle of the month.

It resulted in many Repealer gains – a development both alarming and surprising to many British Conservatives, Peelites and Whigs. With O'Connell dead and his party in disarray, it was certainly remarkable at first glance to observe how the Repealer cause more than doubled its numbers in Parliament. More careful examination, however, would have revealed that the disunity so deleterious of influence upon Russell over matters like Irish Poor Law and so obvious over Lord George Bentinck's scheme for Treasury backing of ambitious Irish railway schemes still persisted. It would also have shown how very important the Tenant Right and public-relief issues, not to mention something as secondary as the Colleges Bill, had proved at the local level. These gains therefore registered discontent upon things of immediate interest having been substantially exploited by individual O'Connellites, rather than a resurgence of self-conscious patriotic fervour under the lash of famine and fever. Maria was uncertain whether Ireland should be 'glad or sorry' or 'between both'[3] as the potatoes became ready for harvesting. Similar feelings must have governed her thinking upon the election in county Longford. Contrary to the current trend the Repealers as such had lost so much impetus there as to leave the progressive fight in the hands of two advanced Whigs – Major Samuel Wensley Blackhall of Colombar, Edgeworthstown, whose opinions Maria had quoted with respect at the height of the famine, and Richard Maxwell Fox,[4] the son of a Church of Ireland clergyman and great-nephew of the 2nd Earl of Farnham, resident at Fox Hall, Rathowen, county Longford. The former

---

[1] Ibid.
[2] ME to the Rev. Richard Jones, 15 Aug 1847 (Edgeworth Papers).
[3] Ibid.
[4] The nephew of Barry and Charles Fox!

declared himself a Liberal 'favourable to the consideration of the Repeal question, in favour of an extension of the franchise and an ambitious Tenant Right Bill'. The latter had lately been a government inspector for the union of Dungannon in county Tyrone under the terms of the Irish Relief Act, a member of the county bench and one of its deputy-lieutenants. Describing himself as a Liberal, he advocated Repeal from outside the Repeal party and favoured an extension of the franchise, but remained strongly opposed to endowment of the Catholic Church. Against these two the Conservatives ran Anthony Lefroy and the Hon. H. L. K. Harman. Without success, for the 'Liberals' won handsomely. Blackhall received 447 votes and Fox 433, compared with only 352 for Lefroy and a mere 323 for Harman. That the ardent Tenant Righter did better than the more avowed Repeal man was surely not without significance?

The Edgeworths did nothing for the Conservatives beyond voting, and Maria felt the thanks offered them by Lefroy were somewhat undeserved. Had there been a real sense of urgency they would certainly have done more, even against Whigs of such impeccable background. There was an air of anticlimax and almost of irrelevancy about the whole contest. Lefroy reported an absence of rioting or 'disposition to riot at Longford' during the polling, and she observed that there did not seem to be 'any ill-blood'.[1] A judgement like this would have been impossible during the preceding two decades and, although Russell depended upon Peel for his parliamentary majority, placid acceptance of Whig government, run at that moment without the support of coercion, was nothing short of remarkable. O'Connell was dead and the true power of his party done for. That was the great fact, and from it this state of affairs had sprung. Gentlemen Repealers uncommitted to the 'Patriot' cause made Conservatives feel safer than had the Whites of the Irish world. A phase was beginning where reform causes would be in the hands of 'enlightened' gentlemen loosely attached to the Whigs. Things seemed in some ways back to the pre-Clare by-election era. The people were to be led by their 'friends'. Repeal seemed a long way off with O'Connell dead and the country laid low by famine. Promising

[1] ME to HE, 14 Aug 1847 (Edgeworth Papers).

the earth was therefore all the easier for some ladies and gentlemen, and losing no sleep over its having been promised no effort
for other ladies and gentlemen. It was as though a new frame of
reference in Irish politics had been created. Everyone seemed
to realise solid reconstruction and modest reform were going
to be the order of the day, especially with the prospect of Whig
administration going on for no little time very, very strong
indeed. Maria had found that even the priests had been 'well-
enough inclined' to Lefroy and quoted the words spoken by one
'when he had taken a glass extra': 'Ah, if you'd have said that
little word we'd rather have had you than any of them.' 'No
doubt this was a lie', she commented, and added, 'though they
say there is truth in good wine, not in whiskey punch.'[1] A lie,
maybe, yet no such incident had been recorded just before,
during or after any other election she had experienced in the
post-Emancipation period. And then another indication of the
state of the political barometer should be considered – the cost
of the election. In the times of great popular hubbub the
Whites had spent money like water. According to Maria the
expenses in 1847 of both victors combined had not exceeded
£1500 at the close of polling. Certainly times had changed,
but not so much as to uphold our heroine's beliefs about the
good that had come out of evil living on.

Over in county Mayo, George Henry Moore had reversed
his by-election defeat of the year before and been elected by a
thumping majority. Instead of defending coercion plans, he had
turned all his guns on the Russell administration for its famine
policy and the failure to back the Bentinck railway scheme.
The principal keynote of his campaign had been the need for a
truly independent Irish party. In other words the Repealers
were tarred with the brush of alliance with the Whigs, and
Moore, a 'People's Friend', had emerged as a strong patriot
espousing the type of policy Maria and her like tended to want
in their heart of hearts. Of course Moore was a Catholic, yet his
notion of patriotism was not so much anti-British as Grattanite.
That is, it embraced the notion of putting pressure on the
British, not for the indulgence of extremist purposes, but to
secure what he and his like considered urgent reforms in
Ireland. In other words a bold move was to be made with the

[1] Ibid.

object of preserving the basis of the social system by the introduction of salutary improvements. Maybe Maria would not really have liked such a course. Nevertheless the object it had in mind was without doubt the one she had long craved for. Writing to Moore's mother the month before the election, she had, like many moderates before, then and since, refused to face up to methods that would have to be adopted if her dreams were to stand even a chance of coming true. And she missed the point about the future by thinking only in terms of improved British-Irish and Catholic-Protestant good will and not of the changes that would have to be wrung from Britain in order to maintain it.

Moore must have found it little short of infuriating to be told that 'too little had been said at the elections about English generosity and too much despair expressed'. Conditions in county Mayo just then did not lead active men of reforming disposition to dwell upon how much the people had to be thankful for, nor allow them to be lulled into contentment by the thought that whatever their errors the British governments had meant well. Maria's statement 'I am no politician'[1] could only have evoked ironical laughter had it not been for the friendship felt for her at Moore Hall and the respect a man of George Henry Moore's gentlemanly stamp would undoubtedly have felt for her age. His success showed how weak the Repeal movement had become and yet proved once again how very strongly the general desire for drastic change was bitten into the political outlook of those Irish Catholics able to vote under a narrow franchise, let alone into that of the great excluded unwashed. Perhaps O'Connell's bid for undoing the Union had lost its immediate appeal amongst large sections of the masses. Nonetheless, criticism of the *status quo* still had an unrivalled attraction for them, and Moore had illustrated very well that where there was a lead to better things it would be followed. Economic recovery and Tenant Right might be less exciting at first blush than Repeal. For a desperate people with its eyes forced to attend to bread-and-butter matters, they were exciting. When linked to the notion of a determined Irish pressure-group free from entanglements with corrupting official influences, they were glamour itself.

[1] Hone, *The Moores of Moore Hall*, pp. 143-5.

Although Parnell was to have more radical policies, his party strategy was the same as Moore's. That Moore failed to keep an Independent Irish Brigade afloat for long was to some extent a reflection upon him. That 'enlightened' gentlemen were hardly the best material to work upon and with must also be borne in mind.[1] For the immediate purposes of our story the fact that a friend of Maria's took up the last substantial bid to combine moderate demands with a tough political strategy within the constitutional framework is highly significant. The tradition of trying to make Ireland like England was strong amongst the Whig and Peelite sections of the Irish landed class. Maria was a grand intellectual exponent of it, but Moore *was* a practical politician, albeit something of an amateur. Through their friendship the links between 'enlightened Protestant' and the 'liberal Catholic' can be seen at their best. The essentially Stanleyite autocratic streak in the one was not matched in the other. Moore's Whiggery had in it a greater element of flexibility and the explanation of this lay partly in his being a Catholic. He was bound spiritually to the masses and their traditions in ways Maria could never have been. She was irretrievably above them. He was at once above and alongside them. So while their overall design for Ireland was essentially similar, her panaceas rested far more than his upon 'Men not Measures'. For Ireland to have become as she wanted it, human nature would have had virtually to change. Moore saw the way through as prising new laws out of the Westminster Parliament. Differences of disposition and background – and age – therefore pushed an old woman into a cul-de-sac, where she lamented the folly of her countrymen and lauded English ways, and drove on a young man to lead the next phase of Irish self-assertion.

Maria was never to see the rise and fall of the Independent Irish Brigade in the 1850s, but the blueprint was clear to her long before any substantial construction took place in Moore's machine-shops. The election over, she took refuge in the intricacies of theoretical politics and economics and consoled herself with plumbing the depths for 'truth' through correspondence with the Rev. Professor Jones. The world began to pass her by. Interested though she was in its ways, her own garden now seemed to offer ample recompense for failure to see

[1] For his career, see M. G. Moore, *An Irish Gentleman: George Henry Moore*.

the Ireland she wanted spring up. 'The Irish tenant farmers had lost their enthusiasm for repeal, and they were not prepared to fight for a republic; but they were beginning to see the value of open and legal combination for the furtherance of their own social and economic interests.'[1] Back in February a Tenant Right Association had been founded in county Cork. Responsible agitation for limited objects had become unfamiliar to Maria. Catholic Emancipation seemed an age ago. What gave Moore a grand opening left her completely uninterested. In November fewer than half the enlarged Repeal party opposed the Government's Crime and Outrage Bill. At over eighty even so enterprising a person as herself found the end of O'Connellism and outbreaks of violence more stimulating than vague rumblings of ordered reform activity. As the next year brought further O'Connellite humiliations and fresh treason, her choice seemed well justified.

[1] Beckett, *The Making of Modern Ireland*, p. 348.

6

Repose and Death

IN 1847 John Mitchel,[1] a Protestant from Ulster and the most
extreme of the leading Young Irelanders, had founded a
journal with the ominous name the *United Irishman*. Inspired
by Fintan Lalor's root-and-branch approach to the land question,
he had worked hard for the twin policy of agrarian reform and
armed rebellion. Once Young Ireland finally left the Repeal
movement in 1848, the horror with which his fellows had
tended to regard such aims gradually wore off. The February
revolution had apparently carried all before it in France,
Chartism seemed very formidable over in England and to
judge from positive results the uses of peaceful pressure in
Ireland had proved limited in the extreme. Russell acted
promptly. A Treason-Felony Bill was passed during April
1848, with Smith O'Brien alone of the Irish Members raising
powerful protests. In May, Mitchel was arrested and charged
with sedition. Found guilty, he was sentenced to transportation,
and Young Ireland responded by beginning active preparations
for armed rebellion. Maria's part in all this was modest in the
extreme. Her only contact with the participants had been to
present Baron Lefroy, Mitchel's trial judge, with some rose-
trees. 'He did well for Queen and Country at the late trial of
Mitchel', she told the Rev. Professor Jones, and went on to
describe how he had been 'really in great danger from the mob
when' leaving 'the court house in Dublin after pronouncing
sentence'. Apparently it had been 'the utmost that a party of

[1] See Dillon, *Life of John Mitchel.*

dragoons along with his carriage could do to prevent the mob from tearing him out. At first' he had desired 'that the military should not attend as he thought the Civil authority should not call upon the military without absolute need.' 'But', he had been warned, 'that he would be torn to pieces unless he had military escort – and, with much ado the military' had 'got him safe through'. The mob had, 'of course', thrown 'dust and stones etc. – One woman having nothing else "Convanient" had thrown a dog at the judge as he got out'.

So, while unwilling to undertake armed insurrection at Mitchel's bidding, the Dublin masses were as ready as ever for a spot of 'thrubble'. Maria, on the other hand, was for once quite an extremist the other way. Law and order had always commanded her deepest loyalty. Still, it was no small thing for her to quote with approval the view that 'General Cavaignac' had 'done great and good service in putting down the Anarchists in Paris'! But there had been another important factor making for improvement. 'The assassination of the Archbishop of Paris' had, she claimed, 'produced a great salutary effect' in France. A great comfort to her and presumably fairly cheap at the price with only a Catholic archbishop lost, particularly as 'It has done the same in Ireland – at least in our neighbourhood – especially among the Catholic clergy, for the priests put it to themselves in the rule of three inverse – if an archbishop be so dealt with by the Anarchists, how would they deal with a priest or the priests?' Another encouraging piece of news had come from her friend Judge Jackson, lately back from the Roscommon and Leitrim Assizes. He had told of how 'as the *best* sign of the times that a Jury where there were nine Catholics brought in without hesitation a verdict of guilty against one of Major Mahon's murderers – a proof that general opinion in Ireland *begins* to go with Law'. But, and here she showed some understandable signs of caution, this feeling for law had 'a great way to go with the generality and the greatest numbers before it' could go 'regularly'.[1]

The Government shared this opinion to the full and were taking no chances. Although the Repeal Association had been dissolved in June, the suspension of Habeas Corpus was rushed through Parliament in one day. That this was possible is in

[1] ME to the Rev. Richard Jones, 18 July 1848 (Edgeworth Papers).

itself a remarkable proof of the total collapse of the thirty-nine stout parties of the previous general election. Supported and comforted by a strong sense of government power and disorganisation at least amongst the agitators, Maria turned increasingly to her garden. Not that she was losing interest in life. She wrote of what ought to be done to her roses over the next year or two, commenting, 'Think of my talking of a year or two at nearly eighty-two and in the present state of Ireland thinking of roses when we should be thinking of Habeas Corpus. But as thinking of mine could do no good in that line, I stick to "Cultivons nos jardins".'[1]

Meanwhile Young Ireland lived in hopes of proving to the world just how far 'the feeling for law' was from going 'regularly'. Their outbreak, in fact scarcely more than a skirmish with the Royal Irish Constabulary, actually occurred in the first week of August.[2] On 30 July Maria felt sufficiently diverted from her roses to inform Jones that everyone at Edgeworthstown was all right 'in spite of rain and rumours of massacres'. 'The latest rumors of burning etc. in the south' had originated, or so she claimed, 'in a very foolish and worse than foolish stock-jobbing manœuvre – all, which, as the newpapers' had already made clear, had been 'a complete fabrication'. Unfortunately it had had a dire effect 'upon the common people', even at Edgeworthstown. They had 'sat up the whole night expecting to be massacred', only to find themselves 'very safe' in the morning. 'As to the actual real danger' she knew nothing more than could be seen in the newspapers. But her eyes had as usual been open 'as to the signs of the times' in the immediate neighbourhood.

> I can only tell you that at the town of Longford, seven miles from this, they attempted to form a Repeal Club and failed. And that at Navan in the county of Meath, about forty miles from this, the meeting of the Club failed in a peculiarly happy manner. The orators proposed that the value of the harvest should, when reaped, be appropriated to the Repeal fund – on which all the farmers rose and sneaked off, saying they did not like that sort of Club at all. When it comes down to the pockets of blusterers, matters appear in a very different light from what they did when it concerned only the pockets of others.[3]

1 ME to the Rev. Richard Jones, 25 July 1848 (Edgeworth Papers).
2 See Gwynn, *Young Ireland and 1848*.
3 ME to the Rev. Richard Jones, 30 July 1848 (Edgeworth Papers).

A harsh and inaccurate judgement upon the Catholic masses whose pence had sustained O'Connell's two great crusades, yet a telling comment on the state of affairs that lay behind the financial and organisational collapse of the Repeal Association.

As the trend went more and more against the agitators, Maria's optimism became bolder. 'Public opinion seems now all in favor of law and power, so well supported by Lord Clarendon. Long life to him! The suspension of the Habeas Corpus Act being so unanimously and so promptly granted must be doubly, quadruply efficacious. When crime goes beyond law, the law must turn round to meet it, or it must be extended or made to act.' Not only had the Catholic priests been chastened by 'the confusion' and murder in France. 'All classes of the laity' had allegedly seen the point as well.[1] And whether this was true or not, the effect was virtually the same. Ireland only just managed to be represented as a participant in the Year of Revolutions. Very wisely, the Government refused to treat a skirmish as a full-blown revolution. No risks were taken, yet no martyrs made. For though Smith O'Brien was actually condemned to death, the sentence was commuted to one of transportation to Australia. To a stickler for clarity like Maria the Government had taken all too long to decide between rigour and clemency. Pardon would lose its grace and punishment its use. Russell and his ministers had, she told the Moores, 'given encouragement, time and opportunity to rebels and knaves and fools to sprout themselves into martyrs and heroes and honest men, which last I do believe O'Brien is – though a fool, as he always was. . . . If these people had fools' caps upon their heads and were made ridiculous, they would have no followers!'[2] Again the same old faith in reason and again the same old refusal to perceive the truly profound and age-old nature of Irish Catholic national feeling. Her estimates were almost certainly badly out and the Government came relatively well out of the affair. Had things been otherwise George Henry Moore would never have kept his criticism within the limits of good advice and supported the official coercion policies. He thought Russell should improve his relief programmes, but with outrages such as those going on in county Tipperary

[1] Ibid. The 4th Earl of Clarendon, at this time Lord-Lieutenant of Ireland.
[2] Hone, *The Moores of Moore Hall*, pp. 147–8.

rampant, he felt no doubt as to where a responsible reformer's sympathies should lie. Such was Moore's considered opinion, and he wrote defending it to none other than Archbishop MacHale of Tuam, an ardent and nationalist 'Patriot'.[1]

During the course of a long life Maria had had many personal griefs to bear. Fanny's death on 4 February 1848 had proved particularly painful to her. She spent as much time as possible at Trim with Harriet and Dean Butler. There was a home from home where she could enjoy the company of two of her favourite relations. With them she passed the late winter and spring of 1849. The third bout of serious famine had passed, and business affairs at Edgeworthstown and Trim gave her lively satisfaction. 'Our rents are tolerably well paid', she reported, 'and we have some hopes that our potatoes will come back again – enough to save us from famine, but not to be again our staple food, which I hope agrees' with the rules of sound 'political economy'.[2] That was in February, but back at her real home in April she repeated her concern about Ireland's future food supplies. 'The people here are very busy and very happy planting potatoes, spite of English statesmen's denunciations against their folly. I think it would be folly to give potatoes up altogether, or to depend upon them as the principal food of the people. Truth often falls between two stools.'[3] It does indeed, and perhaps more often than usual in the Ireland of the nineteenth century. This she had learned and at much cost since her first contacts with the public scene. Disappointment had not, of course, reduced her devotion to any of the lost causes she had espoused. Very suitably, the last letter on matters public that she is known to have written was to the Dean of Clonmacnoise, commending him for his new pamphlet upon the need for 'united education for Catholics and Protestants'. From the school Lovell had run for ten years on this very principle had come many 'valuable members of society belonging to both religions'. 'Harmony' had prevailed amongst them while at school, and their training had stood them in good stead during later life. As for the latest pronouncement of Archbishop MacHale[4] upon education, it was 'the most curious

[1] Ibid. p. 148.

[2] ME to the Rev. Richard Jones, 28 Feb 1849.

[3] ME to the Rev. Richard Jones, April 1849 (Edgeworth Papers).

[4] John MacHale (1791–1881), Archbishop of Tuam and a formidable protagonist of the Catholic and nationalist faiths over a long period.

the most extraordinary, the most outrageously exaggerated and
preposterous specimen' she had ever seen 'of what may be
called by English neighbours Irish eloquence'.[1] Little did she
know what a deal of 'Irish eloquence' was destined to flow on
every public question over the next seventy years. Her educational dreams were doomed never to be translated into reality,
for although the increased grant for elementary education
begun in 1844 led to a rapid retreat of the Irish before the
English language among the masses, English words were not
matched by 'English' thoughts. Sectarians were to continue
ruling the educational like so many other Irish roosts.

To the very end the 'state of Ireland' question loomed large
in her thoughts. What Bentham would have made of contemporary legislation; what her 'dear deceased friend Mr
Ricardo' would have said about the enquiry in Berkeley's
Querist as to 'whether potatoes have been an evil or a blessing
to Ireland'[2] – this was the type of problem occupying her mind
during the last weeks of life. And it was a mind largely unim-
paired by age. Indeed, on the very day of death her conversation
remained at its usual sprightly level. Whether the excitement
about setting out again for Trim (where she was due next day)
accelerated her end is impossible to say, but on the morning of
22 May 1849 she was assailed by sudden heart pains and died
very quickly. So passed one of the most remarkable characters
from a country of remarkable characters.

Though lacking her father's scientific gifts, Maria Edgeworth had proved the aptest of pupils for his precepts on
public affairs. Though his role had in some ways been that of a
Don Quixote, it is strongly evident from what has gone before
that Maria was no mere Sancho Panza. Frequent and deferential
in tone as her references to her father always were, the contribution she made to the maintenance and improvement of
conditions at Edgeworthstown and the thoughts she threw out
on public affairs generally marked her out as a person of
considerable intellect, outstandingly fine feeling and no mean
practical skill as a manager of human beings. Apart from the
1798 rebellion, the father had had to face far less social unrest

[1] ME to Richard Butler, the Very Rev. the Dean of Clonmacnoise, 9 April
1849 (Monteagle Papers, NLI, MS 13346).
[2] ME to the Rev. Richard Jones, April 1849 (Edgeworth Papers).

than the daughter, and nothing like the Great Famine had ever come his way. She lived in hard times and coped magnificently with the trials and tribulations, public as well as private, that descended upon her. Though a very small person in physical stature, she assumed considerable proportions in so many other ways. The range of her contacts and her skill as a mixer with men and women, from the highest to the lowest degree, were also quite remarkable. Yet with all this achievement there was an element of anticlimax. The greatest activity – that of imaginative writing for publication – declined somewhat in the second half of her life. Day-to-day duties and profound disappointment about the direction Irish affairs were taking were both vital factors in bringing this about. Her fact was nonetheless almost as valuable as her fiction. It has given us what for Ireland are well-balanced and just accounts of the everyday working of an estate under enlightened control and the consequences in public affairs stemming from oasis-type economic, political and social conditions. Had her energies been devoured by new literary projects we might never have had the chance to trace an important aspect of Irish life. The role of the 'liberal White' in a non-Black country has a high significance in the study of race relations and revolutions. Misfortune liberated someone of talent at a crucial time in Irish history to provide the wherewithal for unravelling situations of often baffling complexity. From a minute person came a major commentary upon her times.

Epilogue

THE Ireland of today is a far cry from that of Maria Edgeworth. Partition has divided the bulk of the Catholics from the bulk of Protestants. Full independence for the south and west had largely dissipated the nationalistic resentments against Britain, and devolution in the north has met the practical difficulties created by the ending of Dublin-based administration in the area. British power and southern realism have prevented substantial trouble arising out of partition. An agrarian revolution, carried out largely under British auspices during the later stages of the Union, has contributed very substantially towards lowering the political temperature on the nationalist issue in the post-separation period. With politics and the social system approximating to popular wishes among the Catholic masses, religious bigotry seldom finds an outlet of sufficient importance for provoking any major or persistent crises. The Catholic minority of the north undoubtedly has some cause for complaint, but at the same time enjoys considerable material advantages denied to its 'free' brethren of the south and west. Most interesting of all, however, and something of an irony, is the position now accorded to the Protestants of the Catholic domain. Seven per cent of the population and mainly of the former ruling class, they actually command quite a genuine popularity and respect of a sort Maria Edgeworth would have given her right hand to obtain. Politically and economically disarmed, a ruling class can be allowed social prestige – a prestige the snobbery endemic among the Catholic masses finds welcome. Under a democratic peasant republic the stalwarts of a 'foreign' royalism constitute an enormous piece of decoration, and heresy can be forgiven in gentlefolk. There is, after all, enormous virtue in a cultural and educational superiority, fox-hunting, racing and benevolent behaviour, not to mention distinction in the armed services of the United Kingdom.

No doubt Maria Edgeworth would have found the changes leading up to this situation uncongenial in the extreme. Yet such was the way things happened that the final result occurred with one factor present which would have provided her with vast consolation. Ireland in 1849 was strictly speaking a country at a modest level of civilisation.[1] By 1921, when the south and west acquired dominion status as the Irish Free State, this was no longer the case. Pursuit of a reformist line had more often than not been foisted onto the British by agitation and violence. Improvement had therefore frequently been accompanied by coercion, but this had meant that the direction given to reforms could all the more easily cut across the fatuous elements in public opinion among the Catholics. The country's economy was reshaped according to British concepts before there was any embarking upon peasant proprietorship. The Irish language suffered blows at the hands of an English-orientated educational system from which all the efforts of the neo-Gaels have been unable to effect a convincing recovery. Gradually, albeit haphazardly, the Catholic masses became more and more like the northern Protestants and their British counterparts. Like the men of the true colonies in Asia and Africa they were being civilised and educated. As the British went on from Encumbered Estates Acts, freeing land for sale to more efficient owners, to compensation for improvements and the granting of Ulster Tenant Right, so the foundation was laid for belief in general property rights among a peasantry long addicted to admiration for general disorder and feckless modes of life. The northern Protestants had long enjoyed special agrarian privileges: now Ireland had one land-system instead of two. From this uniform basis the transference to peasant ownership and the training of small farmers in modern methods were begun. In the background were good elementary schools and more university education.

---

[1] For an interesting account of Ireland four years earlier, see C. de Cavour (the Cavour), *Considerations on the Present State and Future Prospects of Ireland.*

Ireland began to sport an educated class outside of the Ascendancy and Presbyterian groups, amounting to a set of prospective rulers in the liberalised democratic tradition.

All the time then, while Irish Catholic nationalism proved the pacemaker, British influences formed the patterns of life resulting from it. So, much though she would have deplored it, the function Maria Edgeworth singled out for the Ascendancy was rendered superfluous. She had wanted to save the system of which she and her family were part. For her, charity began and almost always ended at home. Few of her kind saw things her way, and in any case the trend of events was such as would have overwhelmed even a sustained and united reform-from-above campaign by the Anglo-Irish aristocracy and gentry. Their history, their numbers and the views of their tenants were all virtually guarantors of failure. Just as the Grattan experiment had come to grief without the immediate presence of British might to sustain it, so the reform of Ireland and its transformation into an 'England' could be carried out only within a framework where this same might was a paramount factor. The Edgeworth family regarded the Union as the best means to civilisation, and events proved them right. Their great mistake was to hope that this great end could be attained without drastic changes within the Irish economic and social scene – changes going way beyond those of approach by which they set such store. Ireland needed a vital series of operations, not bottles of medicine. Catholic nationalism, the varying British responses to it and to some extent mere chance all played a part in dictating what particular operations took place. They also determined on what date the patient was discharged from hospital. The British doctors insisted upon the amputation of the northern limb as their final prescription, a course never really accepted by the Irish independence party. Still, an incomplete Ireland 'free' was better than further treatment under British control. Civilised Ireland was therefore incomplete. O'Connell's dream of a united free state was not realised, and yet the Union had been repealed. Repealed, however, at such a time and in such a way as not to violate all of Maria Edgeworth's favourite nostra.

Timing is vital in almost all historical processes. What makes nonsense today often approximates to excellent sense tomorrow.

Looking at Ireland in the period of this book and seeing the poor grasp of its problems by the Repeal party, it is hard to resist the notion that the Union had at least the advantage of assuring some chance of ordered improvement and sustained outside aid in times of need. Looking at Ireland some seventy to eighty years later, one can see that circumstances were much changed. Ireland was a very different country, and its predominantly Catholic part was provided with the means for carrying on an existence as a separate state. This is not to say that a continuation of the Union would necessarily have been a bad thing from some pre-eminently Irish points of view. Nevertheless, whereas in Maria Edgeworth's time independence for the south and west would have meant almost certain disaster and prolonged backwardness, dominion and later full sovereign status in the twentieth century could be taken without risk of any such fatal consequences. The Republic of Ireland has already abandoned policies of narrow economic nationalism. Whether or not it manages to become part of the European Common Market, it is already on the way to becoming part of one embracing the British Isles. Partially successful experimentation with native industry has created the confidence and sense of proportion necessary for good Anglo-Irish trade relations. Yet another element of 'Englishness' has entered the Irish scene.

Time has enabled the centrifugal to turn to the centripetal. And while it would be both presumptuous and downright incorrect to claim that Catholic nationalism was a disease which had to work itself out of the Irish system, it is worth remarking that, once the masses of the south and west acquired full independence and felt their pride satisfied, they could estimate more rationally just what sort of relationship with Britain their real interests required. But in the time of their struggles for what they considered their political rights and in the first decades after it was achieved, much had occurred which was to make the subsequent reconciliation with Great Britain all the easier to secure. Maria Edgeworth, like so many able people, saw the attitude the country required, but failed to appreciate the best methods for attaining it. In many ways she was as before her time as her insistent devotion to the hope that the existing system modified could solve all difficulties proved her to be well behind it. While often inconvenient and even infuriating that the truly gifted are frequently denied the opportunities necessary for them to shine, there are the compensations associated with a complete understanding of their situations. Comprehension brings in its train a sense of proportion. A sense of proportion is the key to exploiting most human gifts. Seeing Maria Edgeworth and the contemporary public scene in perspective is a real step towards understanding so many historical situations. A situation understood by the right people can mean numerous problems solved.

Appendix 1

Maria Edgeworth's Thoughts on her Profession

AN interesting instance of how Maria Edgeworth felt on the matter of her 'profession' is provided by a letter she wrote to the 6th Duke of Devonshire (William George Spencer Cavendish – 1790-1858 – who had succeeded to the title in 1811) on 14 August 1837. Maybe the fact of his being a great magnate influenced her into adopting a somewhat self-mocking tone. If it did, that alone would be of no small significance. Authors thinking of themselves primarily as productive artists would very rarely, if ever, make comments about their occupation of the sort recorded here. Of course Maria had by this time long passed her truly productive period; nevertheless the life she was then living merely served to reinforce what had always been her earlier attitude. Here she is most pointedly casting herself in the role of a gentlewoman with literary gifts, not as someone relying solely upon 'professional' prestige.

Her opening remarks were well-contrived and likely to make a favourable impression. She wrote:

> A few words of praise and many acts of politeness by which some years ago Your Grace distinguished the author of the *Absentee* have remained indelibly impressed upon her vanity and upon perhaps some better feeling. But the vanity is certain, for she has now the boldness to hope that you will incline a not unfavourable ear to a request of hers – of great importance to her happiness.

Her propitiation made, she came straight to the point:

Will Your Grace permit me – will Your Grace *encourage* me to apply to Captain Corry for employment as a subordinate agent on any of your estates for a brother of mine. My brother (Francis Beaufort Edgeworth) can produce testimonials of his fitness for the situation better, of course, than any which could be given by a partial sister; and, of course, all the security would be forthcoming which men of business must require.

Next, with the skill of a born story-teller, she explained what was behind the application:

I am tempted at this moment to try to apologise for one intrusion by committing a greater indiscretion (in true Irish fashion); I want to interest Your Grace for a person whom you do not know by telling you a family story for which you cannot care – *cannot* – as anybody would pronounce who does not estimate your capacious benevolence and the capability of your sympathy, even with an Irish stranger, as I do. Now – will Your Grace indulge my novel writer's propensity and allow me to tell you about a bit of family history?

Then came an account of a virtually penniless, yet worthy young couple – Francis Beaufort and his well-connected Spanish bride. The latter had apparently done great wonders with dress material for the wife of another great Whig magnate, the Duchess of Sutherland, and all that was now wanting to make life perfect was 'the means of earning honorable independence' in what must be regarded as 'a most liberal profession'. The blarney spent, she turned at last to the great intellectual interests of her family. 'I wonder at my own unreasonableness. I hope Miss Martineau will never see this note.'[1] His Grace was therefore able to see that his correspondent was the true daughter of her father – every inch (albeit they were few) an Edgeworth.

[1] Devonshire Papers.

Appendix 2

Isaac D'Israeli on Maria Edgeworth

An interesting glimpse of how Maria Edgeworth struck at least one contemporary during her London stay of 1822 is included in a letter from Isaac D'Israeli to Lord Byron of 10 December that year. The relevant extract ran:

> The literary comet in our *conversazioni* this season was Maria Edgeworth, who took up an odd whim of introducing and being introduced. It was all Souls' Day with her. She is monstrously ugly, and I saw her in a Shepherdess's hat. She says nothing, but a great deal. In her father's lifetime, when she came up to London, she was like a sealed fountain; but now, being on her own bottom, she pours down like the falls of Niagara. She is very short, and Sir Humphry Davy observed to me: 'Poor woman, she is on *representation*, and is *not up* to it!'. She promises another novel, and if she can write it without her father, which the continuation of his life excites suspicions that she may not, her criticisers may be criticised.

Certainly a harsh and uncharitable portrait; and certainly a good piece of evidence in favour of the view that Lord Beaconsfield did not inherit all his vast reserves of malice from an unsympathetic mother. Byron himself would appear to have valued Maria's literary merits more highly. He expressed admiration for the 'profound' impression of 'intellect and prudence' left on him after reading her novels, despite their failure to arouse any 'feeling' in him. When Sir Humphry Davy told him of how the scene of the French valet and the Irish poor boy in the novel

Ennui was taken almost word for word from his description of a happening on the way to Edgeworthstown passed on to the Edgeworth family, the poet did not condemn. On the contrary, he enthused: 'So much the better – being *life.*'[1]

[1] Isaac D'Israeli to Lord Byron, 10 Dec 1822, ed. R. E. Prothero *Letters and Journals of Byron.*

Appendix 3

Ministries of the Period

THE ministries in office during the period covered by this book were as follows:

The Government formed under Lord Liverpool in June 1812 still held sway when our story began and continued to do so until his death in 1827. He went out of action following a paralytic stroke in February, but it was not until April that the new Canning ministry was created. When Canning himself died that August he was succeeded by Viscount Goderich, who took over the following month. Internal dissensions and weaknesses were rife in this ministry, and it gave way in January 1828 to one led by the Duke of Wellington. This lasted until the last quarter of 1830. All these ministries had been predominantly, and in one case exclusively, Tory.

November 1830, however, saw the formation of the Whig-dominated Reform ministry of Lord Grey, which lasted through fair weather and foul until the middle of 1834. In July of that year Lord Melbourne, a former follower of Canning, took the premiership of another, more distinctly Whig ministry, but resigned in November and was succeeded by Peel. The new administration was a minority one and the first rightly called Conservative. Not surprisingly in view of its position, it was soon ejected and Lord Melbourne led the Whigs back into office. They were to stay there well into 1841 and it was only in September that Peel began his great second ministry. It was to last almost six years and only in July 1846 did Lord John Russell come in at the head of another Whig government, backed by the forces of Peel against the rump Conservative party under Lord George Bentinck, the Stanleys and Benjamin Disraeli. Maria was to die well before Russell fell at the beginning of 1852 and was replaced by the first of the Derby rump Conservative administrations.

Bibliography

Unless otherwise stated the place of publication is London

A. MANUSCRIPT COLLECTIONS

This book is based very substantially upon the materials listed below.
To their owners and custodians I owe my best thanks.

The Devonshire Papers, at Chatsworth House, Derbyshire.

The Edgeworth Papers. Those up to 1817 in the National Library of
Ireland, Dublin; those after 1817 at present in the keeping of Mrs
H. M. Colvin, but due eventually to be deposited in the National
Library of Ireland, Dublin.

The Edgeworth-Beaufort Papers. Those up to 1817 in the National
Library of Ireland, Dublin; those after 1817 at present in the keeping
of Mrs H. M. Colvin, but due eventually to be deposited in the
National Library of Ireland, Dublin.

The Monteagle Papers, in the National Library of Ireland, Dublin.

B. NEWSPAPERS AND PERIODICALS

1. NEWSPAPERS
Dublin Evening Mail.
Dublin Evening Post.
Nation.
The Times.

2. JOURNALS
Edinburgh Review.
Quarterly Review.

C. WORKS OF REFERENCE

Boase, F., *Modern English Biography* (Truro, 1892–1921).
Burke's Landed Gentry.

Burke's Peerage, Baronetage and Knightage.
Burke's Landed Gentry of Ireland
Complete Baronetage
Complete Peerage.
Debrett's Peerage.
Debrett's Baronetage.
Dictionary of National Biography.
Directory of Directors.
Dod's Parliamentary Pocket Companion.
An Encyclopaedia of World History, compiled and edited by W. L. Langer, rev. ed. (1948).
Freeman, T. W., *Ireland: A General and Regional Geography*, 3rd ed. (1965).
General Register of Ireland.
Hansard.
MacCalmont, F. H., *Parliamentary Poll Book of all Elections* (Nottingham, 1910).
MacLysaght, E., *Irish Families: Their Names, Arms and Origins* (Dublin, 1957).
Newspaper Press Directory.
Philips' County Atlas of Ireland (1881).
Systems of Land Tenure in Various Countries. A series of essays published under the sanction of the Cobden Club, ed. J. W. Probyn, new ed. revised and corrected (1881).
Webb, A., *A Compendium of Irish Biography* (Dublin, 1878).
Who Was Who.

D. BIOGRAPHIES AND AUTOBIOGRAPHIES

This section of the bibliography is not exhaustive. Only those works I found especially useful are listed. Most of them are referred to at some point in the text.

Aspinall, A., *Lord Brougham and the Whig Party* (Manchester, 1927).
Bartlett, C. J., *Castlereagh* (1966).
Brock, W. R., *Lord Liverpool and Liberal Toryism, 1820 to 1827*, 2nd ed. (1965).
Byron, Lord George, *Letters and Journals*, ed. R. E. Prothero (1922).
Cecil, Lord David, *Melbourne* (1965).
Clarke, G. Kitson, *Peel* (1936).
—— *Peel and the Conservative Party*, 2nd ed. (1964).
Clarke, Isabel C., *Maria Edgeworth: her family and friends* (1950).
Edgeworth, Maria, *Life and Letters*, ed. A. J. C. Hare, 2 vols (1894).
Edgeworth, R. L., and Edgeworth, Maria, *Memoirs of Richard Lovell Edgeworth, Esq.*, 3rd ed. (1844).
Edgeworth, Mrs R. L., *A Memoir of Maria Edgeworth*, 4 vols (1867).
Gash, N., *The Life of Sir Robert Peel to 1830: Mr Secretary Peel* (1961).
The Greville Memoirs, ed. H. Reeve, 2nd ed. (1874).

Gwynn, D., *Daniel O'Connell* (Edinburgh and London, 1894; Cork and Oxford, 1947).

Hamilton, John, *Sixty Years' Experience as an Irish Landlord* (1894).

Hone, J., *The Moores of Moore Hall* (1939).

Inglis-Jones, E., *The Great Maria* (1959).

Jones, W. D., *Prosperity Robinson: the life of Viscount Goderich, 1782–1859* (1967)

Lecky, W. E. H., *Leaders of Public Opinion in Ireland*, 2 vols, new ed. (1903).

Le Fanu, W. R., *Seventy Years of Irish Life* (1893).

Lockhart, J. G., *Life of Sir Walter Scott* (1837–8).

Maguire, J. F., *Father Mathew: a biography* (1863).

McCaffrey, L. J., *Daniel O'Connell and the Repeal Year* (1965).

Moore, M. G., *An Irish Gentleman: George Henry Moore: his travels, his racing, his politics* (1913).

New, C. W., *The Life of Henry Brougham to 1830* (Oxford, 1961).

Newby, P. H., *Maria Edgeworth* (1950).

O'Brien, R. B., *Thomas Drummond: life and letters* (1889).

Daniel O'Connell: nine centenary essays, ed. M. Tierney (Dublin, 1948).

O'Connell, J., *Life and Speeches of Daniel O'Connell, M.P.*, 2 vols (Dublin, 1846).

Oliver, G., *Maria Edgeworth* (Boston, 1882).

Sir Robert Peel (from his private papers), ed. C. S. Parker, 3 vols (1891–9).

Petrie, Sir Charles, *George Canning*, 2nd ed. (1946).

Rolo, P. J. V., *George Canning* (1965).

E. OTHER PRINTED BOOKS AND PAMPHLETS

This section of the bibliography is also not exhaustive. Only those works I found especially useful are listed. Most of them are referred to at some point in the text.

Ball, J. T., *The Reformed Church of Ireland, 1537–1886* (Dublin and London, 1886).

Bamford, F., and Wellington, The Duke of, *The Journal of Mrs Arbuthnot*, 2 vols (1950).

Beckett, J. C., *The Making of Modern Ireland, 1603–1923* (1966).

The Black Book of Edgeworthstown and other Edgeworth Memories, 1585–1817, ed. H. J. and H. E. Butler (1927).

Black, R. D. C., *Economic Thought and the Irish Question, 1817–1870* (Cambridge, 1960).

Blake, A., B., F., and Blake H., *Letters from the Irish Highlands of Cunnemarra by a Family Party* (1825).

Bolton, G. C., *The Passing of the Irish Act of Union: a study in parliamentary politics* (Oxford, 1966).

Borrow, G., *Wild Wales* (World's Classics edition: 1920.

Butler, J. R. M., *The Passing of the Great Reform Bill* (1914).

Carleton, W., *Traits and Stories of the Irish Peasantry*. new ed. (1872).

Cavour, C. de., *Considerations on the Present State and Future Prospects of Ireland*. Translated from the French by 'A Friend to Ireland' (1845).

Chadwick, O., *The Victorian Church*, part I (1966).

Connell, K. H., *The Population of Ireland, 1750–1845* (Oxford, 1950).

The Creevey Papers, ed. Sir Herbert Maxwell, 2 vols (New York, 1903).

The Croker Papers, ed. L. J. Jennings, 3 vols (1884).

Cullen, Luke, *Insurgent Wicklow*, ed. M. V. Ronan (Dublin, 1948).

Davie, D. A., *The Heyday of Sir Walter Scott* (1961).

Davis, H. W. C., *The Age of Grey and Peel* (Oxford, 1929).

De Beaumont, Gustave, *Ireland – Social, Political and Religious*, ed. W. C. Taylor, 2 vols (1839).

de Tocqueville, Alexis, *Journeys to England and Ireland*, ed. J. P. Mayer (1958).

Dickson, C., *Revolt in the North: Antrim and Down in 1798* (Dublin and London, 1960).

Dillon, W., *Life of John Mitchel*, 2 vols (1888).

Duffy, C. G., *Four Years of Irish History* (London, Paris and New York, 1883).

——*The League of the North and the South* (1886).

——*Young Ireland* (London, Paris and New York, 1880).

Edgeworth, Maria, *Castle Rackrent*, ed. G. Watson (Oxford, 1964).

—— *Collected Edition of the Novels* (1832).

—— *Helen* (1834).

—— *Orlandino* (Edinburgh 1848).

—— *Practical Education,* (1798).

—— *Stories of Ireland* (1886)

Edwards, R. D., and Williams, T. D., *The Great Famine: studies in Irish history, 1845–52* (Dublin, 1956).

Essays on The Repeal of the Union, ed. J. O'Connell, W. S. O'Brien and T. Davis (Dublin, 1845).

Flanagan, T., *Irish Novelists, 1800–1850* (New York, 1959).

Fox, J. A., *A Key to the Irish Question* (1890).

Freeman, T. W., *Pre-Famine Ireland* (Manchester, 1957).

Gash, N., *Politics in the Age of Peel: a study in the technique of parliamentary representation, 1830–1850* (1953).

—— *Reaction and Reconstruction in English Politics, 1832–1852* (Oxford, 1965).

Godkin, J., *Ireland and her Churches* (1867).

Green, E. R. R., *The Lagan Valley, 1800–1850* (1949).

Gwynn, D., *Young Ireland and 1848* (Dublin and London, 1949).

Halévy, E., *The Liberal Awakening, 1815*, 2nd ed. (1949).

—— *The Triumph of Reform, 1830–41*, 2nd ed. (1950).

—— *The Age of Peel and Cobden, 1841–1852* (1947).

Hobsbawm, E. J., and Rudé, George, *Captain Swing* (1969).

Ingram, T. D., *A History of the Legislative Union of Great Britain and Ireland* (London and New York, 1887).

The Irish Pound. Introduction and a Reprint of the Report of the Committee of 1804 of the British House of Commons on the Condition of the Irish Currency—with Selections from the Minutes of Evidence Presented to the Committee, with an introduction by F. W. Fetter (1955).

Johnston, E. M., *Great Britain and Ireland, 1760–1800* (Edinburgh, 1963).

Kraus, H., *Irish Life in Irish Fiction* (New York, 1903).

Lecky, W. E. H., *Historical and Political Essays* (1908).

—— *A History of Ireland in the Eighteenth Century*, new ed. 5 vols (New York, 1893).

Macaulay, Lord, *Critical and Historical Essays*, 2 vols (Everyman Edition: 1907).

Machin, G. I. T., *The Catholic Question in English Politics, 1820 to 1830* (Oxford, 1964).

MacIntyre, A., *The Liberator: Daniel O'Connell and the Irish Party, 1830–1847* (1965).

Madden, R. R., *Antrim and Down in '98* (1947).

—— *Ireland in '98*, ed. J. B. Daly (1888).

Mansergh, N., *The Irish Question, 1840–1921*, 2nd ed. (1965).

Martin, R. M., *Ireland Before and After the Union with Great Britain*, 3rd ed.—with additions (Dublin and London, 1848).

Maxwell, C., *The Stranger in Ireland* (1954).

Maxwell, W. H., *History of the Irish Rebellion in 1798; with memoirs of the Union and Emmett's insurrection in 1803* (1891).

McCarthy, J. H., *Ireland Since the Union* (1887).

McCulloch, J. R., *A Descriptive and Statistical Account of the British Empire*, 2 vols 3rd ed. (1847).

McDowell, R. B., *British Conservatism, 1832–1914* (1959).

—— *Public Opinion and Government Policy in Ireland, 1801–1846* (1952).

—— *The Irish Administration, 1801–1914* (1964).

McHugh, R., *Carlow in '98: a contemporary narrative* (Dublin, 1949).

Milner, The Rev. J., *An Inquiry into Certain Vulgar Opinions Concerning the Catholic Inhabitants and the Antiquities of Ireland* (1808).

Mitchell, A., *The Whigs in Opposition, 1815–1830* (Oxford, 1967).

Murray, A. E., *A History of the Commercial and Financial Relations between England and Ireland from the Period of the Restoration* (1903).

Nowlan, K. B., *The Politics of Repeal: a study in the relations between Great Britain and Ireland, 1841–1850* (1965).

O'Brien, W. P., *The Great Famine: a retrospect of fifty years, 1845–1895* (1896).

O'Connor, Sir James, *History of Ireland, 1798–1924*, 2 vols (1926).

O'Hegarty, P. S., *A History of Ireland under the Union, 1801–1922* (1952).

Oliphant, M. O. W., *Memoir of Count de Montalembert*, 2 vols (1872).

O'Rourke, The Rev. J., *History of the Great Irish Famine of 1847* (Dublin, 1902).

Paterson, A., *The Edgeworths: a study of later eighteenth-century education* (Cambridge, 1914).

Peel, Sir Robert, *Speeches Delivered in the House of Commons*, 4 vols (1853).

Pim, J., *The Condition and Prospects of Ireland and the Evils Arising from the Present Distribution of Landed Property—With Suggestions for a Remedy* (Dublin, 1848).

Plowden, F., *The History of Ireland from its Union with Great Britain in January 1801 to October 1810*, 3 vols (Dublin, 1811).

Reynolds, J. A., *The Catholic Emancipation Crisis in Ireland, 1823–29* (New Haven, 1954).

Richey, A. G., *The Irish Land Laws* (1881).

Sadler, M. T., *Ireland: its evils, and their remedies*, 2nd ed. (1829).

Salaman, R. N., *The History and Social Influence of the Potato* (Cambridge, 1949).

Senior, H., *Orangeism in Ireland and Britain, 1795–1836* (1966).

Senior, N. W., *Ireland: journals, conversations and essays*, 2 vols (1868).

Sheil, R. L., *Speeches*, 2nd ed. (Dublin, 1853).

Thompson, H. S., *Ireland in 1839 and 1869* (1870).

Trench, W. S., *The Realities of Irish Life*, 2nd ed. (1868).

Trevelyan, C. E., *The Irish Crisis* (1848).

Two Centuries of Irish History, 1691–1870, ed. J. Bryce (1888).

Whyte, J. H., *The Independent Irish Party 1850–2* (Oxford, 1958).

Woodham-Smith, C., *The Great Hunger: Ireland, 1845–9* (1962).

Woodward, E. L., *The Age of Reform, 1815–1870*, 2nd ed. (Oxford, 1962).

Woolf, Virginia, *The Common Reader*, 2nd ed. (1925).

F. LEARNED ARTICLES

Alger, J. S., 'The Irish Absentee and his Tenants, 1768–92', in *EHR* x (1895).

Armytage, W. H. G., 'Little Women', in *Queen's Quarterly*, LVI (1949).

Aspinall, A., 'The Canningite Party', in *TRHS* 4th ser. XVII (1934).

—— 'The Last of the Canningites', in *EHR* L (1935).

—— 'The Use of Irish Secret Service Money in Subsidising the Irish Press', in *EHR* LVI (1941).

—— Canning's Return to Office in 1922', in *EHR* LXXVIII (1963).

Best, G. F. A., 'The Religious Difficulties of National Education, 1800–1870', in *HJ* XII (1956).

—— 'The Protestant Constitution and its Supporters, 1800–1829', in *TRHS* 5th ser. VIII (1958).

Blackall, H., and Whyte, J. H., 'Correspondence on O'Connell and the Repeal Party', in *IHS* XII (1960).

Bourke, P. M. A., 'The Scientific Investigation of the Potato Blight in 1845–46', in *IHS* XIII (1962).

—— 'Notes on some Agricultural Units of Measurement in use in Pre-Famine Ireland', in *IHS* XIV (1965).

—— 'The Agricultural Statistics of the 1841 Census in Ireland', in *EcHR* 2nd ser. XVIII (1965).

Burn, W. L., 'Free Trade in Land: an aspect of the Irish Question', in *TRHS* 4th ser. XXXI (1949).

Cahill, G. A., 'The Protestant Association and the Anti-Maynooth Agitation of 1845', in *CHR* XLIII (1957).

Clark, G. Kitson, 'The Electorate and the Repeal of the Corn Laws', in *TRHS* 5th ser. I (1951).

—— 'The Repeal of the Corn Laws and the Politics of the 1840s', in *EcHR* 2nd ser. IV (1951-2).

—— 'Hunger and Politics in 1842', in *JMH* XXV (1953).

Clarke, R., 'The Relations between O'Connell and the Young Irelanders', in *IHS* III (1942).

Connell, K. H., 'The Colonisation of Irish Wasteland, 1780–1845', in *EcHR* 2nd ser. III (1950-1).

—— 'The History of the Potato', in *EcHR* 2nd ser. III (1950-1).

—— 'Some Unsettled Problems in English aud Irish Population History, 1750–1845', in *IHS* VII (1951).

—— 'Peasant Marriage in Ireland after the Great Famine', in *P&P* no. 12 (1957).

—— 'Land Legislation and Irish Social Life', in *EcHR* 2nd ser. XI (1958-9).

—— 'The Potato in Ireland', in *P&P* no. 23 (1962).

Drake, M., 'Marriage and Population Growth in Ireland, 1750–1845', in *EcHR* 2nd ser. XVI (1963-4)

Dreyer, F. A., 'The Whigs and the Political Crisis of 1845', in *EHR* LXXX (1965).

Fairlie, S., 'The Nineteenth-century Corn Law Reconsidered', in *EcHR* 2nd ser. XVIII (1965).

Gash, N., 'Peel and the Party System', in *TRHS* 5th ser. I (1951).

Goldstrom, J. M., 'Richard Whately and "Political Economy" in School Books', in *IHS* XV (1966).

Graham, A. H., 'The Lichfield House Compact, 1835', in *IHS* XII (1961).

Gray, M., 'The Highland Potato Famine of the 1840s', in *EcHR* 2nd ser. VII (1954-5).

Greaves, R. W., 'Roman Catholic Relief and the Leicester Election of 1826', in *TRHS* 4th ser. XXII (1940).

Green, Mrs J. R., 'Irish National Tradition', in *History*, NS II (1917-18).

Hall, Mrs S. C., 'Edgeworthstown: Memories of Maria Edgeworth', Art. 28, 1 July 1949.

Hill, F. H., 'Pitt and Peel, 1783-4; 1834-5' in *TRHS* NS XIII (1899).

Inglis, B., 'O'Connell and the Irish Peers, 1800-42', in *IHS* VIII (1952).

Johnson, J. H., 'The Population of Londonderry during the Great Famine', in *EcHR* 2nd ser. X (1957-8).

Jupp, P. J., 'Irish Parliamentary Elections and the Influence of the Catholic Vote, 1801-20', in *HJ* X (1967).

Kennedy, B. A., 'Sharman Crawford and the Repeal Question, 1847', in *IHS* VIII (1956/7).

—— 'Sharman Crawford on Ulster Tenant Right, 1846', in *IHS* XIII (1963).

Kerr, B. M., 'Irish Seasonal Migration to Great Britain, 1800–38', in *IHS* III (1943).

Large, D., 'The House of Lords and Ireland in the Age of Peel, 1832–50', in *IHS* IX (1955).

—— 'The Wealth of the Greater Irish Landowners, 1750–1815', in *IHS* XV (1966).

McCourt, D., 'Infield and Outfield in Ireland', in *EcHR* 2nd ser. VII (1954–5).

McDonagh, O., 'The Irish Catholic Clergy and Migration during the Great Famine', in *IHS* V (1947).

—— 'The Registration of the Emigrant Traffic from the United Kingdom, 1842–55', in *IHS* IX (1954).

—— 'Emigration and the State, 1833–55', in *TRHS* 5th ser. V (1955).

McGrath, K. M., 'Writers in the *Nation*, 1842–45', in *IHS* VI (1949).

Machin, G. I. T., 'The Catholic Emancipation Crisis of 1825', in *EHR* LXXVIII (1963).

—— 'The Maynooth Grant, the Dissenters and Disestablishment, 1845–7', in *EHR* LXXXII (1967).

McNeill, W. H., and Kogan, A. C., 'The Introduction of the Potato into Ireland', in *JMH* XXI (1949).

Mulhauser, M., 'Maria Edgeworth as a Social Novelist', in *Notes and Queries*, 17 Sept 1938.

O'Neill, T. P., 'The Scientific Investigation of the Failure of the Potato Crop in Ireland, 1845–46', in *IHS* V (1946).

Palmer, N. D., 'Irish Absenteeism in the 1870s', in *JMH* XII (1940).

—— 'Sir Robert Peel's Select Irish Library,' in *IHS* VI (1948).

Raifeartaigh, T. O., 'Mixed Education and the Synod of Ulster, 1831–40', in *IHS* IX (1955).

Robinson, O., 'The London Companies as Progressive Landlords in Nineteenth-century Ireland', in *EcHR* 2nd ser. XV (1962–3).

Rudé, G., 'English Rural and Urban Disturbances, 1830–31', in *P&P* no. 37 (1967).

Smith, A. W., 'Irish Rebels and English Radicals, 1798–1820', in *P&P* no. 7 (1955).

Times Literary Supplement, 20 May 1949: 'Humours and Moralities'.

Whyte, J. H., 'Daniel O'Connell and the Repeal Party', in *IHS* XI (1959).

—— 'The Influence of the Catholic Clergy on Elections in Nineteenth-century Ireland', in *EHR* LXXV (1960).

—— 'Landlord Influence at Elections in Ireland, 1760–1885', in *EHR* LXXX (1965).

Willcox, W. B., 'Lord Lansdowne on the French Revolution and the Irish Rebellion', in *JMH* XVII (1945).

Index

Neither Maria Edgeworth nor Ireland feature as such in this index. As each is ubiquitous throughout the book it was thought wiser to present a list of everything else featuring on its pages. Through it all matters relating to them can easily be traced. Unnecessary duplication has thereby been avoided.

A Fragment on the Irish Roman Catholic Church, 143
A Passage to India, 53
Abbotsford, 47
Aberdeen, 4th Earl of, 115
Absenteeism, 37, 43, 46, 47, 137
Africa, 182
Agrarian question, 174, 181
Allen family, 59, 60, 61, 62, 63
Anarchists, 175
Anti-Corn Law League, 28
Ardagh, 121
Ardagh, Dean of, 61
Armagh, 116, 163
Arnold, T., 142, 143
Ascendancy, 183
Asia, 182
Australia, 177

Bacon, F., 96
Ballybonane, 120
Ballyglass, 152
Beaufort family, 45, 56, 65, 79, 80, 119, 162
Bentham, J., 179
Bentinck, Lord G., 153, 168, 170, 191
Birmingham, 35, 67
Birmingham Relief Committee, 161
Blackhall, S. W., 157, 168, 169

Bowood House, 39
Boyne, Battle of the, 32
Bristol, 138
Bristol mob, 67
British Constitution, 81, 88
British industry, 38
British Review, 96
British troops, 121
Brittaine, G., 65
Brougham and Vaux, Baron, 40, 133
Browne, Lord G., 152
Burdett, Sir F., 133
Burgoyne, Sir J., 158
Burke, E., 43
Butler, H., 51, 76, 94, 113, 114, 116, 128, 135, 151, 155, 160, 163, 178
Butler, the Rev. Richard (Dean of Clonmacnoise), 64, 76, 80, 96, 113, 114, 122, 144, 178
Byron, Lord, 188

Cahirciveen, 44
Canada, 73
Canning, G., 39, 45–7, 115, 190
Cantwell, Bishop, 108
Carlow College, 67
Carlow, county, 100
Cassidy, Mr, 95, 97, 99
Castle Forbes, 58, 101

Castle Rackrent, 28, 33, 52
Catholic Association, 36, 48, 50
Catholic Emancipation, 16, 22, 26, 32–5, 39, 40, 42, 44, 45, 47, 48, 50, 65, 101, 112, 153, 173
Catholic farmers, 80, 106
Catholic priests, 44, 60, 63, 66, 71, 76, 82, 90, 96, 98–101, 119, 121, 128, 130, 144, 145, 149, 169, 170, 175, 176
Catholic Rent, 105, 106, 130, 164
Catholics, 22, 26, 34, 37, 46, 50, 52, 59, 60, 61, 62, 63, 68, 70, 73, 74, 77, 86, 92, 96, 98, 101, 110, 118, 126, 128, 129, 143, 145, 146, 166, 171, 177, 178, 181–4
Chambers' Miscellany, 161
Charity, 134
Charles the Second, 56
Charleville Court, 108
Charleville, Lord, 108
Chartism, 21, 28, 174
Church of Ireland, 22, 26, 53, 101, 102
Church Rates, 21, 54
Clancy, the Rev. W., 67
Clare, county, 50, 52
Clare, county by-election, 36, 169
Clarendon, 4th Earl of, 177
Clontarf Meeting, 127
Cobbett, W., 133
Coercion, 72, 73, 152, 153, 173, 175–7
Colleges Bill, 168
Common Prayer, Book of, 88
Comprehension, 185
Connell, Mr, 68
Connemara, 72
Conservatives, 74, 76, 86, 88, 95, 96, 99–101, 116, 117, 123, 145, 153, 168, 169, 190, 191
Cork, 19
Cork, county, 173
Corn Law, 153
Corn Law Repeal, 153
Corry, Captain, 187
Crawford, S., 103
Curran, J. P., 51
Curtis, Mrs, 138

Daly, D., 86
Davy, Sir H., 188
De Gaulle, President, 87
Democracy, 100
Demoralisation, 107
Denman, 1st Baron, 40

Dermod, Mr, 78–84, 94
Devon Commission, 125, 136
Devonshire, 6th Duke of, 186
Disraeli, B., 153, 191
D'Israeli, I., 188
Doyle, Bishop, 73, 130
Drummond, T., 53, 74, 93, 98, 101, 110, 111
Dublin, 45, 47, 75–8, 103, 119, 121, 123, 138, 154, 164, 174, 175
Dublin Castle, 119, 162
Dublin Corporation, 121
Dublin Evening Mail, 157
Dublin Poor Law Commissioners, 103
Dudley and Ward, 1st Earl of, 115
Dudley and Ward, 2nd Earl of, 126
Dummond, 124
Duncannon, Lord, 74
Dungannon, 169

Ecumenicalism, 112
Edgeworth, C. S., 34, 40, 45, 59, 77, 78, 80, 81, 85, 86
Edgeworth, F. B., 34, 187
Edgeworth, Mrs F. B., 157, 187
Edgeworth, L. (II), 34, 57–64, 67, 68, 72, 84, 118
Edgeworth, R. L., 16, 30, 33, 79, 80, 82, 92, 152, 179, 187
Edgeworth, Mrs R. L., 40, 41, 45, 49, 55, 56, 58–64, 73, 74, 77, 87, 97, 105, 137, 155, 157, 163
Edgeworth, W. (II), 44
Edgeworthstown, 29, 32, 45, 49, 52, 60, 66, 67, 68, 75, 90, 93, 94, 99, 104, 108, 119, 120, 123, 124, 151, 155, 156, 160, 164, 168, 176, 178, 179
Edgeworthstown Estates, 119
Edgeworthstown Fairs, 54
Education, 24, 25, 44, 49, 102, 134, 178, 179, 182
Election Petitions, 71, 97
Election Recriminations, 77
Elizabeth the First, 30
Encumbered Estates Acts, 182
England, 37, 39, 125, 135, 174
England, Lord Chief Justice of, 131
Ennui, 27, 189
Erysipelas, 135
European Common Market, 184

Famine, 20, 56, 141, 142, 147, 153, 163–5, 180

Famine relief, 150, 154–6, 159, 161, 165–8.
Farnham, 2nd Earl of, 168
Farrall, Mr, 113
Farrar, Mrs, 94, 120
Fascism, 71, 123
Ferral, Mr, 75
Fetherston, Sir G., 95
Fever, 163
fFrench, Lord, 121
Field Garden scheme, 136
Fitzgerald, Father, 108
Fitzgerald, Lord E., 67
Fitzherbert, R., 76
Fixity of Tenure, 125
Forbes, Lady, 100
Forbes, Viscount, 58–64, 68, 70–2, 74–6, 86, 88, 94
Forster, E. M., 53
Forty Shilling Freeholders, 26, 35, 36, 49, 51
Fox, B., 61, 77, 79–81, 84–6, 156, 165
Fox, C., 61, 64, 86, 94, 95, 97–101, 116, 124
Fox, M. A., 160
Fox, R. M., 168, 169
Fox Hall, 168
France, 174, 175, 177
Franchise, 1793 Act, 26
Franchise extension, 64, 169
Franco, Caudillo, 87
Freeman's Journal, 150
French Chamber of Deputies, 41
French Revolution, 49, 129

Gaffery, Mr, 71, 85
Gahan, Mr, 139, 160
Galway, county, 19, 89
Gaullism, 159
General Election of 1826, 27, 36, 44, 49, 50, 52
General Election of 1830, 55 et seq.
General Election of 1832, 69 et seq.
General Election of 1835, 75 et seq.
General Election of 1837, 95 et seq.
General Election of 1841, 116 et seq.
General Election of 1847, 168 et seq.
Geneva, 126
Genoa, 163
George the Third, 32
Gladstone, W. E., 99
Goderich, 1st Viscount, 34, 47, 190

Granard, 26
Granard, Earl of, 58
Grand Jury, 54
Grattan, H. (Sen.), 32, 183
Grattan, H. (Jun.), 65, 76
Grattan's Parliament, 28, 31, 32, 121
Grattan's Parliament, the foundation of, 1782, 16
Gray, Father, 71, 90, 91
Great Britain, 32
Grenville, G., 133
Grey, 2nd Earl, 74, 102, 190

Haileybury, 103
Hall, Mrs A., 120
Hall, Captain B., 49
Hamilton, J., 21, 23
Hanging Gale Rent, 77 et seq.
Harman, Mr, 169
Harvey, Mr, 155
Hawtrey, Dr, 114
Health, Board of, 155
Helen, 37, 75
Hinds, G., 34, 59, 68, 69, 71, 75, 78, 80, 83, 90, 91, 95, 107, 110, 156
Holland, Dr, 129, 130
Holland, Sir H., 51
House of Commons (Ireland), 26
House of Commons (United Kingdom), 35, 38, 41, 73, 74, 98, 163
House of Lords (United Kingdom), 38, 103, 133
Hull, 138

Independent Irish Brigade, 97, 172
India, 48
Ireland, Bank of, 50
Irish Confederation, 163
Irish County Franchise Act, 1850, 27
Irish Free State, 182
Irish land system, 18, 136, 182
Irish landlords, 82, 125, 135, 148, 166
Irish language, 182
Irish municipal question, 75
Irish Poor Law, 46
Irish railway scheme, 168, 170
Irish tenants, 125
Italy, 163

Jackson, Judge, 175
Jones, the Rev. Prof. R., 72, 103, 105, 133–6, 150, 164, 166, 167, 172, 174
Jury List, 131

Keating, the Rev., 68, 90, 91
Keegan, Garret, 59, 61, 62, 71, 139
Kelly, Mr, 94
Kent, 55
Kerry, county, 19, 150
Kildare Place Society, 25
Knox, G., 52

Labouchere, H. (1st Baron Taunton), 158
Laisser faire, 134
Lalor, F., 174
Land Act, 1778, 19
Land improvement, 137
Landlord, role of, 84
Lanesborough, 26
Langan, Abbé, 51
Langan, M., 52, 83, 85
Lansdowne, 3rd Marquess of, 38, 45, 52, 71, 86, 87, 130, 133
Lansdowne House, 67
Lazarus, Mrs, 42, 43, 66, 88
Leagued People, 148
Lecky, W. E. H., 56
Lefroy, A., 58, 59, 61, 62, 70–2, 74–6, 86, 101, 117, 169, 170
Lefroy, Baron, 174, 175
Leibig, Dr, 149
Leinster, 156
Leitrim Assizes, 175
Liberals, 87, 169
Liberal Unionism, 159
Lichfield House Compact, 75, 98, 105, 106, 117
Life of Christ, 118
Limerick, Treaty of, 96
Liverpool, 2nd Earl of, 39, 45, 138, 190
Lockhart, J. G., 46, 47
London, 39–41, 99, 118, 123, 131, 133, 151
Londonderry, 40
Longford, 26, 59, 61, 63, 64, 69, 100, 169, 176
Longford Assizes, 72
Longford County, 26, 27, 29, 44, 56, 68, 74–8, 86, 94, 113, 116, 117, 150, 156, 163, 168
Longford, county by-election, 1836, 96
Lorton, Viscount, 58, 86
Louth, county, 44
Lushington, Dr, 128
Lyons, Mr, 107, 108
Lyons, Mrs, 108

Macaulay, Lord, 23, 131, 145
MacDonnell, J., 152
MacHale, Archbishop, 178
McNally, Mr, 160
Mahon, Major, 175
Malthus, the Rev. T. R., 104
Manchester, 67
Martineau, H., 100, 104, 133, 134, 187,
Mathew, Father T., 112–14, 118, 121, 138–40, 151
Maynooth College, 66, 98, 113, 136, 145, 153
Mayo, county, 19, 33, 120, 170, 171
Mayo county by-election, 152
Meath, county, 56, 64, 76, 150
Melbourne, 2nd Viscount, 74, 92, 93, 98, 101, 110, 190
Methodist Magazine, 112
Methodists, 112
Middlemen, 31
Mill, J., 23
Mitchel, J., 174, 175
Mobs, 55, 175
Moilliet, J. L., 126
Molly McGuires, 145
Monaghan, county, 19, 44
Money troubles, 72 et seq.
Montgomery, Dr, 147
Moore, G., 33, 96, 97, 173
Moore, Mrs G., 108, 118, 149, 152, 171, 177
Moore, G. H., 97, 120, 152, 170–2, 177, 178
Moore Hall, 96, 97, 171
Mullaghmast, 121, 132
Mullins, Mr, 58, 61, 63
Municipal Government Act (Ireland), 1840, 110, 113
Murray, Dr, 161
Murtagh, Mr, 160

Newtown Forbes, 100
Nicholls, Sir G., 102–5
Nicholls Report, 102
Nimmo, Mr, 114
Norbury, Lord, 108, 109
Nugent, Sir P., 117

O'Beirne, Miss, 126
O'Brien, S., 163, 174, 177
O'Connell, D., 18, 33–5, 44, 45, 50, 52–4, 56, 57, 66, 68, 70, 71, 73–4, 76, 92, 93, 97, 98, 101, 103, 105,

106, 112, 117, 120, 121, 123, 124, 126, 128, 130–3, 139, 143, 146, 150, 151, 157, 158, 163, 166, 168, 169, 171, 177, 183
O'Connell, J., 104
O'Connell, M., 76
Oldham, Mr, 113
Orangeism, 128
O'Rourke, Mr, 70
Oscott College, 97
Overpopulation, 136 et seq.

Pakenham, T. (Earl of Longford), 58
Pakenham Hall, 113
Palmerston, Lord, 115
Panza, Sancho, 179
Paris, Archbishop of, 175
Parnell, C. S., 172
Partition, 181
Party, 110, 111
Patronage, 28, 54
Peel, Sir R., 17, 40, 47, 67, 74, 75, 87, 88, 93, 97, 98, 117, 127, 136, 150, 152, 153, 169, 190, 191
Peelites, 153, 159, 168, 172
Pennefather, Mr Justice, 132
Poland, 76
Political Economy, 104, 158, 165
Poor Law, 72, 74, 102–5, 133, 138, 142, 167, 168
Poor Law Act (Irish), 1838, 101, 102, 114
Potatoes, 141, 142, 147, 153, 155, 159, 165, 168, 178
Powell, Miss, 156
Powell, Mrs, 157
Powell, the Rev., 155, 157, 160
Practical Education, 67, 113
Precursor Society, 106
Presbyterians, 26, 59, 61, 62, 183
Priestley, J., 133
Protestant clergy, 130, 166
Protestants, 22, 34, 37, 46, 52, 53, 68, 86, 90, 97, 101, 118, 128, 129, 143, 178, 181, 182

Quakers, 113, 154–7, 167
Queen Victoria, 133
Queen's Bench, Court of (Dublin), 133
Queen's Bench, Court of (London), 132
Queen's Colleges, 26, 146
Querist, 179
Quirk, J., 28

Quirk, T., 28
Quixote, Don, 179

Radicals, 88, 153
Railways, 137, 151
Ralston, Mr, 151
Rebellion of 1798, 38, 67, 179
Rebellion of 1848, 176
Reform Act, 1832, 26, 54, 55, 69
Reform Bill, 1831, 66, 67
Reform Registry Political Union, 69
Registration, 95
Rent, 67, 68, 77, 119, 123, 135,137
Repeal, 16, 21, 28, 33, 34, 53, 60, 74, 86, 92, 105, 121, 125, 127, 137, 147, 152, 163, 169, 173, 175, 176
Repealers, 58, 61, 69, 73–5, 94, 96, 98, 100, 101, 105, 106, 110, 116, 122, 146, 151, 153, 162, 168–70, 173, 174, 176, 184
Republic of Ireland, 184
Ribbonmen, 20, 147
Ricardo, D., 40, 72, 133, 165, 179
Riots, 169
Rome, 163
Romilly, Sir S., 133
Rosanna, 27
Roscommon, county, 19, 145
Roscommon Assizes, 175
Rousseau, J. J., 23
Royal Irish Academy, 120
Royal Irish Constabulary, 176
Rugby School, 133
Rule of Law, 36, 81, 91, 92, 102, 106, 127, 152, 175
Russell, Lord J., 153, 154, 157, 163, 169, 170, 177, 191
Ruxton, Miss, 95, 121
Ruxton, Mrs (*née* Margaret Edgeworth, sister of R. L. Edgeworth), 36

St Johnstown, 26
Schweitzer, A., 23
Scotland, 39
Scott, C., 114–16
Scott, Sir W. 46, 47
Secret Ballot, 54
Shakespeare, W., 43
Shelburne, 2nd Earl of (1st Marquess of Lansdowne), 133
Siéyès, Abbé, 129
Sligo, county, 19

Smith, Sir C., 88
Smith, the Rev. S., 128–31, 137, 143, 145
Smuts, J. C. (Field Marshal Lord Smuts, etc.), 149
Social gospel, 104
South African Progressive Party, 28
Spencer, 2nd Earl, 137
Spring-Rice, T. (1st Baron Monteagle), 38, 41–4, 46, 48–50, 56, 69, 74, 77
87, 89, 102, 113, 114
Stanley, Bishop, 151
Stanley, Dean, 142
Stanley, Lord E. G. G. S. (later 14th Earl of Derby), 77, 87–9, 191
Stanleyites, 92, 97, 105, 110, 117, 159, 172
Starvation, 104
Strickland, G. E., 96
Sutherland, Duchess of, 187

Tamworth Manifesto, 74
Tara, 121
Temperance, 112–14, 122, 139, 151
Ten Pound Freeholder, 26
Tenant Right, 22, 31, 168, 169, 171, 173
Tenantry, 57, 77, 82, 94, 95, 104, 148
Tenants' Act, 1816, 20
The Absentee, 28, 70, 186
The Packet, 139
Thirty-nine Articles, 131
Timing in history, 183
Tipperary, county, 177
Tithe Act (Ireland), 1832, 102
Tithe Act (Ireland), 1838, 101, 102
Tithes, 21, 54, 75, 90, 91
Tone, W., 164
Tories, 39, 47, 53, 57–9, 61, 69, 74, 128, 190
Treason Felony Act, 1848, 174
Triennial Parliaments, 54
Trim, 64, 76, 113, 121, 135, 144, 178, 179
Trinity College Dublin, 26
Trevelyan, C., 150
Tuite, H., 105–7, 158, 162, 163
Tullamore, 160
Tyrone, county, 19, 169

Ulster, 50, 174
Ulster Tenant Right, 20, 182
Union, Act of, 1800, 16, 32, 35, 37, 38, 54, 93, 106, 137, 166, 171, 183, 184
United Irishman, 174
United Kingdom, 57, 76, 182, 184
United Kingdom Parliament, 66, 93
United States of America, 49, 100, 160, 161

Vansittart, N. (1st Baron Bexley), 40
Vestry Cess, 54
Violence, 148
Vivian, 27

Waterford, county, 44
Wellington, 1st Duke of, 39, 47, 48, 50, 67, 87, 103, 116, 153, 190.
West, Mr, 109
West Meath, county, 44, 107, 113, 121, 150
West Meath Assizes, 107
Westminster, 42, 74, 106
Westminster Review, 113
Whately, Archbishop, 161, 162
Whig Arms Act, 1838, 121
Whiggery, 128, 131
Whigs, 36, 39, 41, 45, 47, 52, 53, 55, 57, 59, 61, 67, 69, 74–7, 85, 86, 92, 97, 102, 105, 109, 110, 117, 118, 153, 163, 168–70, 172, 190, 191
White, Col. H., 61, 74, 76, 101, 117, 169
White, L., 58–61, 70, 74, 75, 94, 95, 97, 99, 101, 116, 117, 169
Whiteboys, 20
Whitefeet, 148
Wilberforce, W., 40
Wild Geese, 17
William the Fourth, 97
Wilson, F., 47, 49–51, 58, 62, 101, 122, 125, 138, 142, 143, 145, 148, 149, 160, 178
Wilson, L., 157
Woods, J., 62, 71, 85
Workhouses, 155

York, Duke of, 43
Young Ireland, 146, 163, 164, 174, 176